Climbing Up the Downward Spiral

Climbing Up The Downward Spiral

Hard Times, Drug and Alcohol Abuse and Addiction,
Mental Illness, Suicide

DEAN C. JONES
AND
MICHAEL JOSEPH

RESOURCE *Publications* · Eugene, Oregon

CLIMBING UP THE DOWNWARD SPIRAL
Hard Times, Drug and Alcohol Abuse and Addiction, Mental Illness, Suicide

Resource Publications
An Imprint of Wipf and Stock Publishers
199 W. 8th Ave., Suite 3
Eugene, OR 97401
www.wipfandstock.com

ISBN 13: 978-1-60899-629-2

Manufactured in the U.S.A.

*We dedicate this book to Norman J. Jones
and all of those who struggle in the downward spiral and everyone who is
climbing up the downward spiral.*

Welcome this pain, for some day it will be useful to you

—OVID

Contents

Acknowledgments

W E ARE DEEPLY IN debt to many people for their contributions to this book. Most important are those who have shared their stories with us. Unfortunately, many of these people will never hold this book in their hands. We have either lost touch with them as in the case of Sam and Joan or they have died as in the case of Harlan and Karen.

Many professionals have contributed both to our lives and to this book. Their names appear in the text. The book would not have been possible without their input either in printed form or in interview material. A considerable body of information relates to the topics covered in this book. Only a small part of this literature surfaces in these pages. We are thankful for the resource list that appears as appendix material. Much of this list was shared with us by Dr. Doug Jowdy. A number of people assisted us in the process of doing this book. This includes those who reviewed the material and gave us encouragement, including Father Don Rickard, PhD, who reviewed chapter 3 and Jon Wade who reviewed chapter 4. We are very thankful for the excellent work of Christian Amondson and everyone at Wipf and Stock Publishers who have helped to make this book possible. A very special acknowledgement must go to Nancy Shoptaw for both her editorial skills and her personal encouragement during the editing phase of the project. This book in final form would not have been possible without her assistance.

Finally, we need to acknowledge again those who can personally relate to some kind of downward spiral, the ones whose stories we share, plus those who will read this book and consider in a new way their own climb up the downward spiral.

Introduction

IN THE PAGES OF this book we bring new images to old social problems: hard times, drug and alcohol abuse and addiction, mental illness, and suicide. We have a preference for personal stories. Sit with us as we talk to Sam and Joan about what it is like to claim a camper parked in a Walmart parking lot as home. With them we reach for some insight into how people survive in hard times. Go with us to New Orleans after hurricane Katrina as we again learn from those going through hard times. The journey also takes us to places like Aberdeen, Washington, where many men and women experience major financial loss at a time when the timber industry falls into hard times. You are also invited to journey with us as we share stories of those who are homeless in different cities.

In the chapter on drug and alcohol abuse and addiction, come with us as we take you into an oversized doghouse in a typical suburban neighborhood where some teenage boys are experimenting with cocaine And join us on a long overnight drive with two drug addicts looking for new life in a treatment center. Walk into an emergency room at Tacoma General Hospital as a young man shares his near-death experience after a near-lethal dose of illegal drugs.

The chapter on mental illness begins with the personal story of a long journey with bipolar disorder as experienced by Michael Joseph. The pages of this chapter also include personal experiences of Dean Jones as he shares the story of his brother who has lived with schizophrenia for some fifty years, and work with the mentally ill during twenty years of late-night, downtown ministry reaching out to men and women who struggle to function. Dean also includes stories from interviews for a book he wrote on the mentally ill offender, people with mental illness who have spent time in jail or prison.

The personal stories of both authors continue to have a prominent role in the last chapter of the book on the topic of suicide. You are invited to consider what it might be like to sit in your car with the motor running and a hose feeding exhaust into a car window as you slowly fall asleep with the strong intention of never waking up. Other experiences are included in this chapter, along with strong suggestions about how to become better tuned to the likelihood of suicide. Professional advice is shared including comments from the person in charge of suicide prevention at the University of Colorado in Boulder.

Each chapter of this book includes specific references to spiritual issues. Spirituality becomes important in many ways as people climb up the downward spiral. This may take the form of simply looking in a new way at the marvels of nature. New hope can come from formal services of worship, as suggested in chapter 1. A very personal awareness of God in life can also become a major touchstone for people as shared with respect to a homeless man who wants a "blessing."

A final common thread in this book is that we share from different places in the journey of life. Dean is seventy-eight and Mike is twenty-nine. We know that we look at life differently. Hopefully this adds to our understanding of major problems. It also invites further inquiry into how people can best communicate and support each other. All of us at one time or another will face the experience of climbing up some form of downward spiral. Our hope is that this book will become a positive resource for you. And that it will help you see how others with very different life experiences can add to your understanding.

Dean C. Jones
Michael Joseph
January 2010

1

Hard Times

Dean Jones

*"I made it through the rain and kept my point of view.
I made it through the rain and was respected by others
who were rained on too"*

—Barry Manilow

FINANCIAL LOSS IS NOT a topic to be covered in a few paragraphs. For some it is a long and very difficult journey. All of us can learn from down times even if we do not experience them personally. I invite you to prolong this chapter with reflections of your own. Valuable lessons come from times of financial crisis; lessons that remain important long after the time of crisis has passed.

It has been hard to keep up with the bad economic news coming out during the time of the writing of this book. On April 9, 2009, Pam Belluck reported on the first page of the *New York Times* that anxiety was "sweeping into everyday lives." Her report included a story of a woman living in Cambridge, Massachusetts, who began having panic attacks over the economy.[1] A prominent article for the *Boulder Camera* on May 11, 2009, by Alicia Wallace noted that, "At 7.5 percent, Colorado in March notched its highest unemployment rate in nearly 22 years."[2] The rate would climb higher in the months ahead. It is obvious that many people in our country do not have a comfortable lifestyle today. Maybe it is a man or woman who has gone through divorce. Or perhaps it is

1. Belluck, "Recession Anxiety Seeps," A1.
2. Wallace, "Reviewing the First Quarter."

someone who has lost a job. For seniors getting by on a fixed income, life can become a struggle for basic survival, including decisions about whether to pay for prescription medications or to buy food for the day.

Too many families today face the pain of losing their homes through foreclosure. The "R" word (recession) has come back into the common language with some talking about the Great Depression. As a sign of the times, in 2008 I drove past a man and woman standing on a street corner near a gas station. She held a large, red gas can. He held up a sign reading, "Mom and Dad out of gas." On a hot day in June 2009, another man stood on this same corner. His sign read, "Father Lost Job . . . Five Children . . . No Food." The front cover of *Time* magazine for June 28, 2010, came with the picture of a battered, generic state license plate with the bold letters, BNKRPT. The lead article for that edition of this national magazine was on "The Broken States of America: How the financial crisis of the states affects all of us."[3] For the immediate and near future the story gave little basis for being optimistic. Unfortunately, many individuals in our country could wear old T-shirts with the letters "BROKE," printed on both front and back of the shirt.

In July of 2008 the daily news coverage on TV included photos of police in California monitoring a long line of people waiting to withdraw their funds from a failed Indy Mac bank. In the week of October 6, 2008, newspapers around the country carried headlines with the news that markets worldwide tanked as fears of a wide-scale recession spread. As this book enters into its final stages of editing, the economy continues to be high on the list of concerns for Americans. Lynn Bartels, a writer with the *Denver Post* reported in a front-page article appearing on June 21, 2010, that "no matter their political leanings, a majority of Coloradans believe the most pressing issue facing the country today is 'jobs and the economy.'" In the automated poll by SurveyUSA, the jobs issue topped other popular issues such as immigration and medical marijuana.[4]

In its 2009 third-quarter report, RealtyTrac, a web-based firm that tracks and markets foreclosed homes, tallied 937,840 properties, a 5 percent increase from the previous quarter and an increase of nearly 23 percent from the third quarter of 2008. Foreclosures in September 2009 showed a 29 percent increase over September 2008, the third highest monthly total, behind only July and August of 2009, since the RealtyTrac

3. Von Drehle, "Broken States of America," cover.
4. Bartels, "Poll: Coloradans say jobs," A1.

report began in January 2005.[5] A lot of material and non material losses accompany every foreclosure situation. In May of 2008, *USA Today* featured an article by Stephanie Amour giving a very personal look at the mental health toll from foreclosures.[6] The article begins with an account of Raymond and Deanna Donavan of Prineville, Oregon. In October of 2007, this couple closed all of the doors to their home except the one to the garage and left their car running. Toxic fumes did their work. Sheriff's deputies found the bodies when they were called to the scene. A relative blamed a pending foreclosure for the suicides. Amour also said that crisis hotlines were reporting an increase in calls from worried homeowners and that mental health groups were giving more information on how to handle the emotional stress triggered by the real estate meltdown.

It would be all too easy to relax under the impression that it is only the low-end real estate market that is threatened by foreclosure. But growing evidence suggests that the sagging economy is having an impact in a wide range of markets. The front page of the *Rocky Mountain News* in Denver, Colorado, for Saturday, July 12, 2008, shared color photos of homes valued at over one million dollars on the foreclosure list. One of these homes with a large swimming pool was assessed at $1,100,000 with the owners owing $1,162,500. High-end foreclosures are also posing a threat to senior centers, office buildings, and even churches. The *New York Times* for Sunday, July 13, 2008, included stories of problems faced by people in New York City looking for apartments selling for over one million dollars. A large down payment did not guarantee a mortgage if someone was working in the troubled and unpredictable financial sector. When foreclosure action is pending the major lenders including Countrywide are simply not organized to take calls giving advice. In the first week of 2009, German billionaire Adolf Merckle took his own life, his spirit broken by financial fears. He is only one of other high profile casualties of the global economic crisis. The front cover story for *Time* magazine on September 21, 2009, came with the bold headline: "Out of Work in America: Why double-digit unemployment may be here to stay—and how to live with it."

Many sources tell us that being unemployed today hurts more than in past times of high unemployment. I recently talked with a woman in her forties who is now unemployed. I was surprised by her very negative

5. RealtyTrac, "Foreclosure Activity," lines 4–11.
6. Amour, "Foreclosures Take Toll."

view of her future. She does not see how she can get a job that will last for any length of time. I think that this attitude may be encouraged in part by the stimulus package in place at the federal level. Most of the jobs created by this measure are by nature short term, like fixing the highways. The unemployed woman added that many of her friends are out of work and that one friend told her he was simply going to use up all of his money and then go up into the mountains, never to return. Such a direct comment about suicide was not part of the unemployment picture in the not-too-distant past. Today the problem is also increased by the sheer amount of debt most people have and also the inadequacy of healthcare for those who do not have regular employment.

The shadow of the recession has fallen on many parts of life in our country. My wife and I are members of a program called Golden Retriever Rescue of the Rockies (GRR).[7] This program rescues dogs that for one reason or another are not able to remain in their original home. In an email to volunteers in July of 2009 the director, Mary Kenton, points to the economy as creating lots of problems for dogs and their owners.

> So many of the Goldens we have coming into GRR this year are because of this economy we are all struggling with right now. Some are forced to give up their Goldens as they are having trouble caring for their children. Many have lost their jobs, their homes and are suffering while giving up their Goldens that they can no longer afford to give medical care, house or feed. I have spent many hours on the phone listening to them while their hearts are breaking as they talk about why they can't keep their Goldens.

I assume that this situation can be found in other states and for other breeds of dogs. We can all help by becoming volunteers, doing what we can in these hard times for dogs as well as people. The impact of a recession on household pets is always difficult to determine, but newsletters and word of mouth from those directly involved can become very emotional.

For some in our country, home ownership is only a distant dream, no matter what happens on the national economic scene. We can learn from those who have seen poverty on a personal level as a chronic condition. Now is the time to listen to folks like Sam and Joan. It is unlikely

---

7. For more information about Golden Retriever Rescue, see info@goldenrescue .com.

that they will ever have a home of their own. "We live at Walmart," Sam says. A forty-one-year-old man, he wears a faded blue ball cap frayed at the edges. He lives in a small camper, a "cab over" that rests on the bed of an old pickup parked in a Walmart parking lot. He shares this cramped living quarters with the love of his life, a thirty-year-old woman named Joan. Living at Walmart is a twenty-four-hour exercise in survival. There is constant fear of being forced to move by authorities, of losing everything as their "home" is towed away. When I talked with this couple on the last day of May in 2008 the weather was turning toward a time of daily temperatures in the nineties. It is hot in a small camper in the summer and very cold in the winter. Propane bottles attached to a portable heating element do give some heat for the freezing winter but there is no air conditioning for the summer. No electricity, no running water, none of the things that make life pleasant.

After my visit with Sam and Joan, I went home to adjust the thermostat in our townhouse. With ceiling fans and central heating plus central air conditioning, a touch of the finger automatically adjusts the temperature. The morning after my visit with Sam and Joan, I went out on the trail near where we live for a walk with our dog, a Golden Retriever. We walked past one large home, some four thousand feet of living space with several bedrooms. I am sure that this spacious house overlooking a friendly, free flowing creek and trees newly decorated with the greenery of spring had empty bedrooms. A deck from the second floor looked out on a garden spot where a new sack of peat moss waited on the owner as he began a garden for the season. This surround of living space was more normal for our time—having all of the perks that sustain a positive life. Then I thought of Sam and Joan. I also thought of them as I crawled into our king-sized bed and as I showered with soap, shampoo, and conditioner in the morning and used a handheld dryer to blow dry my hair before using a bottle of soft style Paul Mitchell hair spray. I could not imagine a day without these conveniences. Then I thought of Sam and Joan, living at Walmart.

How does one become homeless, claiming a parking lot as "home?" There are many roads converging on the highway leading to homelessness. For both Sam and Joan, health issues are paramount. Sam has migraines, lower back pain, bad knees, an enlarged prostrate, and high cholesterol levels. One goal for both Sam and Joan is to get her back on disability. On good days, Sam can lift thirty-five pounds. Then he has days when he cannot lift a gallon of milk. It is very hard for him to pull himself up the three feet into his "home" in the pickup. Sam takes seven pills every day at set intervals. He has been declared unfit to work, so draws disability (SSI) of $637 a month. He also sells his blood at a local blood bank and recycles scrap whenever he can. Sam is proud of his eight years of sobriety. This gift of life came when a friend took him to his first AA meeting. At one low ebb in his life, he threw his bicycle off a cliff and intended to follow it to his death but a friend intervened. Both Sam and Joan struggle with emotional downs. Joan takes fourteen pills a day and uses two inhalers. She has back problems, asthma, and diabetes, and also struggles with a weight problem. At one time Joan was on disability. But now she has no income. She looks forward to her monthly receipt of food stamps. Joan has only meager work history and no special work skills.

Health issues are only one of the major problems faced by Sam and Joan as they survive in the suburbs of a large city throbbing with life. Another difficult input into their immediate situation is a tragic turn of events in family affairs. Joan has been left with no effective family support. When Sam was nine years old his dad, then thirty-eight, became involved with an eighteen-year-old and married her. This young lady, turned step-mother, proceeded to beat Sam brutally with her bare hands. One day he showed up in school with black and blue marks all over his body. While his step mom was beating him, she shouted at him that he would never amount to anything, that he was no good. The school nurse alerted authorities and Sam was placed in temporary housing before entering Colorado Boys Ranch. In the temporary housing for dependent children, Sam was raped by an older boy. Given the nature of his family situation it is not surprising that Sam never completed high school. Now he is fearful of getting his GED, thinking that it may jeopardize his status on SSI. Another hurdle for him is that he has problems reading some words.

The day after I listened to the litany of a very painful family situation for Sam, I attended an end-of–the-year dance recital for a five-year-old granddaughter. I sat with several hundred people in a comfortably air-conditioned auditorium while watching children of all ages perform graceful dance steps before adoring family members. The costumes were elegant. Each child had been given personal and loving care to ensure the best display of hair and general appearance. After the performance most children posed for photographs as they were informed that they "were lovely" and that their performance was great. All of these normal expressions of love in the family stand in sharp contrast to the beatings and verbal abuse suffered by Sam.

"What keeps you going?" "How do you make it through the day?" In asking these questions I was hoping that something might come up that would be helpful for others. For Joan, hope is a big factor. Plus a heavy dose of faith. She carries a copy of the Lord's Prayer with her at all times. And she prays. She does not go to church because she "fidgets" and is uncomfortable. Sam talks a lot about the need to focus on the positive. As he says, "If you look at the negatives, you don't get anywhere. You must look at the positive and what you can do, try to make your life better." He goes on to say that he has "been down there, with absolutely nothing." Now he does have a camper. He knows a lot of people who have nothing, who live on the streets winter and summer. Sam gives to the community. He knows many homeless street kids through his direct involvement as a volunteer. One girl of twelve Sam helped had been raped and battered by her dad before ending up on the streets. A final important part of the survival strategy for Sam and Joan is their love for each other. During a visit with them, words like "I love you" and "baby" surface. Sam reaches out to give Joan a hug and a kiss. Living at Walmart—how many folks are doing this around the country today?

As a final comment on this couple, I want to add, as Mike will suggest later in this chapter, that everyone must do what he or she can to improve their situation. It is true that Sam and Joan have a long legacy of turning to others for help. The issue for each of us is, "What can I do realistically in my situation?" Not simply, "What can I get others to do?" On the other hand, I learned in my work with people at night in different cities that many people are unaware of how to access programs available to them. Based on my personal contacts, I take issue with those who write off all of the homeless as simply "shiftless" or "lazy." A number of factors often merge to produce homelessness, as in the case of Sam and Joan. One of my contributions was to help folks obtain any assistance or benefits they were eligible for. When someone is unable to work, SSI is a reasonable resource. The issue of dependency is very complex. We must be careful in judging someone else who is not "independent" as we interpret the term. As I report in the next chapter, it is possible for someone to fall so far below others that he or she honestly feels unworthy of any "free" service. This can include emergency shelter or a public detox facility.

LOSING HOME SWEET HOME

During these difficult times we can learn from many different situations where major loss has occurred. In the case of devastating hurricanes many people lose everything. How they manage to survive can help others no matter what the specific situation of financial loss. When Hurricane Gustav slammed into the Gulf Coast on September 1, 2008, it came as a reminder of Katrina and our vulnerability to severe weather and other "natural disasters." We must listen to the lessons from Gustav and Katrina. And we can learn from the more recent total devastation of lives and property after the earthquake in Haiti in January of 2010. We have no way to know when some form of loss may come thundering or steal silently down the street where we live. Katrina was labeled as the single most damaging natural disaster in the history of our country, with block after block of the city left in ruins when it hit on August 29, 2005. The city of New Orleans once known for Cajun food, music with soul, and good times has become a memorial to loss of possessions and loss of life itself. It is hard to imagine the crushing personal and psychological blow coming unexpectedly to residents of the city. There was flooding in most of the city with the coming of Katrina. With no electricity and no running water, some residents survived temporarily on peanut butter and bottled water. Former living residences were flooded and ripped apart, sustaining "bomb-like devastation." Then came Hurricane Rita bringing more rain. No one is prepared in any way for such an event. How does one survive? Victor and his eighty-one-year-old mother Bernice are among the survivors. In April of 2008 they could look back at that historical moment when flood waters rose waist high in their living room.

"The water was so high . . . we just had to get out, we had to climb up to anyplace higher than the water," Victor speaks as he sits in his wheelchair, near his mother who is also confined to a wheelchair.[8] Three years ago, before Katrina, an old pickup truck was parked in front of the house. This truck was not working but it did hold several sheets of plywood and some old automobile tires. When the floodwaters came, Victor, his brother, and a neighbor used the tires and wood to fashion a raft. This gave some assistance for those unable to stand in the water.

8. Mission team members of Light of Christ Ecumenical Catholic Community in Longmont, Colorado, who traveled to New Orleans in 2007 to assist in hurricane Katrina relief efforts relayed these personal comments to author Dean Jones.

Those who were able held onto the sides of the raft, guiding it to a place below a bridge. Bernice held on to her son's neck for hours in the water. At the bridge, Victor heard his name called out from somewhere above. To this day he is convinced that the call came from God. Whoever the caller was, this became a turning point for Victor and his mother. They were transported by ambulance to a place of safety and were given much needed clothing.

It was dark in the house at around 5 a.m. when Victor watched in shocking disbelief as the water began to rise in his bedroom. One of his immediate concerns as he looked out from his bed to see objects floating in the water was the safety of his blood pressure medication. He was able to retrieve his medication before it floated away. As he was doing this he noticed a snake swimming by in his room. After the water receded and Victor was able to return to the house he found a man who offered to fix up the residence.

Victor gave him a total of twelve thousand dollars but no work was done. He also had a major problem with swelling and discoloration in one leg. Years before he had injured this leg. It did heal with a scab remaining as a form of protection. But hours of soaking in the dirty aftermath of Katrina water tore off the scab and re-infected this old wound. A doctor told him that if he did not treat the leg the result could be fatal. The prescribed antibiotic was not covered by Medicare or Medicaid and it was very expensive. Victor paid for and dutifully took sixty lifesaving tablets, another cost of Katrina.

Roosevelt was not in his house in New Orleans when Katrina came. He had lived in the house for thirty-seven years with his wife and five children. Retired now, Roosevelt was north of the city in Mississippi when the floodwaters came. Water came up to a level of about five feet in his living room. The house, built in 1939, sustained considerable damage. Like his neighbors, Roosevelt "lost everything."[9] He had to throw away damaged furniture. Clothing and everything else was gone by the time he was able to return and when the water was pumped out of his house. Now lots of work must be done. Roosevelt cannot leave the house because it is not secure. So he must stay, trapped in the building until more work is done and normal windows and doors are in place. But he considers himself lucky because he is alive. As he looks across the street at some vacant houses he knows that some of the elderly former

9. Ibid.

residents of these houses survived Katrina but were so stressed by the whole ordeal that they died weeks after the disaster.

Miss May lived in her house in New Orleans for thirty-three years before Katrina hit. After the hurricane she had "hard times," but was more concerned about the losses of others. Her daughter lost everything and then moved in with her. Miss May lives by the philosophy that "we just have to live in hope one day at a time." She wishes that everyone could get back on their feet. The day after the storm her only concern was to get away, as she said, " we got the hell out of here."[10] She spent some time in Jackson, Mississippi, before she was able to return to the neighborhood. Not unlike others going through a natural disaster, Miss May is no stranger to loss. She was married in the 1950s but went through a divorce in 1979, living alone since then. A twenty-six-year-old son was shot in the head while sitting on a levy across town and never recovered. Another son lives on a limited monthly disability check with a bad back and was recently found to have cancer. Miss May has buried her sister and her mother. Looking at her situation in April of 2008, Miss May admits that she does not have much but says that she is satisfied with what she has. She has had lots of hard times since the divorce, but thinks more about others than herself.

A small measure of the feelings of New Orleans residents became evident in many personal messages written in bold black letters on commercial buildings and the remains of private residences after the floodwaters receded. One neighborhood store was left like a discarded, half-eaten sandwich in a sprawl of debris. Someone scribbled in dark letters on the front of this demolished store: "Katrina You Bitch." Another storefront once anxiously courting passing potential customers hoping they would come inside to view displays of rugs became a fortress, warning all who passed to stay away with the following words:

> Don't Try
> I am sleeping inside with a big dog,
> An ugly woman, two shotguns and a claw hammer
> Hey, throw me something mister

After Katrina, men and women walked as in a dream, passing house after devastated house to line up for a free health exam at Audubon Park

10. Ibid.

or to stand in a line waiting for a food handout from the Red Cross. Signs on wrecked houses told part of the story:

10/3 8 cats, 2 dogs, all DOA
9/12 DB (dead body)
U Loot, U Dead

Lessons from Katrina come at great cost, but they can help all of us. One strong message is that there is a real hierarchy of needs. Some needs become very compelling, such as the basic need to survive, to live. Standing in water waist deep is no time to reflect on emotional imperatives. First, it is all important to get out of the water, to somehow move to higher ground. If you have ever gone through a major loss of any kind you can perhaps relate to the importance of looking first at the basics. This is true, for example, if you are forced to move across the country after a divorce or if you have lost a job. In the first case, issues around how to move yourself and how to get a job in a new town have priority. In the latter situation, loss of immediate income may call for a look at local food banks. At some future time there will be energy for considering how the loss is changing all of life. Another example of the importance of keeping a hierarchy of needs in mind is the situation of the death of a loved one. In my role as a minister I often officiated at funerals. Sometimes it was important to consider the health status of surviving family members. In cases where there is a history of heart problems, some kind of medication may be called for before the funeral. Obviously bereavement processes are important. But first the family member must make it through the service.

Another way to look at Katrina is to view it from the eyes of volunteers who have gone there to help in some way. In April of 2007 a team from Light of Christ Ecumenical Catholic Community in Longmont, Colorado, gave one week of service. Their major goal was to assist in the reclaiming of a building owned by Catholic Charities. Considerable work was needed in this building, but first living spaces needed to be cleaned out. Volunteers went into places once the warm homes of others. The former tenants had reduced their tangible, earthly effects to whatever could be fitted into a two-bedroom apartment—all of their mementos collected over a lifetime.

One volunteer looked into a room with one chair in the center and small tables placed around this chair. All items had been arranged for easy access from a sitting position. The team member held back tears as she remembered that this was the way her mother lived before she died, too feeble to hunt down personal items. All must be kept in easy reach. When the group cleaned this life space a Bible was found at the bottom of a stack of miscellaneous things—a Bible held in close reach. Where was the woman who held the Bible in reverence? The volunteers from Colorado had no idea what happened to those who had lived in the facility. Perhaps they were now too sick or too poor to return for their belongings. Or maybe they had died in the wake of the Katrina disaster.

A number of teams from different churches and other organizations have now helped in the time since the hurricane of the century. All have been impressed by the many failures of government bureaucracy. Individuals and small groups, including churches, are really making a difference. Perhaps this is a good lesson for any kind of major loss. Another message is that we must not become too attached to material possessions. In the end we will leave it all. If you have ever had the occasion to clean out the living space of a relative who has died you are very aware of this reality. It pulls us to consider what is truly valuable, truly worthwhile in life.

During a service given for the congregation at Light of Christ the following words were shared by the volunteer team as their way to talk about what they learned from the New Orleans experience:

> Life is precious
> We are all vulnerable
> People and family are more important than things
> Together we can do anything
> God is good

Post-Katrina life calls us to remember that there are individuals who will take advantage of other individuals in times of loss and deep personal tragedy. When at a low ebb in life it is imperative to be on the alert for vultures. I heard, for example, the sales pitch of a man selling a wooden box with electrical wires as an "effective cure" for cancer at a price of one thousand dollars when I was struggling with a loved one in the final stages of cancer. Some are ready to reach for anything if there is even a small chance that it might help. There have been unscrupulous people for ages. In these first decades of the twenty-first century we are seeing the continuing growth of a strong mix of political and corporate power to work both ends of the problem/solution equation.

Unfortunately, some have found that they can gain both by creating a problem and then by offering a solution. At the system level it is possible to imagine much more harm than would ever be possible at the level of single individuals. This danger is now intensified with the power of the mass media and modern technology. One survival technique is for people of good will to become more active in affairs at the community, state, and national levels.

Squeezing Into Tight Quarters

My background includes some twenty years of direct contact with the problems covered in this book while serving as the director of a program of night ministry called "Operation Nightwatch" in different cities within the United States. This work came immediately after holding academic appointments at different universities as a sociologist for thirteen years. In a previous book, titled *Face To Face With Society's Lepers: Downtown Night Ministry,* I wrote primarily to help others working in this type of ministry.[11] And also as a way to call attention to the work to encourage people of the community to give support. The current book takes a different approach. I have often said that we can learn from those who have walked a road very different from our own. This book is for you. It is about surviving, even thriving, in very difficult situations, drawing on my personal experiences plus the experiences of many others. Perhaps it would be best to think of this book as a complement to general living, not simply a guide toward survival in difficult times. Part of the excitement in writing this book is working with a new friend, Michael Joseph. His personal journey, compelling insights, and enthusiasm are inspirational and offer new ways to look at and survive serious problems. This is a cooperative writing project, with both of us equally involved. Our hope is that something in these pages will be helpful to folks who are going through one or more of the problems mentioned. Or that our efforts will be of assistance to those working to help others during what we see as difficult times.

When talking about downsizing, it is imperative to give attention to the spiritual dimension. In reality, it is not so much about where we live but how we approach our situation. Some deliberately turn away from the more common grasping for more and more things as they look

11. Jones, *Face to Face.*

inward and upward, to claim a higher calling. All of us need to examine our lifestyle in this regard. Life is much more than money and what it can buy. As you reflect on your situation today, you may be someone who sits in a fairly comfortable financial situation. But it must be acknowledged that for too many in our country, life has become a very difficult financial struggle. When the hard times come there are too few resources to draw on. It is unlikely that someone going through an economic downturn will face the problem of how to furnish a five thousand square-foot home with ocean or mountain views. With hard times one of the most immediate results is a change in living space. Sometimes this change is very drastic. How can one handle a shift into more meager lodgings?

The popular media often gives images that only add to the hurt. There is a strong preference for displaying primarily lavish lifestyles in movies and on TV. One situation comedy shows a man working as a delivery truck driver in New York City while living in a personal space that would cost over one million dollars in real life. If your concern is how to purchase basic housing, this image will not help. One of the strong lessons for survival is that not everyone lives in a gated community with an inspiring view. Perhaps a parallel can be drawn to images around other situations. I know from personal experience that it can be very pleasant to take a basic class in ballroom dancing. But I have never seen a class that in any way resembles the TV show *Dancing with the Stars*. It is not helpful for beginning dance students to become enamored with the artful display given for entertainment purposes on this TV show. It can also be very depressing for someone going through a personal financial crisis to fixate on row after row of elegant homes in the suburbs. Not everyone has an easy time of it.

In my work of night ministry I saw the "other side" of life, seldom seen by people in the regular flow of work. This view can serve as a balance when the hard times come unexpectedly. It is a strong reminder that not everyone is "well off." While commuting by bus from Seattle to Portland, Oregon, to start a program of Operation Nightwatch for Portland twenty-five years ago I stayed on two different occasions at an old hotel off Burnside called the Estate. At that time the price for one night's lodging was four dollars plus one dollar for a key deposit. Permanent "residents" paid ninety dollars a month. My stay was brief, an attempt to better understand some of the people of the night I wanted to help. But this faded hostelry, a relic from the past, was a permanent home for many men. As I climbed the stairs up to my room I stepped over a pool of matted, blood-stained material on one stair landing, very likely wasted vomit, part of the physical trauma of late stage alcoholism. Before going into my room, I helped a man next to my room to open his door. He was too drunk to coordinate this simple task. Turning on the bare overhead light in my room, I surprised an army of cockroaches that fled in disarray up the walls and out of sight, away from the flood of light. My room had a single bed, a few old blankets, a small chest of drawers, plus a metal folding chair. The common bathroom was down the hall. In the middle of the night I was awakened by the sound of emergency vehicles sending an eerie horn blast out over the dark, empty streets below. This room had no accommodations for cooking or storage of food and no TV. This must have been difficult for permanent residents because they were afraid to go out at night. The streets around this downtown hotel were not safe, day or night. One night three men attacked an older man while looking for something of value. When they found nothing worth taking they threw him to the ground and pried dental work out of his mouth, attracted by the lure of shining silver or gold. Personal safety was also problematic inside this "hotel." One night a man was shot through one of the doors to a room. I pushed the chair up under the door knob inside my room before climbing into bed for the night. In my prayer by my bed that night I thanked God for the opportunity of service.

More recently, while attending classes as a Visiting Scholar at the Graduate Theological Union in Berkeley, California, I was given another look at some very unusual housing arrangements. Every morning I ran down University Avenue to the marina on San Francisco Bay and back. On my way down the avenue I ran under a major bridge taking traffic into downtown San Francisco. A man had assembled a makeshift "home" on the dirt under this bridge. For Howard, a few blankets and some odds and ends of trash made up his living space. Every morning I made two sack lunches, one for myself and another for him. I handed him a lunch as I passed his home, plus one dollar so he could buy a cup of coffee. Midway into my one-year stay in Berkeley this man disappeared from his normal haunt under the bridge. When I saw him on the street later he told me that the police had taken him to jail. He was held only for a day or two but they trashed his belongings. He then found a secret spot where he would not be bothered. I made arrangements with him to drop his sack lunch at a mutually agreed upon location. I never saw him in person again.

Along the same Berkeley street, I ran past another man, Pete, as he was beginning his workday of pushing a grocery cart in search of bottles or cans to return for the meager money he lived on. This man was old but not yet eligible for minimal social security. He lived under an overhang that protected the front entrance of a commercial building no longer in use. He did have an old sleeping bag but nothing else to protect him from weather changes or to give him some privacy. Like the man under the bridge, this man did not have a living space that offered at least a token of "inspiration" or uplift. One issue in such a situation or in other less-than-desirable accommodations is how to build in some kind of outlook that will be positive.

One of the strong lessons for situations of financial reversal with the need to live in less-than-optimal living conditions is that it becomes important to reach for experiences giving some inspiration not offered in the immediate living space. As I write this, my wife and I live in a townhouse in the greater Boulder, Colorado, area. We have no mountain view from our home. But the Coal Creek Trail is only a short distance from our front door. When I go out on this trail I can see the distant foothills of the Rockies. The free flowing, billowy white clouds often add to the beauty of the sky. Before my writing in this book I often walked by the small river that runs through this trail area. It was only when I stopped to really look at the ever-flowing water that I noticed tiny bubbles on the water's surface in places. One winter morning I was captured by the small world of a patch of new-fallen snow glistening in the sun of a new day. In the distance the snow-covered peaks of the Rocky Mountain range pulled me into their grip. I felt like I was one with this entire embrace of nature.

An early morning walk along the border of the county designated open space on this trail has become a time of inspiration for me. I delight in the sight of a pair of mallard ducks swimming in the clear water. The male holds high a proud head of green and blue hues that shine in the reflection of the sun like precious gem stones. The female wears her camouflage uniform of different hues of brown in keeping with her role to sit protectively on the new life waiting inside frail egg shells after mating season. At 6 a.m. on a winter morning, the white outline of the moon hangs high in the western sky while in the east a new day dawns with shades of pink and red held on unique sprays of cloud formation. All of this is visible over open fields and up on a small hill. And I become part of this natural community. No matter what your financial situation might be, everyone can be blessed by the marvels of our natural surround. This is very important in the general spiritual quest.

One of the most inspiring accounts of deliberately walking into the magical surround of nature as a way to deal with loss comes from the work of Julie Davis, a talented musician and storyteller. Living in the mountains of Colorado, nature has been an important part of her daily life for years. When she experienced painful losses, including the loss of both parents in death, she planned a two-month hike on the Colorado Trail. Walking with her dog and two pack goats, she became one with the free offering of nature's wonders. At night she stretched out to sleep on the spine of the Continental Divide, captivated by the living theatre above her as timeless starry galaxies called to her from out of the past. This truly remarkable journey of Julie is available on a ninety-minute cassette with original flute music titled "Journey to the Fluted Mountain: Stories and Music from the Colorado Trail."[12]

Many people over the years have discovered the mystery of strength in silence which includes the experience of being alone in the marvelous theatre of nature. Writing about Centering Prayer, Thomas Keating reaches back to some words of St. John of the Cross as he addresses the importance of silence:

> St. John of the Cross wrote: "The Father spoke one word from all eternity and he spoke in silence, and it is in silence that we hear it." This suggests that silence is God's first language and that all other languages are poor translations. The discipline of Centering Prayer and the other traditional practices are ways of refining our receptive apparatus so that we can perceive the word of God communicating itself with ever greater simplicity to our spirit and to our inmost being.[13]

In his extensive writings, the Trappist Monk Thomas Merton includes many references to the inspiration to be found in the small things of nature. One of the most interesting books coming from the legacy of Merton is the small book *When the Trees Say Nothing*. In this book we

---

12. Davis, *Journey to the Fluted Mountain*. The ninety-minute cassette is available from Winter Wind Music, P.O. Box 1302, Nederland, Colorado 80466.

13. Keating, *Intimacy with God*, 55.

are drawn closer to nature and to creation as we walk anew in the forest, see the flowers and trees, animals and birds against the background of changing seasons. We need to listen to the words of Merton as we appreciate the small things that can get lost in our busy rush to right an economic reversal. Words such as the following:

> Sweet afternoon! Cool breezes and a clear sky!
> This day will not come again.
> The bulls lie under the tree in the corner of the field.
> Quiet afternoon! The blue hills, the day lilies in the wind.
> This day will not come again.[14]

This chapter looks at hard times in terms of such situations as being unemployed, having disabilities that preclude employment, and/or losing a house to foreclosure. In these situations it is good to consider a range of coping mechanisms, including embracing silence in the surround of nature. But hard times in our country do not compare with what people in other countries are going through today. What about a country where death and destruction parade down the main streets of cities on a regular basis or come from the sky in the form of high tech bombs that shatter all life-forms with no warning? A country with a history of violence and bare survival as illustrated today in Afghanistan? A place where a man may survive on a pension of four dollars a month after being discharged with wounds from the military?[15] A country where the plea is for a better life for the next generation as parents feel the daily struggle to survive with little food, poor housing, and no schools for their children?[16] Greg Mortenson describes these conditions in his latest *New York Times* bestseller, *Stones Into Schools.*[17] As he retraces some of the recent history of this country he mentions conditions in 1996 when the Taliban controlled most of the country. Severe edicts were enforced forbidding such normal behavior as listening to music, playing cards, and laughing in public.[18] Mortenson describes in some detail the horrible condition of women in Afghanistan under the Taliban. A survey conducted by Physicians for Human Rights in 1998 found that 42 per-

---

14. Merton, *Trees Say Nothing*, 121.

15. Mortenson, *Stones Into Schools*, 55.

16. Ibid., 63.

17. Mortenson, *Stones Into Schools*.

18. Ibid., 71.

cent of the respondents could be classified as having post-traumatic stress disorder. Fully 97 percent showed signs of major depression and 21 percent had thoughts of killing themselves.[19]

To read the report of Mortenson is to read a story of war and death and killing. When he walked into Kabul in 2002, it was at a precarious place. The population was traumatized, "its infrastructure destroyed, its suffering and its horrors etched upon the gray and shattered surfaces of what had once been its architecture."[20] One of Mortenson's close friends in Afghanistan has been Sadhar Khan, a commander in the fight against the Soviets. Khan has known what it was like to bury a friend since grade school after this man bled to death in his arms. For the purpose of this book, it is interesting that Khan found refuge in solitude as he sat on the bank of the Warduj River. Even in the midst of the kind of extreme hard times institutionalized in Afghanistan, silence in nature had a healing affect upon him. This is strong testimony for such an experience, even in the face of lesser hard times like unemployment in our country. Sadhar Khan wrote a poem describing his experience of the river that appears in full in Mortenson's latest book.[21] In this poem he explains why he sits by the side of the river, doing nothing in spite of the fact that there is much to be done, there is so little food for his people, and so few have jobs. He says simply that he is here . . . "to listen to the quiet, the water, and the singing trees." For him this was the sound of peace. His last words in the poem are "I am so weary of war.[22]

As you read the above paragraphs, they may seem far removed from the problems you or others face during difficult times. But look at them again. There is new hope, new inspiration in purposely allowing ourselves to really experience a freely offered embrace of nature and to truly appreciate the present, the "now." We are part of an ongoing, eternal process. Another dramatic illustration of the power of such an experience comes from the diary of Anne Frank. Hiding with her Jewish family in Holland during the horrible time of the Holocaust, she could never go outside. Before she was found and died in a German death camp one of the most important single things that gave her hope was a large tree growing just beyond her bedroom window. She watched the changes of

19. Ibid., 74–75.
20. Ibid., 79.
21. Ibid., 99–100.
22. Ibid.

leaves, feeling that all would be okay as long as the tree lived. Recently, it was determined that this tree was deceased. The official verdict was that it should be given a merciful death. But the common people, realizing its symbolic significance, launched a strong protest. This tree was a living presence in view just beyond a self-imposed prison. All of us need the equivalent of such a tree.

I am interested in the many different things and experiences used by people in a reach for daily hope, even inspiration. One woman hung a framed picture of an elderly woman in a prominent place in her small apartment after going through divorce and then facing the prospect of looking for work in a new city. For her, this single picture spoke a message of encouragement. For others, a stuffed animal or loved pet may provide important moments of a positive feeling that all will eventually be well. One senior citizen sometimes reflects on her childhood at a time when living conditions were not ideal. One high point in her life at that time was to slip into the unlocked front door of a large Roman Catholic Church where she sat or walked in silence on a weekday. My father died last year at the age of ninety-six. The last thirty years of his life were spent in a small apartment in a building for seniors and finally in one room in an assisted living facility. Except for the last few years he had the company of his wife of seventy years, my mother. He also lived across the street from a major shopping mall in north Seattle. One of his favorite activities was to walk to the mall and stroll around inside. He did this twice a day. He was not one of those who walked the mall for exercise. He watched other people. It was his way to reach for new experiences, new touches of life. He could not understand why others in his building never went to the mall.

THE HUMAN SPIRIT

People are important during times of major loss and for life in all of its ups and downs. It is very helpful to talk to someone about a loss or any major change in life, good or bad. Unfortunately, when hard times come it can be difficult to develop a new circle of acquaintances. Back in the late 1960s when Rev. Bud Palmberg started the Operation Nightwatch program in Seattle, he told the story of a man he met downtown late one night. This man had recently gone through a divorce. He moved into a cheap apartment downtown near his work. And he was lonely. On many nights he took a roll of quarters with him as he walked the streets. Every time he passed a homeless person he offered this stranger one of his quarters, hoping that a conversation would follow. It is normal to need people in our life. I worked for a chain grocery store located in an interracial district of Seattle while going to graduate school. Some of the customers using this store lived across the street in a low-cost apartment building. A few of the women who were senior citizens made it a practice to walk across the street several times a day, buying one item at a time so they could talk to one of us in the store.

Loneliness was one of the major problems I saw at night on a regular basis while doing night ministry. Sometimes seniors living alone go to a downtown tavern at night to find people. Unfortunately, the body handles alcohol differently as it ages, making some of these women and men vulnerable to alcoholism as part of their search for someone to talk to or someone who will listen. Another aspect of a change in relationships with downsizing, for some reason, is that a person can become preoccupied with thoughts of better times, believing that warm relationships are no longer possible. It is important to both honor the past and to let go, allowing for new relationships. At 5 a.m. in the darkness before dawn on the downtown streets of Aberdeen, Washington, I met a man walking aimlessly along a sidewalk. At the time I was working with local clergy trying to start a night ministry. When I reached out a hand to Kevin and invited him to sit with me in my car, he shared his story. He was preoccupied with feelings of loneliness, saying things like, "I don't have any friends; I am all alone." He volunteered the information that he had "cried so much" that he could not cry anymore.

Kevin had gone through the experience of his wife leaving him while he was living in Seattle. He then lived with his three daughters after his wife's death. The oldest was nine years old. The building they were living in caught fire. Two of the girls burned to death. He jumped out of the window, hugging the nine-year-old. Homeless at the time of our meeting, Kevin told me that he was "dying of AIDS," contracted from his careless use of needles as a drug addict. An alcoholic, he was declared unfit to care for his daughter. She was taken from him by the court. As he wandered the streets of a strange town he said that he did not want his nine-year-old daughter to see him "dying like this." Energy for reaching out to new friends was drained as he poured all of his feelings into memories of the past. Given his physical condition, new relationships would be difficult. For others it is an emotional block from the past without the physical barrier. An important lesson here is that we must honor the past but go on with the present. Kevin had been a musician. He said that he wanted to sing a song for me as I sat with him in my car, a song he wrote for his wife. With this, he started beating a hand on his side of the dash to simulate some kind of musical instrument and then sang the following song—a sad song of love lost that could be sung by many others as they struggle in a less-than-desirable situation, or those who have lost a loved one without the surround of homelessness:

> I thought about you all night long
> Couldn't get no sleep.
> We used to have a love so right
> My love was oh so deep.
> Oh, must have been a year or so
> Since I laid eyes on you.
> I've been so miserable.
> I've been so blue.
> Oh, everybody keeps asking me
> Why I feel this way.
> In my mind I can't be free
> Till you come home to stay.
> Oh, I threw away your picture
> I tried to forget you.
> In my mind I hear you laugh
> Lord, what can I do?

How much of a struggle is it for people who have moved down the social register or who have simply moved to a new town to find new relationships? First, it is important to acknowledge that social relationships are important. A woman in her fifties who went through divorce and then moved across the country alone is a good example of how to reach out for new people. She first worked hard at different jobs to bring in the basics for living. Then she joined a single's club in a local church. Next, she found a ski club that featured social events as well as outdoor activity. She first felt very strongly that it was up to her to generate a new social network. She has done that very successfully over the last ten years. It is possible to find new friends in a new place or to reach out for new people if older, "sunshine" friends disappear when times get hard.

Lots of lessons come from our situation today. We can also learn from the past when our country as a whole or some part of the country was going through difficult times. Some in our time can recall personal or family stories around the Great Depression. I was born in the bleak years of that Depression. I remember my Dad talking about how hard it was for him to find work. There have been other troubled times in our country. In 1912 bread lines were feeding thousands of unemployed men in New York City. In that same year the Los Angeles police drove back demonstrators protesting unemployment. The timber town of Everett, Washington, went through very tough times in 1915 when there were so few payrolls that the saloons were overwhelmed by full houses of destitute men. In the same year, Portland, Oregon, gave blankets to unemployed indigents who were sleeping on the cold floor of a public hall.

My contacts during night ministry in Aberdeen, which included reaching out to the homeless, came back in the 1990s. The area was hit hard by a downturn in the timber industry after the spotted owl was declared an endangered species, calling for a renewal of interest in protecting its natural habitat, the stands of tall timber in the Evergreen State. Timber giants like Weyerhaeuser began cutting jobs instead of trees. Talking to people back then, I felt some of the pain of family members. Living without an income is a family affair. "I have disappointed my family" were the first words I heard from Sue, a single mother. With these words Sue began to cry and reached for a Kleenex to restore her appearance. Then she talked about how hard it was to get by on unemployment with little hope of getting another job. Pressed for more of her story, Sue had strong feelings that she had disappointed her mother and her estranged husband. She depended on others to get by and this hurt. Sue lived in a house owned by her mother, paying only utilities. She sat in this old house with no money to buy plants for the yard, no office to dress up for, no work assignments to help her feel needed.

There are many ways in which hard times can become difficult for a family. Survival strategies must give serious consideration to all members of a family. Sue did have a job as a data entry person for a company that moved out of the town. This job did not pay a lot but it was secure. She had medical coverage and paid holidays. At that time her husband worked as an auto repairman in a union shop. Their marriage was "a little stormy." When she lost her job and then he lost his job the marriage took a dive. When I talked with her they had been separated for three years. It was hard for Sue to really rest at night. Drifting off in sleep was very difficult. But then some days she just felt like sleeping all day. It was not easy for her to "get up and get dressed," since there was no one, nothing to dress up for. One of her major concerns in this process was that she felt her daughter was brought into the pain of the situation too much. Sue talked to this twelve-year-old about her down feelings, but she was aware that there was a potential danger in being too reliant on the child to serve as a listening board.

As indicated above, normal roles in the family can change with major shifts in available work. Family roles change with any major shift in work roles. One example of this is the situation where one or both parents change from working in an office away from home to working at home with the assistance of a computer. During the hard times in the timber industry in Washington State a number of men were forced to reconsider their position in the family, not an easy thing to do. Bill, for example, talked with me about how much he enjoyed his work as a manager of men. But when we met he volunteered the information that he was drawing unemployment while his wife worked. He cooked and took care of the house. One of his concerns was how his children were taking the change in roles. He said that he wondered what the kids thought when they told their friends at school that their dad made their lunch. Sometimes he had cabin fever, sitting alone at home all day. He could not wander far from home since he had to be available when the children came home from school in the early afternoon. Late in the day after his wife came home and they had the evening meal he would sometimes take off on his motorcycle for a long ride.

Some of the most poignant references to hard times and the serious impact on all family members come from the words of children. Serious letters to Santa Claus can capture these feelings. Back when I was working in Aberdeen and when times were hard with a decline in the timber industry, Thad, a boy in the third or fourth grade wrote his letter to Santa Claus and it appeared in the *Tacoma News Tribune* in December of 1992. Thad first tells Santa that his dad is not working anymore. He then goes on to describe a family in crisis, with his mom putting food on the table but not eating herself and the house lighted with candles after the lights were shut off by the city. His final plea to Santa is for a job for his dad and then a request that he be taken to heaven so his dad would no longer need to buy him clothes.

More recently, letters to Santa that find their way into the press continue their childhood pleas for help. In 2001 one headline captured attention with the words, "Dear Santa: Letters from children take a more serious, selfless tone this year." Seanna Adcox with the Associated Press shared part of one letter: "Mommy lost her job after Sept. 11," six-year-old

Paris wrote to Santa Claus. "Daddy works two jobs now. Please help."[23] Katherine Roth, again with the Associated Press, shared the following with a dateline of December 2, 1999: "The letters were addressed to the jolly old elf himself, but for those reading Santa's mail, it was hard to keep a joyous face. 'Some of these just break your heart,' said Jean Shaw, her eyes misty as she read a letter from a child in Garnerville, N.Y. 'He says he and his family just want toys and they don't care if they're used, because his mother has no money.'"[24]

The lesson from Thad is heavy; it is imperative to talk to children when a major crisis comes for the family. Too often we fail to recognize that young children can be very perceptive. They need to be told that they are loved and given assurances as much as possible. It is always good to allow time for sharing with children in the home. A family may not be going through financial hard times, but still, sharing is important. Talking is important. Perhaps one form of assurance in the case of unemployment can come from awareness that mom and dad are doing their best to find work. Parents must, however, avoid the temptation to develop strong feelings of inadequacy in their job search. Lots of people are out of work. The actual numbers depend heavily on where the family happens to be living in the country. It may be helpful to consider some approaches to being out of a job that are not beneficial. I list some I have found to be informative, perhaps you can add to this list:

- *Being unrealistic.* This is the proverbial "head in the sand" approach, avoiding to take a realistic look at the situation. Unfortunately, some of the proclamations in the faith community can be misinterpreted in a way that actually encourages this view. True faith empowers one to face real life situations and challenges.

- *Pushing the panic button.* This points to a nervous and frantic attack with lots of emails and telephone calls but no basic, well thought out plan.

- *Failure to do the homework about a place where one wants to find employment.* It is always the case that employers appreciate someone who has taken the trouble to find out about the company, agency, etc.

- *Trying to do it alone.* Failing to use help from natural networks of family, friends, etc.

23. Adcox, "Dear Santa."
24. Roth, "Tragic cases bring tears."

- *Over or underestimating your talents.* Either approach can hurt the job search.

A list of things to do when you have had a gap in employment and are now looking for a new job appeared on Internet on May 2, 2008. I believe these suggestions are still applicable today.

1. *Use your cover letter to your advantage.* In addition to showcasing your experience and skills, your cover letter can answer any questions about an employment gap that a manager might have.

2. *Network.* It's a small world. The more people who know you're looking for a job, the more likely you are to hear about an open position.

3. *Knowledge is power.* Stay abreast of new trends, technology and developments in your industry by attending seminars and courses to prove your time off doesn't put you at a disadvantage.

4. *Volunteer.* Many employers view volunteer work as relevant experience, so don't be afraid to devote some free time supporting a favorite cause. Volunteering not only benefits others, it also allows you to network and beefs up your resume.

5. *Stay positive.* During an interview, emphasize the experience, accomplishments and enthusiasm you can bring to the position. Don't focus on the gap in employment.[25]

On the issue of children and unemployment, some professionals encourage projective probing when it is difficult for the child to express feelings in words. This may include the encouragement to draw pictures or the use of key words that the child can project his or her feeling into. The list below is only suggestive. A specific list must be tailored to match the age and ability level of the child.

- Can you draw a picture of the job your mom/dad had?
- Why did she/he lose the job?
- How did you find out about his/her job loss?
- What do people say about the job loss?
- What would you like to say about the job loss?

25. Rasmussen, www.CareerBuilder.com.

- What do your friends do when they worry about their mom or dad's loss of a job?

- What can you do when you worry or feel bad?

The key to using any device like this is the follow-up by the parent. Perhaps any words given by a child can become talking points. The child should not need to bury feelings about something as important as a job loss.

I see value in giving some kind of projective option for the child to use when talking is difficult. I recall seeing a boy in juvenile detention back when I was working as a caseworker for the State of Washington. This boy had not been seen by anyone working on his placement in a foster home for some time because of an oversight in the system. When I first saw him he was obviously very dejected. I talked for awhile and then gave him a blank sheet of paper and a pen, asking him to draw me a picture. He drew a race car with the driver in the car represented as a small black dot. As I continued to see him and continued to give him the opportunity to draw he stayed with the race car picture but over time the driver grew bigger and bigger until it assumed a normal size for the car. I saw this as one way for him to express how he felt about himself.

JOB LOSS IN PERSPECTIVE

There is a need for general models that are helpful in the process of losses such as the loss of a job. Rev. Jan Friend, a counselor with Lutheran Social Services in Tacoma, Washington, while I was involved in night ministry, gave workshops on losses of different kinds, including the loss of a job. He often shared his own story. His father and mother fled Germany years ago with their seven children, heading for a new life in America. They lost things in the process, arriving in the United States with very few material possessions. During this ordeal the entire family went through a grieving process. "How do you mourn loss?" became a major interest of Rev. Friend. He saw the loss of a job as one of many experiences best understood in terms of a grieving process. When someone loses a job the following will most likely occur:

> There will be a grieving process not unlike that associated with the death of a loved one. Learn to accept it. Recognize that what is happening is going to take its toll. Take stock of your blessings. Try to remember that you are not alone and that it is not the end of the world. Help each other.

In a workshop, Rev. Friend asked, "In all of life what have you lost?" This question introduced an open-ended discussion about loss of things, loss of relationships. Other questions included: "With these losses, how did you do your grieving?" and "Looking at your responses to grief, what do you now see as most effective?" He also used such basic material as a listing of the stages of grief, applying this to job loss. One such list is shared below:

1. We are in a state of shock.

2. We express emotion.

3. We feel depressed and very lonely.

4. We may experience physical symptoms of distress.

5. We may become panicky.

6. We feel a sense of guilt about the loss.

7. We are filled with anger and resentment.

8. We resist returning.

9. Gradually, hope comes through.

10. We struggle to affirm reality.

In his analysis of the pain around job loss, Rev. Friend suggests that people most need to have moral and emotional support—even more than specific help in finding a job.

The reference to financial loss in terms of general conditions of loss and stress invites a look at conditions that foster depression. We all handle stressful situations differently, depending on factors such as genetic background, support systems, etc. For some people, prolonged unemployment can ultimately be part of very serious depression. The neurosciences are teaching us a lot about what happens in the brain during depression.

Unfortunately, when a person is unemployed he or she is also likely not to have health coverage. Some health insurance plans include payment for mental health services. With no income and no health insurance it becomes very hard for the unemployed to access therapy as one way to cope, but this may be a very important need.

One painful part of being out of work is that it can really hurt the sense of self-worth. Twenty-five years ago while trying to start a program of night ministry for Denver I was forced to draw unemployment for a few months. I can remember the long lines snaking around the block outside in warm weather and then inside when winter came. One of my problems was that I was forced to wait on the whims of a man or woman behind a counter who had regular employment in spite of the fact that this person most likely did not have my background which included a PhD and years of college teaching. This experience forces one to take a new look at personal worth. Out in Aberdeen I talked with Dave one day as he sat on the sidewalk in front of the Aberdeen Rescue Mission. He had hit a new low in feelings of self-worth. He did not feel that his opinion was of any value. He was just "hanging on," totally preoccupied with his personal plight. This was evident as he commented about passing cars. He said that he felt that people were "staring" at him. He was waiting for free food. A Gospel service would precede the meal. He would have little emotional involvement with anyone during the evening. Dave was simply waiting for better times, for another chance.

SIMPLE SPIRITUALITY

Changes in life circumstances can have a profound influence on anyone's faith. The *New Yorker* is not known as a platform for the discussion of "faith and doubt." But that was the caption for a collection of short stories appearing in the bleak spring of 2008 when our country was feeling the pangs of recession. One of the short stories, titled "Winter Light," includes the following words, spoken by the minister of a church after the showing of the Bergman film, *Winter Light*:

> . . . Humanity in peril, lonely, afraid, as we seek power and find only more fear and loneliness, hiding from one another and from what we really want and what would give us true strength and friendship and new life, and yet here it is, all the while, knocking on our door.[26]

It is reassuring to know that even in the direst of circumstances reaching for and touching the Divine can be very real. I saw this often in my work at night. While on the downtown streets at night I wore the standard black clergy shirt and white clergy collar. This was appropriate in my case because I was ordained as a Protestant minister after graduating from Bible college before going on to earn my PhD and then to teach college.

26. Wolff, "Winter Light," 70.

After ordination I did serve as the pastor of two different small, rural churches in Oregon. I appreciate the legacy of Protestantism. Some ten years ago I became a member of the Roman Catholic Church. More recently, I became involved in a new expression of Catholicism with no organizational ties to Rome, the Ecumenical Catholic Communion (ECC). I appreciate the legacy of Catholicism. In 2008 I published the first book to be written about the ECC.[27] When invited I now attend different churches and share around the topic of personal survival in hard times. Back to my work in ministry at night, my most memorable encounter on the city streets came on Burnside Street in downtown Portland. Three men arrived in town after riding in an open boxcar going west from the east coast. On first contact these strangers wanted information about places where they might get food in town. Later in the day I saw them again. One of the three said that he wanted to talk with me in private. As I stood with him beside a parking meter he looked at me and uttered the plea "bless me." I put a hand on his shoulder, closed my eyes, and invited him into the prayer. When I opened my eyes I looked at him again and saw a face transformed. I walked away from that chance encounter like walking on a cloud. On another day, I saw a homeless man curled up under a blanket on the sidewalk while reading the Bible. It was not unusual for people to ask me to pray for them or someone else. God can be found even in circumstances that would seem not to nurture faith. On the higher end of things, God can also be found in corporate boardrooms and in homes with a lot of "creature comforts."

It is hard to visualize the chance encounters that are part of the work of night ministry if you are not familiar with the scene. As part of this work, I often walked the downtown streets alone and spent time in taverns between the hours of 10 p.m. and 2 a.m. I also recruited clergy volunteers who were willing to participate at least one night a week. Since I was the director of the program my time was not limited to the late hours of 10:00 and 2:00. I was on call at other times, worked in an office, and on occasion visited the downtown scene at different times. This included my early morning exploration of the downtown turf in Aberdeen while setting up a night ministry for that city.

One of my volunteers was a minister and a retired literature professor from the University of Washington, Rev. Harold Simonson, PhD.

---

27. Jones, *New Light.*

He painted a picture of his impressions after spending some time in the Acme Tavern in downtown Tacoma:

"Acme Tavern"
Getting things together, Lefty?
Lost job, room; pickup smashed; homeless now—
Litany intoned, he nudges his one buddy who,
glass empty, stained fingertip signaling another,
slowly turns his stool to show a graveled face,
spaniel eyes focusing on nothing.
     Down the bar sits a black giant,
arms like aging oak,
every sip a thankful sigh.
How's life, my friend?
     Happy. My mammy
call from New Orleans, say
she's doin' fine—at ninety-one
     Timeless smoke
Smudges walls
muffles coughs
makes halos.
     A sooty parka hunches solitary,
tractor hands fidget dead Buds,
his table centering the littered world.
How you doing tonight?
Whatcha know?
Truth's simple.
What's that mean?
We're talking, that's what.
  Where's Jesus?
Right here.
Man I luvya.
Love you too.
     I raise him to a hug—to eye
my soiled vest, my cross
no bigger than a dime—then
zig-zag out
Hoping something's found[28]

In situations of financial reversal, some of the traditional approaches to things "spiritual" can seem to have little relevance. One of

---

28. As a personal friend, Hal wrote these words for author Dean Jones in about 1995.

the hallmarks of poverty is that attention turns more to the immediate situation, to the demands of looking for work or looking for a place to stay. Formal church services often turn more to the unseen, to the past, or the future. For one who is going through a time of economic hardship astute theological discussions of the nature of God as presented in different books of the Old Testament, for example, seem far removed from immediate, pressing demands. I have not had long periods of unemployment, but I have been in situations where the immediate situation was very compelling. From these experiences, I wonder what would happen if we could truly sense the Divine in all, including the very immediate, personal surround.

While doing my night ministry I ran several ultramarathon distances as benefit events for the program. This was a natural thing for me to do because I had been running marathons since the age of forty, turning then to the ultramarathon distance and once completing the 72-mile run around Lake Tahoe. At this writing I am considering another 26.2-mile marathon to celebrate my eightieth birthday in 2012. While in Tacoma I ran the distance from near the entrance to Mount Rainier National Park to downtown (50 miles) on three different occasions, the last time on my sixty-fifth birthday in a time of eight hours and thirty-five minutes. At 6 a.m. on the morning of that last run I saw a herd of elk as I began running. I was singing to myself "Kyrie Eleison" (Lord be with me). At that time I was a member of the Holy Disciples Catholic Church in Puyallup, Washington, where these words were often sung. I know every foot of the 50-mile stretch of highway down from the mountain. For eight hours and thirty-five minutes I was watching every small patch of the highway shoulder ahead of me. A bottle of water hung from a leather band around my waist. I was immediately aware of oncoming traffic, changes in weather, and the movement of my body under a T-shirt and shorts. I mention this experience to call attention to the fact that at times our focus is on the here and now. Appeals to ultimate destiny, to the "spiritual" in an abstract way can seem to be simply not that relevant. As I read the Gospels, I am continually aware of how Jesus touched immediate situations: healing a blind man, reaching out to a leper, etc. The Divine can enter into our immediate situation. This is a profound "survival strategy" when facing economic hardships.

Twenty years ago I made trips to Los Angeles from Tacoma where I worked with local clergy to start a night ministry. On one occasion I stayed at the YMCA in Hollywood. In this place the accommodations were sparse; I used a communal bathroom. One morning a man standing next to me in this bathroom was doing his laundry in the sink. A tangle of rusted metal held an old TV set up from the floor in my room but the set was not working. At the desk I overheard the clerk on duty tell one of the lodgers that it would be best for him to go directly to the police station to report a theft of two hundred dollars, since they were unlikely to respond if he simply called on the phone.

After staying in the room at the Y, I made my way on foot to a large church serving the immediate Hollywood area. Sitting in an adult forum at this church on a Sunday morning I became aware of how hard it might be for someone who is going through a hard time to simply attend church. On that Sunday I am afraid that I was still too preoccupied with thoughts of my meager sleeping arrangement to really tune into the Sunday morning services. I was comparing my lodgings with the palatial estates in Beverly Hills I ran past during my morning workouts. During the church service I noticed a bug crawling along my arm and began wondering if I had picked up body lice. While in Tacoma doing my work at night I sometimes made the rounds with a local clergy volunteer. One night a Lutheran pastor who was out with me invited a stranger to her church. The man did make it into the building, but only after driving past the edifice three or four times to get his courage up.

There are many ways in which a community of faith can be very helpful during hard times. On Sunday, June 22, 2008, I attended Mass at St. Matthew Church in Orange, California. The Presiding Bishop for the Ecumenical Catholic Communion, Bishop Peter Hickman, gave a homily that was powerful as a message for troubled times. On that Sunday a gallon of regular, unleaded gasoline was selling for $5.15 at Needles, California. A local paper in Arizona ran a front-page article on the increase in the number of homes cut off from utility services because of delinquency in payments. The Iraq war seemed to be going on without end at a cost of several billion dollars a month with the number of casualties growing everyday. Concerns over a possible war with Iran, potential problems because of global warming, major concerns over healthcare in the United States all served to increase anxiety, even fear. And Bishop Hickman rose to the challenge of the times in his homily that addressed fear directly. As he reminded his congregation, hate is not the opposite of love; fear is truly the opposite of love. If we fear we are too likely to simply react in kind when faced with danger. Fearing war we go to war, fearing theft of material possessions we are more likely to steal ourselves. The Bishop also shared his personal anxiety about his ability to pay the mortgage on his house and said that he was now driving slower on the freeway to save gas, a welcome openness to private life challenges seldom heard in a homily. The Gospels challenge us to replace fear with love, becoming men and women who rise up to the problems of our time instead of becoming part of the problem. Rabbi Michael Lerner reinforced this same focus in his book *The Left Hand of God*, where he suggests that we adopt a new worldview, replacing models of domination and fear with hope and love.[29]

Rev. Mary Hardy, Assisting Priest at St. Mary Magdalene Episcopal Church in Boulder, gave another sermon fitting for the times in September 2009. During some of my time in writing for this book I attended this congregation. Rev. Hardy said, in her sermon, that she sometimes found herself parking her car when she noticed a man or woman standing on a street corner with a sign wanting help. She walked over to the stranger to stand with him or her. Rev. Hardy also mentioned that she was still waiting for the sale of her house in another town in Colorado where she lived before taking her new position at St. Mary Magdalene. Under the leadership of the Rector, Rev. Mike Houlik, this church gives 25 percent of its operating budget to needs beyond the local church. As one demonstration of interest in the homeless, youth from this congregation, under the guidance of youth minister Don Martinson together with a few adults, became part of an exposure to poverty experience. They camped out off the streets in Boulder in makeshift, cardboard shelters and then delivered small packages of basic essentials directly to those who were homeless. Reporting to the congregation during a worship service after this event, those who participated shared how they were changed in the process in their attitudes toward the homeless. They spoke, for example, about the reality that homelessness is not always a choice. Some they saw were, in fact, working but not making enough to purchase regular housing.

A powerful message on survival in hard times was given by Rev. Jason Hays, Associate Minister for Pastoral Care and Congregational Life at the First Congregational Church of the United Church of Christ in Boulder on Sunday, January 24, 2010. This Sunday came shortly after the tragic earthquake in Haiti. Rev. Hays titled his sermon "Finding

---

29. Lerner, *Left Hand of God*.

Hope in Despair." His scripture for this message was Psalm 130, which includes the words, "O Israel, hope in the Lord." The sermon had a lot to say about hope in times of despair. Hope was defined not as some external commodity but as part of the fabric of life. And it was placed in the communal setting of the church. Rev. Hays began his sermon that day by referring to a *CNN* news photo of a mother in Port au Prince crying uncontrollably over the loss of her son in the chaos of the city after the killer earthquake. In the sermon, Rev. Hays suggested that often it is the small glimpses of light, of hope that make the difference. To illustrate this he shared his personal journey with depression, saying that during that time it was the small encouragement of friends, the simple act of getting out of bed, and drinking a chocolate shake that made the difference for him. The children's sermon he gave before the main message was very timely. Speaking to the children as they gathered around him in the front of the church, Rev. Hays held up pictures of children, a woman, and a man crying. The children were invited to think about who they could talk to if they were sad, if they were crying. Parents and teachers were held up as possibilities along with the word that God made us to have feelings; they are okay. During this worship service the following words of hope were shared in the bulletin and as those present joined their voices together:

> On this day of wonder and awe, we gather,
> Not in isolation, but in community—a community that cares for
> one another.
> Let us hope when hope seems hopeless,
> When the dreams we dreamed have died.

The experience of God does not require an academic degree or financial status. It is all about the most basic stuff of life as we live it. In Catholic churches and in many Protestant churches a typical worship service includes Communion or Holy Eucharist. Here the common elements of bread and wine are transformed into the body and blood of Christ. Common stuff becomes uncommon. God walks with us in the everyday, mundane stuff that makes up life as we live it. Being unemployed does not remove us from God. Whatever our daily experience brings, it is touched with the Divine. Words, ideas, the spinning of colorful phrases are not the ingredients for a walk with God. Today as never before we need to get back to the basics, to the simple joy of the eating of a crisp apple, the sight of laughter in a child's face, the singing of birds outside our window on a winter day. The meditation tradition offers a lot to us in pushing for the immediate presence of God. I have been involved in Centering Prayer as taught by Father Thomas Keating and find that this gives me reinforcement for quietly settling into a time that becomes sacred.

In his book *Awakenings*, Father Keating makes a strong plea for the relevance of the Divine in all experiences of life. He includes a story of a man who is driving along a highway, feeling fine in every way. Then he has a flat tire and his sense of well-being, including an awareness of God, is lost. He becomes anxious as he tries to fix the tire, more stressed waiting for help, and does not return to his state of calm until he is safely home, the car in its garage.[30] The lesson for us is clear, we must try to avoid the "flat tire syndrome" in which God is put on hold during a crisis time. God does not pull the plug on us. He walks with us when we are working or when things are going good as well as during those times of darkness for whatever reason. It is not unusual for times of serious crisis to become an arena for a dance between faith and doubt.

The best of the long tradition of Christianity has a great deal to do about going through difficulties. This began with the words and actions of Jesus. He brings hope for everyone, as expressed so eloquently in the following words:

> Blessed are you who are poor and lowly and afflicted,
> For the Kingdom of God is yours.
> Blessed are you that hunger and seek with eager desire now,
> For you shall be filled and completely satisfied.
> Blessed are you who weep and sob now,
> For you shall laugh.
> (Luke 6:20–22)

Jesus came at a time of considerable social unrest. There were many poor people and considerable tension between the rich and the poor. The opulence and splendor of the royal court was a source of deep pain for common people. Jesus was part of a stratified social system. The very wealthy made up the royal court, Herod the Great a prime example. Next were merchants, large landowners, tax farmers, bankers, and families of inherited means. Then came the middleclass, retail traders, small tradesmen, and craftsmen—the class Jesus was born into. Finally, at the bottom of the status hierarchy two groups of poor people struggled for

30. Keating, *Awakenings*, 9.

daily survival: those who tried to earn a living as slaves or day laborers and people who lived from some kind of subsidy. Beggars were the very lowest on the scale: the sick, blind, lame, and lepers. There were also the fatherless and widows, victims of misfortune who needed and received the assistance of the community.

Some of the help for the poor at the time of Jesus parallels the type of assistance given today. In his day there were institutionalized processes reaching out to the unfortunate. The poor were allowed to pick the leftovers in the field. Giving to the needy became an expected part of high feast days such as the Passover or Feast of Purim. In Jerusalem up to one-half of the second tithe went to the poor. The synagogue became a welfare center. Food and clothing were given. This system of charity was so well organized that it attracted many proselytes from the Gentile community. But the poor were generally despised by religious teachers. They were excluded from most sacred places, overburdened with laws and taxes, and often subject to search and seizure of goods. People in general were not encouraged to go beyond the law in giving to others.

Jesus walked into this picture with a bold new agenda for the poor, the outcast. He spoke of new hope for the lowly and the needy. His most fundamental appeal was to the masses, the multitudes. Crowds coming to hear him often included the sick and destitute, the suffering poor, and the blind, lame, and crippled. Jesus did not appeal to the upper classes. His last days were a protest, a challenge to the religious and political establishment. In Luke and elsewhere in the Gospels the coming of the Kingdom is described in terms of an eschatological reversal. The poor become rich and the rich poor. The parable of the rich man and Lazarus in Luke 16:19–26 is a prime example of this. Jesus was anointed to preach good news to the poor.

There has been a long line of individuals following Christ in his compassion for the poor. St. Francis of Assisi was a major influence in the thirteenth century. For St. Francis, piety and poverty were not antithetical. As he saw the situation, since poverty was part of Christ's way of life it can be a worthy choice for others. For him, helping the poor was redemptive work. Today as in the thirteenth century, a number of people follow in the tradition of St. Francis. In this tradition, almshouses were developed for the poor, as well as hospitals and wayside hotels to shelter "tramps" and offer meals for the poor. There were also congregations established specifically to serve the poor.

Toyohiko Kagawa was one of the very important individuals serving the poor in the twentieth century. Born on July 10, 1888, in the home of a wealthy family in Japan, Kagawa was given extensive exposure to Buddhism and Classical Confucian texts before his attraction to Christianity while in middle school. The missionaries always treated him with respect. He was drawn to a description of God as one who cares and loves. Memorizing whole chapters of the Bible, he saw as his high calling service to the poor. Leaving his family home with nothing but the clothes on his back, he entered the Presbyterian College in Tokyo in 1905. In seminary he shared his small room with a beggar he picked up along the road. He gave his meager allowance and his shoes and clothes to those in distress while he wore rags. At the age of twenty-one, Kagawa moved into the depths of the Shinkawa slum. Here ten thousand people lived like sardines in "homes" six-by-six-feet square. This space often held a family of five or six with no windows, a communal kitchen, a water hydrant outside, and a common toilet. Living with those he helped, Kagawa was subjected to all sorts of difficulties. He contracted a serious eye infection from his close neighbors. His service included offering burial rites for those who died when surviving family members had no money for such service. And in the midst of his work with and for the poor Kagawa found time to write. At the age of fifty-seven he could point to authorship of sixty books with over two million copies sold.[31]

The work of Liberation Theology by Roman Catholic priests in Latin America came as another major milestone in the work of the Christian community on behalf of people living in dire circumstances. It was direct exposure to unbelievable poverty that inspired these priests to action. They saw people everyday who invoked deep feelings of concern. One woman, for example, went to a priest after a mass to confess in sorrow that she had gone to communion without going to confession first. When the priest asked for an explanation, she replied, through tears, that she had gone for three days without food, only drank water. When she saw the small pieces of white bread she went to communion just out of hunger for that meager amount of food. The priest's own eyes filled with tears as he recalled the words of Jesus at his Last Supper and the true meaning of Holy Eucharist during which bread is transformed into true life. It was experiences like this that compelled priests in Latin America to become involved in Liberation Theology concerns.

31. Axling, *Kagawa*.

There is real danger when people of faith become active in trying to change systems that are hurtful for the disadvantaged. A number of priests active in Liberation Theology suffered for their behavior. Archbishop Oscar Romero, for example, was murdered in 1980 after speaking out against the army of San Salvador. He spoke at a crowded church service, urging the army to stop killing peasants, claiming that this was against God's laws. The Archbishop was not naïve in making these statements. He was aware of the danger to himself. He became one of many martyrs in the revolution for the poor, shot and killed for his antimilitary stand.

Today a different kind of brutality can be unleashed when people try to speak out. Rabbi Lerner and others have formed a promising "Network of Spiritual Progressives." This group planned a major gathering to coincide with the 2008 Democratic Convention in Denver. Working for peace and justice and reaching for an interfaith expression including Jews, Christians, Buddhists, Muslims, and others, this effort runs against those who want a preservation of the status quo and their own place of power and privilege. In April of 2008 the Network was forced to face a modern version of brutality. Some kind of virus infiltrated their computer system, sending out messages in the name of the Network of Spiritual Progressives offering sexual enhancements, financial deals, and other things not connected in any way to the goals or mission of the Network. This could have been the work of anyone who tapped into the system at random. But it would be the way to sabotage a good work today. It is difficult to see how anyone could oppose a united effort by "secular, spiritual and religious people to replace selfishness and materialism with love, kindness, generosity, open-heartedness, nonviolence, and radical amazement at the grandeur of the Universe." Trying to change the bottom line in America, this group calls for a shift from the focus of maximization of money to a focus on love and caring as well as ecological sensitivity.

Perhaps the strongest message of this chapter is that we simply must reach for a new level of understanding where we truly accept the reality that we are one with all of nature including all those who suffer. In one way, we must become one with those in the Mideast who are served a daily diet of bullets and sounds of gun shots instead of an increase in daily bread. We need to know more about places in the world where people try to survive on incomes of less than one dollar a day. Places including the slums of Port au Prince are part of our world. Here men institutionalized the playing of dominoes in public places as a way to pass the time on the days and weeks when there was no work due to the very high unemployment rates even in good times. Now thousands of men, women, and children are still trying to survive in Haiti after a major earthquake shattered the capital city in January of 2010. Stories of bare survival continue with accounts such as that of the thousands misplaced by one of the worst earthquakes in recorded history in Chile in February of 2010. Our world is one, including the cyclone-ravaged delta area of Myanmar where thousands of people have died or gone missing over the last two years. We are also one with the over one million who became homeless and the thousands of children, women, and men who continue to struggle for survival in the aftermath of a killer earthquake in China. And we are one with the record number of some one billion men, women, and children worldwide suffering from malnutrition, a near starvation existence. The high calling to reconsider our individual view of life in general including others very different from ourselves is best expressed in a frequently quoted poem written by the Buddhist monk Thich Nhat Hanh, titled "Please call me by my true names."

Do not say that I'll depart tomorrow
    Because even today I still arrive
Look deeply: I arrive in every second
    To be a bud on a spring branch,
To be a tiny bird, with wings still fragile,
    Learning to sing in my new nest.
To be a caterpillar in the heart of a flower,
    To be a jewel hiding itself in a stone.
I still arrive, in order to laugh and to cry,
    In order to fear and to hope,
The rhythm of my heart is the birth and death
    Of all that are alive.
I am the mayfly metamorphosing on the
    Surface of the river.
And I am the bird, which, when springs come,
    Arrives in time to eat the mayfly.
I am a frog swimming happily in the clear water
    Of a pond.
And I am the grass-snake who, approaching
    In silence, feeds itself on the frog.
I am the child in Uganda, all skin and bones,
    My legs as thin as bamboo sticks,
And I am the arms merchant, selling deadly
    Weapons to Uganda.

I am the twelve-year-old girl, refugee on a
  Small boat.
Who throws herself into the ocean after being
  Raped by a sea pirate.
And I am the pirate, my heart not yet capable
  Of seeing and loving.
I am a member of the politburo, with plenty
  Of power in my hands,
And I am the man who has to pay his "debt
  Of Blood" to my people,
Dying slowly in a forced labor camp,
My joy is like spring, so warm it makes
  Flowers bloom in all walks of life.
My pain is like a river of tears, so full it fills
  All four oceans.
Please call me by my true names, so I can hear
  All my cries and laughs at once,
So I can see that my joy and pain are one.
Please call me my true names, so I can wake
  Up and so the door of my heart can be left
Open, the door of compassion.[32]

Looking back at the above pages, I see a lot of references to looking beyond self, to the glory of nature, to God. This is all important. But I also know that it is extremely important to consider our own moods, strengths, and weaknesses. Keep reading. In the next pages you will be introduced to Michael Joseph. He has the courage to share his own struggles, including times of heavy concern about the lack of finances. I truly appreciate his respect for others, even those like Sam and Joan, the homeless couple mentioned in this chapter. As I read Mike's story, I am shocked by how much things have changed since I was in my mid twenties. I married when I was eighteen. Back then I was going to college full time at Anderson College in Anderson, Indiana. I also worked full time for General Motors at the local Delco Remy plant. I worked the swing shift from 4 p.m. to midnight on an assembly line making automobile horns. That was over fifty years ago. I made $2.85 an hour plus benefits. At the time no one would have dreamed of General Motors declaring bankruptcy! Men I worked with on the swing shift were comfortably raising families on the $2.85 an hour salary. Credit cards were not in vogue, and drugs never complicated down times for anyone I knew. It

---

32. Thich Nhat Hanh, *Please Call Me*. Printed with permission of Parallax Press.

is a different world today, and much more difficult to manage in many ways. Mike's story touches on timely issues that should be given a lot more attention by today's media.

Fishing Down at Rock Bottom

Michael Joseph

"Scar tissue is stronger than regular tissue.
Realize the strength, move on"

—HENRY ROLLINS

I was sitting on my bed with my mind racing, surrounded by bills. I was panic-stricken and suddenly I started to cry. I was twenty-one years old and crying like a child. I had been living on my own now for three short months, forced out of my father's home by my unreasonable behavior and uncontrollable temper. Years later, I would learn that I have a mood disorder and that would have helped me to understand why I was feeling so overwhelmed at the time. I pushed all of the bills off of my bed onto the floor and screamed at the walls, "Screw this!" to no response.

There was no way I would be able to come up with an extra four hundred dollars a month. My irresponsibility with credit cards combined with overpriced rent had finally caught up with me. Were bills and debt the only things I had to look forward to in life? I was supposed to be an adult, however I had been acting like a child with no sense of responsibility. I had been spending money that I did not have and not really planning anything for my future. I had been smoking a lot of pot and it had begun to take its toll on me. Marijuana is a wonderful mood stabilizer, however when used in excess it has a tendency to make people happy with boredom. I would spend my time staring at the TV and had little motivation to do much else.

I had been recently laid off from my job and was waiting to receive some help from the government in the form of unemployment checks. Basically, I was in a slump. I had little money saved at the time and was not prepared for a sudden job loss. I was scared to think about where the bulk of my money had gone. It was up in smoke now, resin in my lungs. I knew that I was being dramatic and that there were people in the world who had far worse financial problems. I did not want to think about them right now, I just wanted to cry and feel sorry for myself. A quote from one of my favorite movies kept running through my head: "Hitting bottom is no weekend retreat." For me these words mean that hitting bottom is not something for only a few days—it has a long run. These words of wisdom were spoken by Tyler Durden, a character created by Chuck Palahniuk featured in the movie (and novel) *Fight Club*. I really thought that I had hit bottom; that I could go no lower. I never realized at the time how wrong I was. I would later learn that life would often present us with "tough times" and it is not the tough times that build character; it is how you handle the tough times as an individual. Your trials define you as a person and develop your true character. As I sat there, on my bed with a pile of bills scattered throughout the floor, I thought of ending it all. I was obviously not handling this properly; I had severe character flaws that required lots of attention, reflection, and work. Escaping the problems was not the right way to handle them, although it was easy, however detrimental. This was not the first time, or the last, I would think about suicide. In retrospect, looking at this situation leaves me feeling sorry for the twenty-one-year-old boy that I was at that time. He had not yet learned how to deal with the shit that life can shovel out and was in for some tough lessons.

You are right in thinking that this was a melancholic time for me and I really had no right reacting this way. I had plenty of good things, but I was subconsciously choosing to focus the majority of my energy on the bad things in my life. That, I would later learn, was my fatal flaw in handling stress. Focusing on the pain that comes along with difficult situations such as money management, relationships, family, and all the other things can obscure our view of the good things around us.

The war in Iraq would start in two short months and gas prices would begin to steadily climb over the next six years. Things were tough everywhere and they were only going to get tougher.

I resented my father for kicking me out of the house while I was in my sophomore year of college and I resented the free world of America for being so damned expensive. In hindsight, I resented myself and I hated everything. It was all due to my attitude, the way that I perceived things. Life is only what you perceive it to be, and I perceived it as very grim with a hopeless future. A few days before this hopeless moment, I was talking with a friend, who happened to be a college professor. He had acquired his PhD in mathematics and was one of the smartest friends that I had at the time. Ray was in his late forties, however he was not your typical college professor. He had long blackish-grey hair and a scruffy beard to match. Not your typical scruffy beard either. I am talking about the kind that father time would grow: long and bushy. He lived in a cheap apartment below me, played music, went on long trips to music festivals, wore ragged clothes, smelled funny, smoked pot, laughed a lot, and hated the government. He was, by every definition that I have ever heard, a true hippie. I gave him my song and dance about my despair over the current situation and he was not sympathetic. He raised his voice and aggressively spoke, "You don't know how easy your generation has it. Sure, you're a sophomore at the University of Southern Colorado but what the hell do you think you know about life? When I was your age they were putting so much damned stress on us to do everything perfect. You've got to be smarter than the Russians! We've gotta figure out how to do this before the Russians!" Ray had started referring to my generation as the "Bart Simpson" generation. He said that we just surfed through life, striving for mediocrity. We did not worry about winning or losing, since we were taught that everyone was a winner. We had missed that huge lesson of competition. We did not know how to handle the defeat or loss that would undoubtedly occur repeatedly throughout life. I let this conversation resonate and it eventually sunk in, but not quickly enough.

Ray was right. There I was, sitting on my bed, feeling sorry for myself, not knowing how to handle my defeat. From where I was sitting, in my comfortable bed, I could not even imagine the feelings that I would eventually have at the real bottom. Then, in the midst of all my sulking and rage, she knocked on the door, and without hesitation or an answer, she entered. Her beautiful mocha eyes, and the way they looked at me, always melted my heart. Immediately upon seeing me, she started crying, empathetic toward my pathetic state, me slouched over on my bed, crying like a baby over some petty bullshit. She told me that she was three months pregnant after she and I had been dating for a month. I stayed with her and eventually held her hand and coached her throughout the delivery. And although the child was not my own, I fell in love with both of them. I knew the relationship would never last; we both wanted different things, but we were there for each other. Right now however, I was not even there for myself. When I felt like this I cared little about myself and much less anyone else.

"Hi," I said in a pathetic whimpering voice, "Where's the kiddo?"

"She's sleeping, Mom's watching her," she replied in her most comforting voice, calm as always, but a bit apprehensive. She had called ten minutes earlier to check on me and I broke down crying and hung up the phone mid conversation, giving her no way to respond. This kind of behavior was a big reason why many people distanced themselves from me. Why should she, or anyone for that matter, have to deal with me projecting my negativity outward? Now she was in my room expecting an explanation. She did not deserve her feelings being pulled around by my overdramatic bipolar behaviors. These thoughts caused the guilt to rise up from my stomach and lodge in my throat. This only made me cry more. She immediately threw her arms around my shoulders and comforted me, her slow beautiful voice commanding me to listen. The soft brown skin of her face pressed against mine as her mocha eyes filled with tears.

"It's not as bad as you think," she said as she tried to comfort me, "We'll get through this."

"That's not what I want. I don't want my problems becoming your problems." We were embraced as I spoke, our faces pressed firmly together. I felt her warm tears start to trickle down my face. "You have a three-month-old daughter to worry about and you don't need a drama queen boyfriend creating more stress in your life."

"I like your drama," she smiled gorgeously. I was twenty-one years old and she was by far the prettiest girl that I had ever dated. When she smiled, she would flash a perfect set of ivory white teeth and the corners of her eyes would crinkle just a bit. I thought that she was adorable, but she was also far too kind to deserve me. Because of my self-defeating feelings, our relationship would eventually dwindle into nothing but memories.

There was something about her optimism that helped me to tune my mode of thinking. Amidst my anger and frustration a moment of clarity came over me. "I just need to get a roommate or something and I can probably just call the credit card companies and work something out, right?" Finally, rational thoughts were coming from my overwhelmed brain. All it took was a little bit of relaxing and some encouragement.

CATALYST FOR CHANGE

I have titled this story "Fishing Down at Rock Bottom" after a line from the Jimmy Buffet song, "A Pirate Looks at Forty." For some reason, I think of this time in my life every time that I hear that line in the song. This experience was by no means rock bottom for me; I would later have experiences that would make this day seem like an ice cream party complete with rainbows, unicorns, dancing, smiling dwarfs, and a fat clown twisting balloons. "Down and out" times are an important part of our lives. How we respond to and handle ourselves during these times defines us as human beings. Far too often I have overreacted and let my emotions get the best of me when faced with obstacles. I have lashed out at others in anger and frustration, when I should have used my time at the bottom to reflect and calmly plot through solutions to my problems. Too many friendships and relationships have been damaged because of this selfish behavior. When faced with difficult problems, it is important that we ask ourselves specific questions and avoid the self-pity. How did this happen? How could I fix this problem? How can I assure myself that this will never happen again?

I mentioned above that "down and out" times are an important part of everyone's lives. They can become a catalyst of epiphany and growth when handled with honesty, humility, and courage. We can easily coast through life defining ourselves by the things we have acquired, the places we have been, and the people that we know, but moments at the bottom will strip us of all of these things. They will cause us to deconstruct and disassociate from everything. However, we can put these pieces back together, if we succeed in understanding what happened and decide to climb out of the pit (as painful as this may be). Eventually we will be able to look into the shadows, stare at the bottom from the top, and smile with a deep sense of accomplishment. These devastating times in life can serve as motivation for change. Much self-improvement and progress can come out of hitting the bottom. If we are honest and courageous enough to look closely at our problems we will often learn things about ourselves that we may have been aloof to in the past. In my story above I felt broken, but I had not lost everything. It was the conversation with Ray, along with the comfort and motivation from my girlfriend that triggered my decision to look at things differently. I simply needed a couple pushes to shift my focus from self-pity to self-reconstruction.

As I said earlier, there were, and still are, people in this world who have hit much deeper and bleaker bottoms. There is much to be learned from these people, especially the ones who have taken it upon themselves to rise from the ashes and discover that losing everything can oftentimes set us free. Sometimes it takes losing everything to find the true person that was hiding behind the material exoskeleton.

SMILING IN THE FACE OF HOPELESSNESS

Now in 2009, nearly seven years later, I have reached a combined debt of over ten times what it was on that dehumanizing day. Four years of college followed by four years of grad school, combined with manic spending sprees have helped me rack up an enormous debt. The credit card companies and lenders love me; I had been dealing with them through my entire college career and still am. However, it does not intimidate me anymore and I have learned that fiscal problems, while encumbering and time consuming, are manageable with a little self-restraint and common sense. I have learned effective ways to handle problems through my own life experiences and in addition I have learned how other people effectively handle their own problems.

While working I see a lot of people suffering from depression, mental anguish, anger, and many, many other types of mental, as well as physical illness. You can find these people everywhere, not just in the grocery store pharmacy where I work. Let me paint a mental picture for you.

Six months after I graduated from college I was employed in a grocery store chain with over one hundred pharmacies to choose from in the state. For the experience, I decided to work the graveyard shift in the one with the highest volume of prescriptions filled. Seven straight days of working eleven- and twelve-hour nights, followed by seven days off. Against the advice of my psychiatrist, I chose to work this shift. He told me that working graveyards is "contraindicated" in a patient with a history of erratic moods.

Contraindicated is derived from the Latin prefix "contra" meaning against, or opposite, and "indicare" meaning recommended or required. Basically contraindicated is doctor talk for "don't do that!"

I am officially diagnosed as bipolar and that means my mood tends to fluctuate from extreme highs to extreme lows, sometimes without warning, which I will elaborate on in chapter 3. But until then let us get back to the mental scenario that I am painting for you. I know that references to my place of work do not necessarily relate to the topic of financial loss. But my work setting is referred to often in this book. I want to introduce this to you so that you can have a better understanding of where I am coming from today.

I was standing behind the counter in the company's busiest pharmacy in the state. It was 11:30 p.m. and the shoppers were still waiting for their prescriptions to be filled. I was the only person working in the pharmacy. I should have been wondering why I had over sixty prescriptions to fill before the end of the night, and currently several people waiting in the cash register line, and one more at the other end of the pharmacy waiting to drop a prescription. This pharmacy was filling more prescriptions than the busiest late afternoons at retail pharmacies in smaller towns in which I have worked. I have become accustomed to being overworked at understaffed pharmacies because there is a shortage of pharmacists in America. There has also been an increase in the amount of prescriptions being written. Each year more and more promising new medications are being released and advertised to correct or help manage more and more medical aliments. Less help and bigger workload are only two of the many reasons why you may find yourself waiting in increasingly longer and slower lines to simply get pills stuffed into a bottle.

You can see why this type of work tends to aggravate many of my colleagues. Truth be known, it aggravates me sometimes too, and when I start to feel bothered I try to take a few moments to simply recalibrate myself to a more positive mind frame; this is one of many effective methods I have learned to handle stress. I had just gotten off the phone with "Suzie Q" a woman in her mid fifties who has been living with mental illness since her early twenties. It is a constant challenge but she chooses to accept her condition as part of what makes her the person that she is. She expressed concern to me over the phone about something she had seen on TV earlier. Apparently Dr. Oz was on the Oprah Winfrey show and asked the audience at home to remember four numbers. After a commercial break he returned and asked the audience to recall the numbers. "Suzie Q" remembered none of the numbers correctly and this caused some disarray. She was very alarmed about this while we spoke over the phone and asked me if she could be suffering from early Alzheimer's disease. I did not think that was the problem so I told her to calm down and I would call her within the hour after things slowed down at the pharmacy. Since she was accustomed to staying up late, she agreed to wait until later to discuss this problem.

At the moment of the call, I had been working hard trying to concentrate on doing things correctly and in a timely manner all while talking to Sam, a regular customer who also happens to be homeless (Dean introduced Sam earlier in this chapter). Sam had just dropped off seven prescriptions for himself and the woman he lives with. They both lived out of their camper in a Walmart parking lot a few miles away. Despite his situation, Sam always appears to be in high spirits when I see him, and interestingly enough his mood is not due to his medications. Because Sam chooses to look at the positive aspects of his life, rather than focus on the negative, he does not see his situation as hopeless, just "temporary." More than anything else however, Sam is deeply in love with his partner, Joan. Love has an amazing way of helping people through difficult times.

"That pill makes me dizzy if I stand up too fast," Sam stated in a matter-of-fact tone of voice. I enjoy discussing effects of medications with my customers. All too often their comments revolve around complaints about the cost, wait-time or our perceptible lack of customer service.

"It'll do that," I laughed. "Do you know why it makes you dizzy when you stand up too fast?"

"Because it's lowering my blood pressure and the blood will leave my head if I stand up too fast," Sam smiled, revealing a gap in between his two front teeth. His over- simplified answer was correct.

"Good answer. Next time that happens, just sit back down, wait a few seconds, and stand back up slowly. You're not going to win a fight against gravity. It'll pull that blood down to your socks if you stand up too quickly."

Sam was describing a side effect of his blood pressure medication commonly referred to as orthostatic hypotension. It is a sudden head rush due to an abrupt decrease in blood pressure upon standing up too quickly. It is not a pleasant side effect, but it does mean the medication is working properly. Earlier in my life I experienced this same side effect when smoking marijuana as it too can cause orthostatic hypotension.

Sam was waiting at the head of the line, with the other two customers behind him. Immediately behind him a rough looking middle-aged white man was waiting patiently. He would eventually purchase a pack of ten hypodermic needles from behind the pharmacy counter where they are kept. It is a rare night that I don't get at least one customer purchasing needles. Customers often refer to them as "insulin syringes" and most of them are used for insulin. Too often though, I believe that I am selling them needles that are to be used to inject illegal drugs, such as heroin, cocaine, and methamphetamines. Legally we have a choice, as pharmacists, to dispense or not dispense a medication or medical supplies. Some pharmacists refuse to sell needles to people unless they have a prescription on file for an injectable medication, but I would rather sell them clean needles than risk the person sharing a dirty one with another drug user. I know enough about drug addiction to realize that a user will find a way to use regardless of whether I am selling them clean needles or not.

On the other end of the pharmacy, waiting patiently at the drop-off window, was a man that I had never seen before whose name I would learn was Armando. He was waiting to drop off a prescription for Percocet and he was a doctor shopper.

When a person becomes addicted to prescription medications often they will resort to something referred to as "doctor shopping." This is the act of requesting the care of multiple physicians simultaneously without informing any of them that you are seeing multiple caregivers. The patient will see a physician and commonly have a scripted story that will most likely end with the physician writing a legal prescription for a narcotic drug. Some patients even go to the extent of self-inflicting, faking, or exaggerating injuries in order to feed their addiction. It is not uncommon for a typical doctor shopper to be seen by more than fifteen general practitioners in one year. Physician and pharmacist education and training on warning signs and the dangers involved in doctor shopping have increased in the past few years, and due to the recent widespread abuse of prescription drugs, many states have criminalized the act of doctor shopping. Many states are now diverting money to fund online prescription drug monitoring programs in order to help crack down on this form of drug seeking. It should go without saying, but I will make mention anyway that the funding for these programs often comes from taxpayer money. And speaking of tax dollars, I would like to mention one last thing that I have noticed about doctor shopping. The patients doing this are often receiving state-funded insurance, such as Medicaid. This means that they are receiving an overabundance of medical care and prescription drugs via the public health system, and passing the bill to you, the taxpayer. I will briefly elaborate on Armando's situation at the end of chapter 2, when I discuss addiction. Allow me to deviate away from the other customers and get back to Sam and Joan, the homeless couple.

I was still filling Sam's prescription, when I was overcome by a sneezing fit. It was early spring and my seasonal allergies were really starting to cause me trouble. Watery eyes, stuffy nose, and that untouchable itch in the back roof of my mouth were all part of my daily life in early spring and fall. "Excuse me," I said, relieved after finishing my final sneeze. "My allergies are killing me. I've been taking Zyrtec, but it doesn't seem to be working for me very well this year." Exposure to allergens causes histamine to be released in the bloodstream. Histamine will activate specific receptors in the body and this in turn leads to the typical symptoms of allergic reactions (runny and itchy eyes and nose, sneezing, etc.). Zyrtec is an antihistamine drug similar to Benadryl but without the sedative effects. This is because Zyrtec, a second-generation antihistamine, does not cross the blood brain barrier. Antihistamines block much of the histamine from landing on the receptor sites and lessen the symptoms. Apparently the antihistamine I had been taking was not doing a good enough job, or my recent exposure to allergens was causing too much histamine to be released in my blood.

"You need to try Allegra," Sam confidently responded. "Have you ever heard of that one?" asking me with a straight face, he wasn't joking. I simply stared at him in disbelief for a moment. A moment later the disbelief was washed off of my face with a smile. "Sam, I'm a pharmacist, of course I know of Allegra, and it doesn't work that well for me, but I'm glad that it works for you." The same drug can show one response for one individual, while seemingly doing nothing for another individual. I did not have the time to go over this with Sam right now as I was overworked and understaffed. "Thanks for the suggestion though, you're the first person to ever come in here and tell me what I should be taking." I had been a licensed pharmacist for nine months and that had never happened. We couldn't help but share a laugh, definitely enjoying each other's company.

At that moment Sam turned around and scanned the other customers. "Whoah! You've got a line here. Why don't I go for a walk around the store and you can help these other people?"

That's the thing about Sam. Despite his situation in life, he is still happier than many middleclass Americans that I have met. He is actually one of the most pleasant customers I have dealt with. What was his secret? I would later discover, upon getting to know him better that he makes it a point to keep an optimistic attitude. When I think about Sam's attitude I cannot help but recall the words of Janice Joplin, "Freedom's just another word for nothing left to lose."

NOWHERE TO HIDE

When we are able to detach ourselves from all of the things that we possess, something amazing can happen, if we let it. Having nothing else to hide behind, the person that is inside will shine through. This is the case with Sam; he is a big happy guy who likes to laugh. Of course he does not act this way with everyone. Many people will treat him differently since he is homeless. I know this because I have done it in the past with other people. This is where attitude comes into play again. Some pharmacists might view Sam as a "problem customer" since he chooses to hold up the line and chitchat. This goes back to attitude. I choose to deal with him with a positive attitude and he reciprocates with a positive attitude. This makes our shared experience a positive one; clearly the opposite of what was more likely to happen.

You may have noticed I have focused on the positive aspects concerning Sam's attitude and neglected to discuss his control over his current situation, so let us take a look at that. When I asked Sam and Joan why they are living under such conditions they replied that their situation is largely due to circumstances outside of their control. This mode of thinking can simply encourage the "not-my-fault" mentality of a lot of people whether they are homeless or not. During a discussion with Sam and Joan, when I asked what gives them hope and makes them happy, they both replied almost simultaneously, "When people give us things." This really surprised me at first, but after some thought, there is no doubt that they both lived very difficult lives that have led them to where they are today. Some of the blame can be due to poor upbringing and the influences of society, but much more than they both realize has to be placed on the decisions that they have both made in life.

I have tried to ask Sam if he felt he could do something more productive with his time. He displayed an enormous sense of pride when confronted with the question and replied quickly, "I help the street kids." He is also actively involved in his church, where he brings many of these "street kids." Of course, these things are a good step in the right direction and it is not my place to tell either of them how they should be living. But I can see the potential Sam and Joan have to climb up the downward spiral. I know that they can do it one day, but they must first realize that they are the true answer. Only they truly know how to most effectively apply themselves in a productive way. By this I mean they must be willing to accept the fact that they must become more responsible for taking care of themselves and they can be successful in life. I believe they do appreciate all of the help they receive, but they are not aware of how it has enabled them to become dependent on someone other than themselves. I truly believe that Sam and Joan have discovered much about themselves while sliding down the spiral. They are trying to climb their way back up but it is not an easy thing to do and they need help other than just being given things.

I would like to close this chapter with a simple suggestion. The next time you find yourself thinking negatively about someone else (we all do it), take a few moments to realize that they too are struggling in life. Their immediate struggle may consist of financial problems, mental problems, addiction problems, or they simply just stepped in some dog poop fifteen minutes earlier. We all have difficulties in life to varying degrees and occasionally we should take some time to distract ourselves from our own problems and help someone else with theirs or simply talk with them. The next time you pass that strange person on the street and you are about to toss them a dirty look, instead smile and say hello. You may surprise yourself and come out of the experience with a new perspective. How often do you complain to a manager after you have been mistreated or not helped to your satisfaction by an employee? How often do you praise an employee to a manager after they have helped? It is said that the squeaky wheel gets the grease and this mentality has led to a population of consumers who complain to get what we want. Happiness is a way of life and it is contagious. If there is one thing that working in the retail industry has done for me, it has made me a better customer. I try to always let retailers know that I appreciate what they are doing for me and the feeling of appreciation is most often reciprocated, creating a positive environment. I will say it once again: happiness is contagious.

CONVERSATION

In the final section of this chapter Dean and I talk together about finances and financial problems. The conversation took place in a large, downtown library as we sat at a small table on the second floor. As we talked we looked down at a busy city streetscape and up at nearby tall buildings that frame our city. Some people below walked eagerly, perhaps hurrying to work. Others seemed to be going nowhere in particular. There is a forty-nine-year difference between Dean's age and my own; he is seventy-eight while I am twenty-nine. Another way to look at it is that Dean is ten years older than my dad. But, despite our differences we find that we can learn a lot from each other. We invite you to pull up a chair and listen as we talk.

Dean: My first question for you, Mike, is how much of a problem do you think credit card debt is for people your age?

Mike: It's definitely a problem. I have a lot of friends who are not responsible with money. Too often I'm not responsible with my money. It's so easy to get out of control and max out a credit card with a high APR and then you'll find yourself spending the next year or two paying it off. It's funny how many credit card companies send me applications for new cards while I have existing credit debt. I hear too many of my friends complaining about money trouble, saying things like, "If I could just have a better paying job, I'd be able to keep my head above water." Not making or having enough money seems to be a commonality among many middleclass youth today. Credit cards are an easy way to very quickly spend money that we don't have. With that said, credit cards can be a valuable asset when used responsibly. It's good to have a credit card in an emergency situation, such as a broken car or missed paycheck.

Dean: Honestly, that's hard for me to understand, since I did not have any debt until I was in my forties. At that time I borrowed money from Household Finance Corporation. I had no credit cards, but I do have a credit card now and have had one for years. You're talking about people in their twenties having major financial problems. It's obviously a very different world today. In thinking about this chapter, it's like we are living in two different cultures. Much of my material for this chapter is memory of the past as I am retired now. I bring up a lot of stuff that happened a long, long time ago. You are more in touch with today as you are working.

Mike: I'm not sure how to elaborate on that. It's a different time. Like you mention in your writing, drugs weren't a problem when you were my age. You were making $2.85 an hour and working with people who were supporting families on that wage. I have friends who are making

$8.00 to $12.00 an hour and they're struggling to support themselves. I've been talking to a lot of people my age about these things since we've started this project and some of them have cynical views about our situation. They think that the government is purposefully making things hard for us, a very mistrusting attitude. Others just try to brush it off, move on, and roll with the punches. They try not to think pessimistically about it and move the conversation toward something else, something more positive.

Dean: Are they able to think about things like marriage and family, or do they simply say, "I can't afford that right now?"

Mike: I have friends who are married and I have friends raising families and that sort of thing. Some of them are struggling. Some of them are on welfare and some of them are happy about their situation. Some of my friends who are on welfare seem very content, actually happier than the friends who are not receiving any government assistance. I find that a bit strange and it's a shame to see this and compare it to those who would like to start a family but refuse to do so due to the current state of their financial affairs.

I have friends who work very hard to try and live comfortably by their standards. One friend who comes to mind is a prison guard. He has been doing this for four or five years now and he makes a good salary compared to others I know. But the things he is seeing in the prison system, the people he has been meeting, both workers and inmates, have really been affecting his attitude. He says that he could easily see himself losing all respect for humanity if he kept at this job for a long time. He has decided to simply start a new career and since then has started buying and fixing foreclosed houses with the help of his father. He just sold his first house and made around thirty thousand dollars. He has a wife and kids right now so he cannot just quit his prison job and lose his benefits, so he is working hard to make enough money to establish himself in his new line of work, but it takes time. I went through four expensive years of college, followed by four even more expensive years of grad school and it was hard to stay optimistic when I was so uncertain about my future. It was the people around me who kept reassuring me that I was "doing the right thing," or "choosing a good career." These people helped keep me focused on finishing school. It is good to not only surround yourself with people like that, but also to strive to be that way yourself. And on the other side of it, I think that it is important to praise your friends and acquaintances when you see them doing well and working hard.

Dean: As I see friends my age, Mike, I know that there is a lot of difference in their financial status. But private finances are never a topic for open discussion. Some in my extended family are having major money problems. One key difference between folks my age and your friends is that we are retired, living on fixed incomes. We know that there is no way we can get a better job, and at my age other concerns can become much more important than financial issues. I know a number of people, for example, who have major health problems. For those over fifty-five who are looking for work the recession hits much harder than for those who are younger. Different sources report that workers over fifty-five are now jobless for longer periods of time than those under fifty-five. Age-bias complaints are up with the recession. The July/August 2009 *AARP Bulletin* included a major article on how the recession is hurting older Americans hard with abuse from both family members and others preying on the sometimes overly desperate anxiety of the elderly about their own financial future.

Mike: In my work at the pharmacy, I see examples of the problems that older folks have. One night, for example, I saw an elderly couple come up to my cash register to pay for some expensive prescriptions, a couple hundred dollars for each of them. They were spending so much money on the medicine that they decided to spend their remaining money on canned cat food. This is what they were going to eat! This was the only way they saw to survive on a fixed income. When I went home that night, I talked about the couple with my dad. He acknowledged that this kind of thing does happen. My question was and is what can we do about it? I couldn't very well give them their prescriptions for free or even discounted. If I did that for them I'd have to do that for everyone and corporate America would quickly take my job away from me.

Dean: We are trying to give some hope in this book. I think that generally we both talk in positive terms and we also both know about some pretty sad situations. Do we need to end this with more hope, more of the positive?

Mike: All of the situations that we have talked about, where the people survived, they just kept going. They plowed through it. They found something to help them. Often it seemed to be something spiritual, something to believe in.

Dean: I think that the spiritual side is very important. Maybe we need a better theology of money. The other part that I think of when reflecting on this is that relationships are important, maybe this is the sociologist in me. I'm thinking of some of the people in my extended family who are having a hard time right now. There have been strains in the relationships between them and their children and grandchildren. When that happens it makes the financial situation much worse. If the financial situation is tough and immediate relationships have gone sour, it makes life much more difficult to deal with. Sadly, I think that many of those in this kind of situation do not have the means to buy this book. I know that they are hurting.

Mike: You've got to pay close attention to relationships. I've ruined too many relationships by reacting to certain situations with a negative attitude. But, on the contrary, when I look at the good, solid relationships that I've had and still have today I notice a trend in the way we've dealt with problems. I expect to have ups and downs in every relationship. "Sunshine friends" are what I call people who leave with the first sign of trouble. These "friends" are only around when things are fun and easy, taking what they will. They're like leeches. A good relationship involves a delicate balance of give and take. Sometimes we need to step back and evaluate our buddy system. I remember reading a book written by Drew Pinsky in which he described the generation of people in their twenties as being extravagant and flashy.[33] The 1960s and 70s were the era of free love and a bohemian lifestyle. What really jumped out at me was his evaluation of my generation. He called my generation a generation of people defined by a series of misguided relationships. I often ask other people what they think of this and it seems common to many people my age. We jump around from one friendship or relationship to the next. If things go sour, we move on. We're all expendable. The best friendships that I've had required a lot of hard work, a lot of patience, empathy, listening, caring, and helping each other. I love my friends although there have been times when I've said that I didn't like them.

Dean: I know that chapter 3 of this book will include references to cognitive behavioral therapy. This approach to life suggests that if we change the way we feel about and perceive situations, we will change our behavior. I think that you have been referring to this process although you have not used the specific term, "cognitive behavioral therapy."

33. Pinsky, *Cracked.*

Mike: I think that encouraging people to talk about things that bother them is a good thing to do. It is also important to have an unbiased, professional opinion and that's what a psychiatrist or therapist can provide. This is someone who does not simply just sympathize with everything you're telling them. They can show you a different way to look at things. My father has always pressed the issue of setting goals in life. Since I was young, he's always told me to constantly set goals and to work hard to achieve them. My philosophy is that once the goal has been achieved, we should set a new one. It's also important to never stop learning, never settle, and to constantly educate yourself on different topics.

Dean: Back to the main topic of this chapter: the money part of life is very important. Financial loss is a heavy thing.

Mike: I agree with you, but we also need to keep things in perspective. I like what you said about the fact that when we die, we don't take the money, the possessions with us. Really all we are when we die is who we are. The relationships that we've had and the influences we've made, these are what we really leave behind. I spend most of my money, and I know that this isn't the wisest thing to do, but I do enjoy doing it. I spend most of my money paying off debt and the rest seems to go toward fun with friends. I like this since it makes me feel good.

Dean: I get the impression that there are a lot of differences in your free expression of things like money in your circle of friends compared to the people I know. As I said at the beginning of this conversation, private finances are never a topic for open discussion in groups that I am a part of. References to money are also conspicuous by their absence in formal church services that I attend. It is in the free expression of personal concerns during the "prayers of the people" that I often hear mention of things like someone being out of work, or someone coping with cancer. The sermon or homily seldom considers anything like the problem of how to survive in hard times.

Mike: As I see it, money and work need to be placed in the context of all of life. I was talking with a friend the other day who expressed significant concern about his financial situation. He is very comfortable and confident with all aspects of his life except his career. He works for a local business framing pictures. He doesn't feel that his job is something that's stable and furthermore, there's not much room for him to advance salary-wise. I admire him in many ways. He's got a lot of interesting things to talk about and is always fun to be around. He tells me that the women he's been dating aren't interested in long-term commitment, primarily because he does not have a solid career. I suggested that he consider some kind of college or vocational training. Of course, he'd already thought about that, telling me that he was pondering going back to school for a few years to study computer technology. This would be a perfect career for him, since he's already very computer savvy and enjoys working with them. People always seem happier when they go into a career that they're genuinely interested in, rather than chasing after something because it pays well, is a secure job, or their parents want them to do it.

Too many of my friends and acquaintances tell me the same thing. They say, "If I was making the type of salary that you're making, I'd be doing just fine." This always makes me laugh. They're only looking at the monetary aspect and not at the situation involving it. I spent eight years of higher education to get the job that I have. It was very hard and stressful to say the least, not to mention the personal struggles I have had with drug use and spells of manic depression. I spent a lot of money for my education; a big part of this is student loans that will need to be fully paid off one day. My education was very, very costly, but do I worry about it? Yes, but not as much as I used to; I've adjusted. Budgeting and planning are important things to do. I'm still learning the ropes of money management and my suggestion to someone having money management problems is to seek out a financial planner or at least speak with someone to get money advice. Every time that I speak with my financial planner, I feel like I've just left a therapy session! It's great.

Dean: How are you ever going to get out of the debt you incurred while going to school? That must be very depressing.

Mike: I'm just going to pay it. In general, people must expect some debt after college, if they walk away from it with no debts, good for them. Paying back student loans isn't a death sentence, it is money invested in your future.

Dean: Every chapter in this book includes a section on "spiritual issues." Looking back at your childhood, Mike, can you recall any important discussions of financial status as part of your experience of church?

Mike: I don't recall specific conversations regarding financial status. I grew up in a Roman Catholic family and attended Catholic school. At church, my mother made it a point to always put her money for the offering in a closed envelope to ensure privacy. I remember that it bothered me when other people sometimes seemed to make a public display of what they were giving. Some of my classmates would brag about how much money their parents contributed to the church. My father was a firefighter and raised myself along with my two brothers. My mother had a full time job raising the three boys. We weren't poor by any means, but we were never wealthy either, at least in comparison to many of my classmates. Eventually I became fed up with many of the personalities that I came across in the Roman Catholic Church and left it behind me. I spent many years in an almost godless state of mind, this possibly contributed to my frequent "acting out" and irrational behavior. I set no boundaries for my behavior and lost much of my sense of self-control. Eventually I found my way back to a spiritual path, but in no defined religious denomination. I don't subscribe to any specific religion now. But I know there's something bigger than this, something bigger than you and me. Just look around, we're all part of something bigger, and we're all connected. Personally I feel that spirituality can be practiced and experienced differently from person to person. I do consider it a big part of my recent happiness.

Dean: I grew up in a family strongly devoted to evangelical Protestantism. My mother and father began their seventy years together during the bleak years of the Great Depression. Dad liked to tell and retell how the church changed his life. His older sister first prompted him to get involved in the church. At that time he was in a cycle of despair over his prospects for work. He really gave up on trying; spending a lot of his time camped out in a local movie theatre. I wonder what movies he watched back in the late 1920s. Then he went to an evangelical, Protestant church and was converted. Immediately, as he told the story, his life changed. He was more diligent in his search for work, primarily painting and paper hanging, and found a good job for those times. He worked hard to feed his growing family, including me. Unfortunately, during the last thirty years of his life he became consumed by an unfulfilled dream of making a lot of money, becoming "important," which made it difficult for him to savor the simple joys of living. He was mostly interested in making money so that he could make a difference in the church, in the world. Unfortunately, my father was never able to sit back and truly feel his importance simply because of who he was, with no need to reach for financial "success." He never considered such material as that of the sociologist Max Weber who wrote about *The Protestant Ethic and the Spirit of Capitalism.*[34] Weber looked at how some people equate their financial status with their status with God. This can result in a lot of frustration over the lack of finances if this is truly seen as a "sign" of disfavor with God.

34. Weber, *Protestant Ethic.*

2

Drug and Alcohol Abuse and Addiction

Michael Joseph

"Just cause you got the monkey off your back
doesn't mean the circus has left town"

—GEORGE CARLIN

I HAVE COAUTHORED THIS book to offer strategies for dealing with some of the most difficult problems in our time. This chapter in particular is intended to provide education on drug and alcohol abuse and addiction. It has been written with the intention of anyone being able to pick it up and read, including adults, children, drug addicts, social users, or clean and sober individuals. I will share several personal stories of drug and alcohol use from my mid teens to the present. Please follow me into my past and allow me to share with you a few of my personal experiences along with my current reflections on drug use and its effects on my life. In order to benefit from this story only one thing is required from you: an open mind. Allow yourself to find a viewpoint where you can maintain a good balance of comfort and vulnerability, because a stubborn and argumentative state of mind will only hold you back from reaping the full benefits of this book. Walk with me and allow yourself to become a part of the story if you can. This was hard for me to write, a lot of this is very personal. I suspect that it will be easier to read if you take it in slowly and read between the lines. This is a taste of what is really happening in our world today from my point of view.

KIDS IN THE DOGHOUSE

Many books have been written concerning addiction. In the limited space of these pages I share some of my personal story. Illegal drug use is not something you are likely to observe at your neighborhood McDonald's. It is something done in underground circles, something teenage boys might do in an oversized doghouse, and I spent time in such a doghouse. To really understand the role of friends, the behaviors around use, and the associated feelings it is necessary to take a look into this world. The full picture can never be drawn from time spent in the comfort of a library. This chapter progresses naturally from the material shared by Dean in the last chapter. He also spent time in strange places and situations getting to know firsthand the issues around poverty. It was not necessary for him to sleep in the cheap, cockroach-infested ho- tel near Burnside Street in downtown Portland, Oregon. As a sociologist, he had the experience of staying in the Hilton Hotel in New York City while waiting to present a paper at a national meeting of the American Sociological Association. He also knew what it was like to sit in a church office, in peace and quiet, preparing a sermon for Sunday. Both of us have been in unusual places that many people try to avoid and in the process we have experienced things that may help to add insight into the world of major problems of our time. While I will focus on illegal drug use, later in this chapter Dean will look more directly at alcoholism. As I have suggested above, perhaps our experiences will help someone who is sincerely trying to climb up the downward spiral. I highly recommend that you also turn to other resources including Alcoholics Anonymous (AA), Narcotics Anonymous (NA), Al-Anon, and other books readily available in bookstores and libraries, and to information accessible on websites on the Internet. A list of resources is included at the end of this book.

Now I invite you to visit a "normal" household in Any Town, U.S.A. It is 8:15 p.m. on a Thursday and the house is quiet. Cydney, a single mother raising two high-school-aged boys, had not been home this early on a weekday in months. She had been working two jobs for the past four years in order to survive. She worked in a real estate office from eight to five and waited tables at a local diner, usually until mid- night. Tonight had been a slow night and she was able to sneak out of the diner early. She had expected to find Kwynn and Chris on the back porch smoking pot when she got home. They had been smoking pot for about two years now and she had never confronted them about it. In fact, both boys thought she was completely oblivious to what they were doing. They would often light incense and smoke cigarettes to mask the smell of marijuana, but the characteristically pungent odor would still bellow through the house. She knew better than to object, she was their age during the seventies and smoked her fair share of pot. That was partially why she ignored it; she knew that teenagers tended to experiment, that it was part of growing up. She did not really think marijuana was as bad as the "war on drugs" had claimed, and much of the negative publicity about it did not hold truth in her mind. Furthermore, the boys had proven that they would not respond to parental punishment and simply acted out further when reprimanded. Besides, she had bigger problems to worry about. Chris had been borrowing his mom's Jeep while she was at work. However, this was abruptly brought to an end when Chris high centered his mother's brand new 1999 Jeep Cherokee on the railroad tracks. Thinking it was no big deal, Chris left the car on top of the tracks while he went to the store to purchase a pack of cigarettes and call a friend to help free the Jeep. When Chris saw the Jeep next, all that remained intact was the stereo; a train running its daily route had demolished the vehicle. Chris's mom was not even sure if the insurance would reimburse anything, "Does auto insurance even cover a vehicle demolished by a train?" she thought. She tried grounding Chris as punishment instead, but he decided to move out. He stopped sleeping there, but in actuality still ate and lived there all day while she was at work. It was then she noticed the same treatment from Chris that she had from all the men she had dated: disrespect.

Tonight she was not going to trouble herself with recent problems. She had just opened a bottle of her favorite wine, pinot noir. It was the elegant taste of this wine that she enjoyed most. This particular wine was made in the best region in the world for growing the certain grapes. The bottle was a gift brought back from Burgundy, France. She carried the bottle into the living room, flipped on the TV, and sat down on the leather sofa to relax. She looked around the room at the pictures on the walls and shelves. They were mostly photographs of her and her two sons throughout the previous eighteen years, and lost in thought, she was almost ready to cry. She examined the color of the wine as she refilled her glass; a deepened hue of cherry red. Cydney felt the blissful vapors as the aroma filled her nostrils. It was a sweet sensation to her olfactory senses.

She enjoyed the aroma again briefly and closed her eyes, just before she slowly took her first sip. This was a rare occasion, Cydney being able to relax with some wine all by herself.

When she opened her eyes the newscaster on the TV was talking about the percentage of cocaine use among high school students. According to the latest data released from an annual survey conducted by the University of Michigan's Institute for Social Research, the percentage of high school seniors who had tried cocaine in the past had jumped from 8.7 percent in 1997 to 9.3 percent in 1998.[1] Chris and Kwynn each had about one hundred other kids in their classes. Kywnn was a high school junior and Chris should have been a senior. If these stats held true, it meant that about 8 or 9 kids from each child's class had used cocaine. She could easily see some of Chris's friends doing cocaine. Those little shits were always causing trouble. The statistics on marijuana use had remained relatively the same; about 49 percent of high school seniors had smoked marijuana in 1997 and in 1998.[2]

The newscaster went on to discuss marijuana being a gateway drug and mentioned the percentage of students who had smoked marijuana and then went on to use cocaine. Cydney's thoughts started wandering to the whereabouts of her two sons right now and what they were doing. She reached for the remote and immediately shut off the TV, the news was too overwhelming and this was her night to relax. She cleared her mind and took another sip from the glass. The wine was marvelous, the house was quiet, and everything was perfect. It was then she began to cry.

Parked in the street outside of Cydney's house, I sat in the back passenger seat of Kevin's grey Nissan Sentra. Jorge was in the back seat babbling about girls. He enjoyed talking almost as much as listening to himself talk. The trouble was that I liked listening to him talk as well. We had too much in common. I had met up with the two of them after a date with a beautiful girl. It was a rarity for me to have a date during my four years in high school. After telling them all about my date, Jorge started his nonsensical babbling, while Kevin lectured me on proper dating etiquette.

"You should've gotten your ass out of the car and walked her to the door at the end of the night," he confidently proclaimed. "Always walk them to the door." After that night I would always walk my dates

1. Johnston, et al, "Life Events," 37.
2. Ibid., 36.

to the door. I had little experience with women and no one as honest in giving advice as Kevin. My dad would simply ask, "Do you have a girl-friend?" Regardless of my answer, he always said the same thing: "Don't get anyone pregnant." To this day he has still not given me the birds and bees talk or lessons on proper male to female communication and the courtship process. It seemed to me that Kevin understood those things better than my dad, or at least he knew how to communicate them to me better.

"You gotta be a gentleman, Mike," he went on. "Women love that shit."

"Put out or get out," Jorge mumbled trying to add some twisted humor to the conversation.

"Hold the door for them; compliment them on their hair, clothes, and nails, whatever the hell they've got going on," Kevin spoke with a great degree of certainty. "Did you kiss her?" He finally asked the question that I'd been dreading. I wanted to tell the truth but instead answered, "Yeah . . . uh, of course." I could see Kevin smile out of the corner of my eye. He knew I was lying, but wasn't going to push the subject. That's how he was; he always knew when I was getting uncomfortable. That's when he'd back off.

My self-imposed insecurities over my inexperience with women caused as much awkwardness for me as my drug use caused. Kevin lit a joint of some of the town's finest dirt weed. Dirt weed is a slang term used to describe really cheap marijuana. At that point in my life cheap pot was all I could afford to smoke. I was seventeen years old, working twenty hours a week for minimum wage in the sporting goods section of a chain department store. It seemed all of my money was stretched thin between food, gasoline, alcohol, and cheap drugs. I tended to party in excess and it drained my bank account quickly. Whenever I had money left over I would take the opportunity to do something extra, such as take a girl out on a date or, more often, see a movie with friends. These were things that I had imagined the sober kids doing all of the time, but frankly it did not appeal to me as much as wasting time doing drugs with my friends.

While my mind drifted Kevin took a long slow drag from the joint and held it in his lungs as he handed it to me. Jorge immediately objected, "Hey the rotation goes to the left, stoner! Pass the joint to the left!"

"It's stoner-right, I always pass my joints to the right," Kevin replied matter-of-factly.

"Too late now man, Kevin screwed it up and I'm reaping the benefits," I laughed just before filling my lungs with the thick smoke. Almost immediately I started coughing uncontrollably.

"You don't get off until you cough," Jorge snickered through the cloud. This expression held some truth. I would often not feel the intoxicating effects of marijuana until I took that one hit that launched a coughing fit. Coughing causes dilation of the capillaries in the lungs resulting in more blood flow to the area. With more blood available the drug is readily absorbed more quickly.

We continued smoking the joint for the next ten minutes and at the time it seemed like the longest ten minutes of my life. We were waiting for Chris to arrive in hopes that he had found some cocaine. It felt as though we were in stasis but unable to remove our minds from what was in store for the night.

Kevin starting giving me more words of wisdom on how to improve my love life, "You know what you need to do Mike . . . " Kevin jumped in his seat as he was startled by a knock on the window.

"What's up bitches?" Chris exclaimed. He had a knack for coming out of nowhere and scaring the shit out of everyone. Chris stood about six foot three and might have weighed one hundred eighty pounds. He was tall and skinny, but still maintained a muscular frame. He had just turned eighteen and was now the official cigarette buyer for our group. He smoked both cigarettes and weed. He had a melodramatic voice and an optimistic attitude that would find the humorous side of any situation. I admired him almost as much as I admired Kevin. We were all great friends.

"Look what I got," Chris said as he pulled a small bag of cocaine out of his pocket.

"Sweet," Jorge exclaimed, "and it only took you three hours!"

"I got held up, besides it's really good shit. I got an eight ball, there's enough here to last me a week. I took a nummie ten minutes ago, and my entire face is still numb, I swear to God." Chris tended to swear when he exaggerated, an eighth of an ounce of cocaine is commonly referred to as an eight ball. This amount will normally produce about thirty-five "lines" of cocaine. However, the four of us would finish it by the end of the night. Later in my life I would see people do several times this much while having "coke parties." Cocaine and the culture that surrounds it scare me, and I prefer to avoid it. I have met many functional members of society, in many different fields of work who claim to occasionally dabble with this seductive drug. But compared to the number of people who claim to use only occasionally and still function I have seen it destroy many more people's lives. This destruction is brought on much more rapidly when the user brings a hypodermic needle or crack pipe into play. When smoking or injecting cocaine, the euphoria experienced is more of a "rush," a shorter, more intense high.

"I scored it from one of my dad's friends." Chris had a father with a drug problem and knew how to exploit the situation. Just as he was stuffing the bag back in his pocket the living room light flipped on inside Chris's house. "Shit dude, I think my mom's home." Panic quickly covering the optimism in Chris's face.

"You sure it ain't Kwynn?" Kevin asked trying to instill a bit of hope.

"No, he's with his girl." Chris was thinking of his options. We were parked just outside of the house and if she were inside the house she would see us soon. We always had the green light to drink and smoke pot at his mom's house, but smoking coke was something else entirely. Chris's dad and mom had been divorced for years now and she worked all the time to support the two boys. We often took advantage of her constant absenteeism.

"Just get in the car dawg," Kevin demanded, "we'll smoke that shit in here." Kevin would often take great risks in order to use drugs. Once he had driven his car ten miles outside of town and parked on the side of a dirt road so we could "safely" do cocaine.

"No," the three of us quickly replied in sync.

"Fine, I got a better idea," Chris said as he got in the back seat with Jorge. "I'll just make a few foils in here and then we're gonna do 'em in my back yard."

"Yeah maybe we can light a bonfire and invite the police over too, Chris," I hassled.

"Just shut up Mike, and trust me. And keep it down; I don't want my mom to know we're out here making foils."

"Foils" or "foily" are what our group of friends, and many others in the drug culture, commonly called smoking cocaine. More specifically, it entailed mixing cocaine, baking soda, and a tiny amount of water on a piece of aluminum foil. The mixture was then glazed over the tin foil. Next, we would heat and dry the mixture by running a lighter underneath the foil to complete the concoction. What I did not understand at the time is that we were conducting a basic chemistry experiment every time we would make a foil. What we were smoking was essentially crack cocaine; the recipe involves mixing cocaine, baking soda (sodium bicarbonate), and water. This mixture is then heated and the "rocks" precipitate from the mixture as it cools. We had simply skipped the "rock" part and had a glaze of cocaine mixed with bicarbonate on each foil. Cocaine hydrochloride, that is cocaine in its normal form, is not suitable for smoking since the temperature at which it vaporizes is very high and also very close to the temperature at which it burns. An amateur mistake would be to try and sprinkle some cocaine in with some marijuana; the user would ultimately burn the majority of the drug and waste much of it in the process. When baking soda, cocaine hydrochloride, and water are mixed and heated, the baking soda breaks down into carbon dioxide and sodium carbonate. The hydrochloride from the cocaine molecule will now react with these chemicals, leaving the cocaine as a free base oil. Completing this chemical reaction enabled us to "properly" smoke cocaine instead of burning it.

Cocaine abuse in general is unsafe, illegal, and highly risky behavior. In my personal and professional opinion this method of cocaine delivery (foils) is unwise as well as unhealthy for a number of physical and psychological health reasons. Smoking cocaine gives the user a high that is quicker and more intense than snorting. However, as mentioned before, the effects of smoking cocaine do not last nearly as long as snorting. This leaves the user wanting more and they often find themselves going through a lot of drug very quickly due to the shorter lasting effects. There are also a number of cardiovascular and pulmonary problems that can be linked to this form of use. I am very glad that I left this lifestyle behind me before it caused any detrimental problems and hope that I can somehow help other people by sharing my experiences with this culture.

Drug addiction is an extremely difficult disease to treat. There is a very high failure rate. People will often relapse even after long periods of sobriety. It is a very deceptive disease and addicts struggle with the thought that they can manage their drug use without help. At first, drug use is fun, new, and exciting but as time goes on using becomes more frequent and it becomes a habit. Finally, it progresses to being something that the brain tells the user is essential for survival and the user feels he or she cannot live without.

Fifteen minutes later we were sneaking into the backyard while Chris delicately carried his three segmented pieces of tin foil each containing cocaine glaze. A few minutes later we were in a doghouse in Chris's backyard, ready to get started. My heart started nervously pounding with excitement.

"Quit it dawg, you're holding the flame too close. Don't burn the shit, smoke it!" Kevin scolded me as smoke enveloped my face. My eyes were burning, my nose was stinging from the stench, and my heart was pounding like a drum. I was doing it all wrong.

"Sorry," I defensively responded. Something jagged was poking my hip. I readjusted my positioning in the corner of the doghouse. My mind was racing and I could not light it without messing things up. "It's not like I'm a pro at this. Why am I even doing this?" I looked up to Kevin; he had it all, I thought: friends, good looks, personality, girls, and besides he was just plain cool. Hanging out with him made me feel cool as well, and he always treated me like I was part of the group. He listened to me and treated me with respect, something I rarely got from other people.

"Here, let me just light it for you and I'll hold the tooter," Kevin finally demanded with a smile. We were terrible influences on each other.

A tooter is drug culture slang for a straw or other thin cylindrical object used to snort or inhale smoke. Right now we were using the hollow shaft of a Bic pen. Kevin and Chris always used the same Bic pen and occasionally scraped it and smoked the resin when they were out of drugs and money. Right now, there was no scraping because Chris had just spent his week's paycheck on what he called "enough coke to last him the week."

"Do you like this doghouse?" Chris proudly proclaimed and continued without giving either of us a chance to respond. "I built it last summer. It's way bigger than most dog houses . . . better too, sturdy." It was big enough to cram the four of us hunched over small bits of tin foil. I started to wonder if Chris had built it in hopes of sleeping a pet polar bear instead of his scruffy mutt or maybe he knew we would find our way inside of it. Chris was bleached-blonde, had a light-hearted attitude, and was a bit on the wild side. He was great at building and fixing things: Nintendos, cell phones, gardens, doghouses, and of course aluminum foil contraptions. I guess that you could say he was a bit like a cooler version of MacGyver with a drug problem, always willing to help. He was never afraid to voice his opinion, which was often outrageous. For that reason he pissed off many people who may have been able to help him through the problems that would arise over the next few years. That is another story though; right now we were still in Chris's doghouse smoking coke through a Bic pen and something was still digging into my hip.

"Come on Mike," Kevin was now holding the tooter for me and lighting the foil from underneath. He kept the flame steady at about a quarter inch below the foil; he was practiced at this.

"All you have to do now is breath in slowly, you can handle that right?" Kevin pleaded with me. I felt like the most inexperienced drug user ever. I could not afford cocaine and even if I could I would not have bought it. Kevin often scavenged his parent's garage, as well as the neighborhood, for things to sell or pawn. He was almost eighteen years old, with no job or source of income aside from his parents. Most of his money was spent on drugs, alcohol, and parties. Despite his bad habits he would always treat his friends with kindness and respect and whenever he had money it would go quickly on a large meal or drugs for the group.

Jorge was also seventeen and lived with his parents. He had a job at the same department store where I was working and this equated to nothing but trouble when the two of us were scheduled together. He was a little bit less experienced than us; tonight was his first time doing cocaine. We were all in our senior year of high school, aside from Chris who had recently dropped out. We should have been applying to various colleges and universities or asking girls to the prom; the type of shit that "normal" kids were doing. Instead, we were hiding in a doghouse and I was being scolded for burning the cocaine. If I knew then what I know now, I would have been at home applying for scholarships or grants for college. College is pricey and it is even more expensive if you plan to have a good time while you are there. I may have been the under-educated drug user of the group, but I was always considered the most book-smart. That is easy to accomplish when you are hanging around with the high school druggies. Right? Wrong. The previous statement is not to discredit the intelligence of Kevin, Chris, or Jorge. In fact, my conversations with them were of a much higher intellectual caliber than the typical "oh my God" meaningless high school chitchat. I would later learn that many addicts tend to have higher than normal intelligence.

So, while they were not bookworms like me, my doghouse companions were very intelligent people. And maybe this disease compelled them to focus their talents and energies toward self-destruction. Addiction is a disease that can take anyone; do not fool yourself by saying you are strong willed or have too much self-control. If the substance exposure is tempting and frequent enough, even the most well grounded individual can get sucked into the downward spiral that is addiction. Of course, some are more prone to get sucked in than others.

At the time none of us saw what we were doing as a problem, because it was not an immediate problem mostly because it was more like a stepping-stone in a trail leading to a world none of us could see or understand. The term flirting with disaster comes to mind. We were all experimenting for different reasons. I was using for a number of reasons. The friends, the feeling of escapism, and the attention it attracted are among the many reasons, but more than anything I was just plain curious. Sure, I went through the Drug Abuse Resistance Education (D.A.R.E.) program. I had a police officer come into my class to talk once a week during my fifth-grade year. He showed us the actual drugs and told us what kind of people to avoid, which essentially taught me where to get the drugs. He also showed us drug paraphernalia that was made from simple household objects. I remember drawing on these memories at the age of fifteen while making my very first bong in my dad's garage. I cannot help but wonder if a healthcare professional specialized in addiction treatment and recovery would be more effective at teaching kids about drugs than a police officer.

But I must take responsibility for myself. I did not have enough control over my impulsiveness and therefore let curiosity get the best of me. It was the solace that I took in academia coupled with the friends that I made later in life which kept me away from repeated drug exposure and probably saved me in the end. But right now I was still in the doghouse smoking crack and something was still digging into my hip.

"Dude, something keeps poking my hip." I complained.

"That's Rio's bone stash you're sitting on!" Laughed Chris. Rio was his mutt of a dog lying in the grass who should have been in the doghouse right now instead of us.

We spent the rest of the night crouched over in a doghouse with a slobber soaked bone digging into my hip. I am not proud of nor do I regret this or the other darker sides of life that I have experienced. I have felt both pride and regret in the past, but have since then resolved my past and accepted these experiences as what has molded me into who I am today. That does not mean that it still cannot come back to haunt me if I let it. I try to draw on these experiences whenever helping people with problems involving drugs, alcohol, and the spectrum of mental illnesses that are often associated with them. This is what is called being "street-smart." Being street-smart, not unlike being book-smart, can only teach you so much. A well-rounded education is necessary to understand all aspects of a problem. I am very grateful for these experiences. I am very grateful for the knowledge I have gained and even more grateful to have survived them.

Kevin, Chris, Jorge, and I would spend a total of two and one-half years drinking and doing drugs together. We would become the closest of friends, but eventually a period of turmoil and mistrust within our group of drug curious friends would overcome. Eventually we all went our separate ways. I went off to college and stepped down to weaker drugs and started dating, which alienated me from the group.

Kevin's urge to steal in order to feed his habits, along with his secretive behavior regarding his drug use would ultimately destroy many of his friendships alongside his family relations. I would later find out that he had waxed and waned through periods of sobriety and drug use but by the age of twenty-six would be incarcerated for drug charges. His experiences with drugs were tough and sometimes overwhelming. I am sad to say that I have not spoken to him in years, but I have heard through a mutual friend that he is no longer behind bars and is staying clean. This, many recovering addicts say, is how recovery is best approached, one day at a time.

Unfortunately, my friend Chris took an even darker road. His charismatic, no bullshit personality gave him the luxury of always being surrounded by friends willing to help finance his drug habits. To the best of my knowledge he never went back to finish his high school diploma. He eventually took solace with a priest in Texas and stayed sober for a year or so. After that he moved back to his hometown and took up company with his old friends, setting himself up for disaster. Old friends and environment usually are not conducive to recovery and this is easy to understand if you think about it logically. The old friends will likely be still using and being around them will allow the recovering addict to have easy access to drugs. The old environment is familiar; therefore, the recovering addict will know from whom and where to find drugs even if they are not immediately within reach. The old environment can also trigger cravings; for example, seeing an old doghouse in which you used to use drugs may spark the memory of the feeling the drug used to provide. Cravings are constant during recovery and can be brought on without warning; therefore, it is important to find a stable and supportive environment conducive for recovery. It is equally important to find friends who are doing more with their lives than consuming drugs.

The last time I saw Chris he was the drunkest guy in the bar and he kept hugging me and telling me how proud of me he was. It felt good to hear praise from my old friend, but seeing the state that he was in and the way people were reacting to it nullified these good feelings. The bartender asked me to get him out of the bar because he was making a scene, so we left and went our separate ways that night and I haven't seen him since. It was good to see him and I hope he is doing well now but I cannot help but wonder if it would have been better for Chris to stay away from his hometown until he had a better understanding of his addiction in addition to several years of sobriety.

MIND OVER MATTER

I miss my friends and I cannot stand what this disease has done to their lives but what bothers me more is the chance that I had to help them. I was their friend, I had their respect and I was the "smart" one, which meant they would often listen to me. My ignorance on the topic often led me to respond to their behavior with coddling. On the rare occasion that they would question their behavior, I would tell them it was not that bad, we were just experimenting. This response was easily accepted, since that is exactly what we were doing, experimenting. The problem was that we were ignoring the fact that experimenting could open the door to a serious problem very quickly.

What is addiction? Where do we draw the line between addiction and drug abuse? I have seen people who have abused drugs and I have seen people addicted to drugs and the line can be very thin. Addiction has strong physiological components, primarily neurological and it is associated with withdrawal symptoms, while abuse is any inappropriate or nonmedical use of a substance.

I am willing to wager that high school students would be more reluctant to admit taking drugs, therefore biasing any survey to reflect a lower number of students taking drugs than reported. With that said, I can assure you that more than nine or ten of Cydney's two son's classmates had tried cocaine. I know this simply because I was hanging out with the kids who were doing the cocaine and many times I was partaking in the activities with them. In fact, the number of kids using cocaine was closer to fifteen or sixteen. And this is simply one high school in America. What I feel is most important here is that these statistics hold much truth, a significant percentage of kids have been and will continue to experiment with drugs, before, during, and after their high school years. Personally, I feel that waging a "war" to completely stop the use of drugs is not the best way to handle the situation. A certain degree of experimentation should be expected; therefore, an understanding of what to do to effectively stop this experimentation from progressing into addiction is needed. If our government, on a federal and state level, could somehow divert the money spent on the "war on drugs" into awareness and prevention then we would have more resources available to detect and treat the problems caused by drug use earlier in people's lives.

What I am simply trying to say is that I feel our society needs a better understanding of what addiction is and how to effectively manage it. Addicts are often viewed as the dregs of society and degenerates that need to be locked away. It seems to me that too often people are looking toward the criminal justice system to handle the addict, when in fact it should be the medical community *combined* with medically trained individuals in the criminal justice system. The question is why can't the average person see addiction, and furthermore mental illness, as something that is manageable and in my opinion in the same realm as diabetes, cancer, or heart disease? The average person has the ability to view things like this; they just require the proper education and an open mind.

Rheumatoid Arthritis is a disease. Asthma is a disease. Schizophrenia is a disease. Addiction is a disease. If you can agree with all of these statements, you are in good company. The World Health Organization[3] and

---

3. World Health Organization, "Lexicon of alcohol and drug terms," lines 268–72.

the American Medical Association also think of all of these as diseases.[4] A disease is treatable and people can go on to live productive and fulfilling lives, while living with disease.

Drug addiction is an extremely difficult illness to understand and treat. Simply put, it is a disease of the brain characterized by a compulsive, often uncontrollable craving or urge to seek out and use a particular substance, even in the face of extreme consequences. Unfortunately, there is no simple definition for addiction, and the extent and effect of the disease differs with each individual. The problem becomes chronic, or long term in many people, and oftentimes reoccurs after a period of abstinence.

This was illustrated in the above story with Kevin. He had gone through periods of sobriety, followed by periods of reoccurring drug use, even in the face of destroying certain friendships and risking possible incarceration.

In my story, I allude to all of us in the doghouse having a disease. At that moment in time none of us had a debilitating form of the disease, however we were all in the experimenting phase. Unbeknownst to any of us at the time, we each had our own predisposing factors helping to push us into the spiral of addiction. In the medical community most diseases have criteria listed as predisposing factors or risk factors. Risk factors for drug and alcohol dependence include: genetics, young age of onset, race and ethnicity, gender (men more than women), employment status and occupation, and educational level.[5] Chris had a father who abused drugs and alcohol and was not always present in his life. Chris inherited his father's genes, meaning he is most likely genetically prone to addiction like his father. Furthermore, the broken family in which he was raised (childhood trauma), along with his mother's attitude on his drug use (she ignored the pot smoking), placed him in a higher risk category for addiction. Of course, no single factor will make an individual an addict, but all of them play a part. One of the biggest features that will put an individual at risk is environment, such as parents, friends, home and school life, etc. Sadly, I must admit that my involvement and encouragement of drug use contributed to Chris's and many other people's addiction problems, just as their attitudes contributed to my problems.

4. American Medical Association, "Alcohol and other drug dependence."

5. Ries, et al, *Principles of Addiction Medicine*, 19. Additional information on addiction found on pages 16–20.

I have already explained some of the reasons why I was experimenting but one of the biggest was the comforting effect that drugs had on my brain, which is why many people take drugs and alcohol. When using a substance to achieve a desired effect a positive feeling will often accompany the experience. Too often people believe that they can control their substance use, however drugs can quickly take control of a person's life. Think of how quickly social drinkers can find themselves making bad decisions while intoxicated; unsafe sex, drunk driving, and fighting are just a few examples. And the repercussions can last for months or years: quick decision, long penalty.

There is a difference in the way an addiction-prone individual's brain responds to drugs and alcohol when compared to a nonaddict's brain. When a nonaddict takes a drug, they feel a nice high and that is usually the extent, unless they continue to repeatedly expose themselves to the substance. When an addict or addiction-prone individual takes a drug, they fall in love. The brain of the addict tells them that they want more, they need more, and they have to have more. Finding and consuming drugs becomes instilled in the brain as part of survival much like finding food to survive. The way the brain functions is changed over time and when exposed to the substance frequently enough, a person feels they need the drug to survive. They feel like shit without it or their mind obsesses over getting more. When they are out of drugs it is always on their mind.

Once more drug is given to the individual, they simply want even more. With continued drug use the everyday activities normally causing pleasure tend to stimulate less and less. This is called anhedonia. Brain studies have shown that individuals addicted to drugs show actual physical changes to areas of the brain critically important to decision-making, control over one's behavior, and judgment.

So over time as someone continues to abuse a substance, the effect becomes less and the need becomes greater. This casual use is how it started for the four of us in the doghouse and almost everyone else. We were unaware of the power these substances possessed. Although I did enjoy it, the feeling that I had while using cocaine did not appeal to me as much as other drugs. For this, I am extremely lucky. It made me a bit more hyper than usual, very jittery, and antsy. I spent a lot of time quickly running my tongue across the roof of my mouth, as sort of a nervous tic. Mostly I just wanted to talk a lot and do more cocaine.

Cocaine essentially binds to a specific part of the neurons in your brain and prevents dopamine (a happy go lucky neurotransmitter involved with feelings of pleasure) from coming into the cell. Dopamine would normally be brought up into the brain cell and removed from action; instead, it stays in an area called the synaptic cleft and is free to bind to dopamine receptors. The dopamine that was supposed to be sucked into the brain cell but could not (due to the cocaine effect) now acts on dopamine receptors and produces more nerve impulses than usual. There is something called the dopaminergic reward pathway, and it is involved in feelings of pleasure. The abundance of dopamine activates the dopaminergic reward pathway. What I am getting at with my drawn out explanation here is that cocaine leads to an excess of available dopamine and more feelings of pleasure and euphoria. The stimulation or pick-me-up effect is caused by another neurotransmitter being activated, norepinephrine, which is similar to adrenaline.

Doing cocaine made me feel like I was doing something terrible and this feeling was instilled through my upbringing. My mother and father both stressed to me the dangers involved with drug use; unfortunately this was not enough to stop me from experimenting. In fact the "don't do that" attitude actually made me more curious and willing to experiment. So while this drug ultimately sucked in two of my doghouse companions, Kevin and Chris, the other two, Jorge and I, escaped its clutches. Jorge had a good family upbringing, no immediate family members with addiction problems, and no mental disorders. He is your typical lower risk individual when drug addiction is considered. This is why it is not hard to believe that he simply walked away from these experiences wondering, *"what was I thinking?"* as he went on to start a career and family. Kevin and Chris both went on to battle their disease as it slowly started to take more and more control over their lives. They had found their drug; it was cocaine, an upper. I went on to find mine, marijuana.

THE NIGHT I FELL IN LOVE

It was 10:30 at night. The sky was speckled with stars and I was marveling at the way it looked. I had spent my first fifteen years living in a crowded suburb in Southern New Jersey. I had only been living in the Midwest for two months now and missed my small suburb and my friends that I had grown up with in Jersey; however, the sight of so many stars at night was one of the few comforts that I had found in my new home. New Jersey was so crowded and lit up with street lights, houses, and traffic that you could see only half of the stars that you would find in the sky while gazing in the darkness that was the Midwest. I was sitting in the middle of a dirt road waving a flashlight around pretending I was Darth Vader. My new stepsister, Devon, and a mutual friend, Miranda, accompanied me in the darkness. It was the middle of nowhere and the stars looked beautiful. It was the perfect night to fall in love.

"No. I am your father," I quoted Darth Vader from *The Empire Strikes Back*.

"You're such a nerd," Miranda giggled.

"He's so annoying," Devon complained, "he's always doing this shit."

Devon had just turned sixteen. She stood four foot eleven and was having a harder time adjusting to living in a new place than me. Our parents had been living together for a year now and I had just moved in permanently. It was an adjustment for the both of us; I never had a sister and she never had a brother. Obviously she was not used to the strange personality traits that gave me my individuality.

"Gimme a break," I defensively responded, "I don't get to play with flashlights too much."

"I think it's kind of funny," Miranda responded. I started to smile, until she added, "In a dorky kind of way." Miranda had a cute smile, blonde hair, and a bubbly personality. In fact I had a crush on her at the time. She liked to laugh and make jokes, and more importantly she knew how to take a joke. A good sense of humor can help a person tremendously throughout life. In a perfect world I might have fallen in love with her that night. Instead I fell in love with something much more seductive.

Earlier that day while on lunch hour in school I had an "appointment" with a new "friend." His name was Joe. I had talked with him the previous day and tried to establish enough trust to ask him to get me a bag of weed. I told him that I had smoked marijuana plenty of times in the past, but in fact this was to be my first time and I think he knew that, but I felt the need to lie anyway. Joe had agreed to get me a dime bag. A "dime bag" is slang for about a gram of marijuana, worth about ten dollars. A dime bag can easily be consumed in one session between three people; it is about two "joints." This term was originated from a dime being worth ten cents, a dime bag being worth ten dollars. A smaller bag was called a nickel and as you have most likely guessed it is worth five dollars.

As I walked through the cafeteria doors to the outside patio the unfamiliar scent of cow manure filled my nostrils. My new high school was located directly across the street from a grazing pasture and I had not yet adjusted to the scent and would not for another year. I looked around outside until I saw Joe sitting on a three-foot wall towards the back of the patio with his back facing me. I stood there awkwardly for a few minutes; he was almost in the "off limits" area of our outside cafeteria patio and I was too nervous to approach him. He turned around calmly and waved me over as if we were friends. I slowly walked over to him with my head down. I had a bad habit of looking at the ground immediately in front of me as I walked. I was depressed to be somewhere new and not at all confident in myself, and my body language illustrated this clearly. These feelings of depression and self-inadequacy helped drive me to seek out drugs as a source of anesthetic. These feelings and behavior, whether conscious or subconscious, are part of something I would later learn to be called the shame-anxiety cycle.

I sat down next to Joe. He was a tall kid, seventeen years old, with a mustache and a considerable amount of hair on his chin. It is amazing how facial hair made a high school kid look cooler. He smiled a crooked grin and said, "Hey."

"Hi," I replied nervously. I had never done a drug deal before and had no idea of the etiquette and proper procedure involved and I was over thinking things. Joe's head motioned to his right shoe, a dirty black Chuck Taylor. I sometimes wonder if this is the most commonly worn shoe in the United States.

"Shoe," he calmly said, while maintaining his crooked grin. He slipped off his shoe, which confused me. "Did he have an itch? What the hell was he doing with his shoe?" I thought.

"Take off your left shoe," he ordered. As he said this, I saw a sandwich bag sitting in his shoe, containing what could only have been my bag of marijuana. A wave of panic consumed me and it must have shown. "Calm down man," Joe said in a comforting voice, "nobody's watching."

He was right. No one could see our feet; we were sitting on a concrete wall, with our feet facing the stinky cow field. I realized this and immediately relaxed a bit. Confident now, I calmly took off my shoe with my other foot. He reached down and transferred the bag from his shoe to mine. I never imagined a drug deal would ensue in this way; a bag of drugs being transferred from one sweaty shoe to another. I hoped he did not have any sort of strange fungus. We stared at each other for a minute and I remember wishing that I had something cool and interesting to talk about, but I didn't.

"Just throw the money on the ground," he said, in a deep monotone voice.

I dropped the ten dollars by his feet, which he didn't pick up until I walked away.

"You'll like it, that's pretty good shit," Joe assured me. It wasn't, but I wouldn't know that until years later, when I would actually try "good marijuana." It was, however, good enough to get myself as well as my two young companions high later that night. I placed my shoe back on my foot, gave Joe a nod and a thank you and walked away. I would not touch the bag until I was at home, in the safety of my room some four hours later. I remember looking at it and thinking "So, this is weed, pot, reefer, bud, marijuana; whatever it's called . . . it looks like some sort of spice." The smell was overwhelming; it radiated from the bag and quickly filled up my room. Over the next ten years that smell would become all too familiar to me, much like a perfume worn by a lover. The sense of smell has a wonderful connection with the memory. To this day, when I smell marijuana in the air, I am immediately attracted to the scent. It is very similar to the feeling you experience when you meet a stranger who is wearing an ex-lover's perfume or cologne.

I had obtained a cheap pipe from another friend at school. I was not exactly sure how to use it, although it seemed simple enough. That is where Miranda and Devon came into the picture. They had both smoked pot before and knew a bit more about the culture than I did. Although I had neglected to tell them that I had not gotten high before, I suspected that they knew. I think that catches us up to where I started. This brings us back to the dark, beautiful, starry night when I fell in love.

"Can you turn off the flashlight?" Devon asked. "We're not that far from our house." I quickly responded by shutting it off. We were only a few blocks from our house and our parents thought we were going for a walk to a local park to "hang out."

"Is that stuff all set?" I asked.

"Yeah, the bowl is packed," Miranda responded. At the time the phrase "packing a bowl" was foreign to me, however it would become all too familiar as the years progressed. Picture a pipe, like the kind an old man would smoke. The bowl is the front portion where marijuana, in this case, is stuffed. Filling this up is commonly referred to as packing a bowl.

I let the others take the first drags from the pipe. By the time it was passed to me I was so nervous, I remember sweating even though I was sitting in the cold November air. I started to fumble around with the lighter. It was childproof and I was fifteen years old, still a child. I finally lit the contents of the pipe and inhaled slowly.

"Haghk . . . ugh . . . gagh," I choked out monosyllabically as the smoke spilled out of my lungs. They told me to try again and I did. I coughed again and again as I tried to hold the smoke in my lungs.

"You'd better keep it down," Devon ordered me, "they might hear us." She was paranoid, most likely from the marijuana. Paranoia is a very common side effect associated with the drug.

I do not know exactly how many hits I took from that pipe or how many bowls it took, but I do remember the instant that I first felt that feeling. "Whoa!" I exclaimed. "It's like I'm dreaming, but I'm completely awake." I started to analyze the previous few minutes of my life. They had gone by slowly and felt as though I was in a dream. I was functioning, but not in control. It was almost as if I were watching myself on TV. The drug was working and it was an amazing feeling for me; a few moments later I started laughing hysterically. I didn't even know what was making me laugh, but Devon and Miranda quickly joined me in the same nonexistent joke. The three of us laughed for what seemed like hours, but it was indeed only a few minutes. Distortion of time is another side effect of marijuana.

ADDICTION AND MARIJUANA

The main constituent responsible for marijuana's pharmacological effect is delta9—tetrahydrocannabinol (THC). How this chemical exerts its effect on the body was not completely explained until the late 1980s when scientists discovered and published compelling evidence for something they named the cannabinoid receptor. THC and other cannabinoid drugs bind to these receptors and activate them, leading to the "high" as well as other effects. That is right; we all have tiny receptors throughout our bodies that are waiting to be activated by THC molecules. Scientists went on to discover that our bodies have an entire endogenous cannabinoid system; cannabinoid receptors can be found in our brain and peripheral tissues. Endogenous translates literally to: endo, meaning "within;" and genous, meaning "generated." Therefore, if something is said to be endogenous it is created within the human body. If you have ever heard the term endorphins, it is referring to endogenous morphine that is released in response to pleasurable activities in life. This causes the "natural high."

In this book I frequently refer to my experience with marijuana as falling in love. A person can be addicted to many different things, but often an addict will have a drug of choice. The best description that I have heard on the topic of the drug of choice came from Kevin T. McCauley, MD. Dr. McCauley is well known in the research field of addiction and I had the privilege of hearing one of his lectures while attending the University of Utah School on Alcoholism and Other Drug Dependencies.[6] He described the drug of choice as the love of the addict's life: their girlfriend, boyfriend, husband, or wife. He went on to say that he would often see a look of dread in an addict's face when they were told that they could never again do their drug of choice. He compared the look to what you would see on the face of a human being as they were informed of the death of a loved one. This comparison could not be more fitting. The thought of never being able to smoke marijuana gives me that exact feeling. I understand that marijuana is not as devastating as heroin or crack, but when an individual becomes dependent on it problems arise.

Dr. McCauley explained how physical changes occur in the mind of an addict as the disease progresses and the substance of abuse is introduced into the body more frequently. The changes specifically occur in the midbrain, the portion of the brain that handles survival. This section of the brain normally drives us to eat, kill (to protect or eat), and have sex. Not the type of sex in which we partake for pleasure. I am referring to procreating; the subconscious desire that all animals have to spread their genes into the next generation. These things ensure survival of our genetic code and they are driven by the midbrain. Dr. McCauley also explained studies conducted by a psychologist named James Olds. Olds

---

6. Dr. McCauley lectured at the University of Utah School on Alcoholism and Other Drug Dependencies in July of 2008.

experimented on mice by designing an apparatus that would allow them to self-administer electrical shocks to the reward center in the midbrain. This would create a sensation of pleasure. Once the mice discovered that they could get some sort of stimulation from this electrical shock, they would continuously only administer shocks to themselves; neglecting all other survival behaviors such as food or sex. This exclusion of all other survival behaviors was noted to the point of death. These mice would become addicted and their addiction would lead to them neglecting all other aspects of life, ultimately killing them unless the option to self-administer stimuli was removed.[7]

Now I would like to take this a step further and relay another excellent point that Dr. McCauley made in his lecture. Mice get addicted to drugs. Do mice weigh moral consequences involved in their decisions? No they do not. Do mice have a mouse god that they pray to in the evening? No they do not. Have you ever seen a sociopath mouse? I have not. Mice do not have drunk and abusive parents. Do mice have mouse gangs with tattoos, guns, and leather jackets? Not that I have ever seen. Addiction takes over the midbrain's survival hierarchy, making drug the new number one: ahead of eat, kill, and sex.

Now that you know the physical traps set for drug abuse, I challenge you to see the addicted human as a human with a disease, not a degenerate, unintelligent, sociopath who invited every problem into his or her life. With that said I must add that I have never had a problem neglecting the necessities of survival because of a marijuana addiction. But I still used in the face of severe consequences, which would have affected my quality of life. I personally believe that marijuana is a mild drug, safer in comparison to the abuse of other drugs. It can still be abused though. When marijuana is used too often, physical effects can be noted, such as adverse impact on learning and memory, and increase in rates of anxiety, depression, suicidal thoughts, and schizophrenia. Research on chronic, or long-term users has shown changes in the brain with regard to dopamine activation and changes in the way an individual responds to stress. These are two characteristics noted in the addicted brain with all substances. When marijuana is smoked it will no doubt affect the heart and lungs by resulting in less oxygen being taken up by the blood. Research has shown marijuana smokers to have the same lung troubles as tobacco smokers.

7. Ibid.

Now that I have briefly covered the science behind marijuana, I would like to explain why I view the drug as such a seductive substance. Despite the obvious positive and negative effects there was one effect in particular that subconsciously, and later consciously, drew me toward the drug. It has a wonderful effect on stabilizing the mood. I am not citing any medical literature for that statement because it is my personal opinion from years of use. As I mention earlier, I live my life as a bipolar human being. My mood can often shift from extreme highs to deep depressing lows at the drop of a hat and marijuana helped to keep this in check. I have only just recently learned that cognitive behavioral therapy (talking with a professional), along with proper legal prescription drugs, can stabilize my mood as well as, if not better, than marijuana. With that said, cognitive behavioral therapy is also an excellent option for someone who is struggling with an addiction to marijuana, as well as any other addiction problem.

I mentioned earlier something called the shame-anxiety cycle of addiction. Shame has a lot to do with an addiction spinning out of control. I learned about this from another effective lecturer at the University of Utah School on Alcoholism and Other Drug Dependencies, Merrill Norton PharmD. As a clinical assistant professor at the University of Georgia, Dr. Norton explained this very effectively. Certain things in life will cause stress, disgrace, anger, fear, and similar problems. These problems lead to anxiety, which starts the cycle. We all have these problems, but some of us are more prone to handle them via escapism, a form of running from our problems. Escapism can be drug or alcohol use, sex, procrastination, or any other form of self-defeating behavior. Dr. Norton refers to these as "stinking thinking." These behaviors do however cause temporary relief to the anxiety felt by the individual, but in the addict, they will eventually lead to remorse, which eventually progresses to shame. Now, this is where the addict will either keep running through the downward spiral or get off and deal with the shame in a more healthy way. Healthy shame refers to the individual embracing the problem and walking down the road of recovery. Unhealthy shame can be: isolation, embracing a false self, codependency, and shamelessness. These feelings fuel the addiction process until the problems are faced in a process of recovery.[8] Now that I have explained that how we handle shame can effect addiction, allow me to bring you back to my life.

8. Dr. Norton made these statements while lecturing at the University of Utah

PARENTS JUST DON'T UNDERSTAND

I had just turned sixteen and learned the ropes of smoking pot. I had a bong that I had built from a water bottle. I got the idea in the fifth grade, while being educated in the D.A.R.E. program. Officer Friendly showed us a couple of suitcases full of drug paraphernalia and how it all worked. The schematics stuck in my head and it did not take long until I was crafting my own smoking devices.

The day was a typical Saturday for me: my parents had just left to check out the local yard sales and Devon and I were in my room packing up a bowl in my bong. Cindy, our faithful black and grey terrier-poodle mix, was also joining us in the room. I had a strange suspicion that Cindy enjoyed the secondhand smoke, because she always seemed to come around when I was smoking pot. After two smoked bowls and fifteen minutes had passed I heard a noise.

"What was that?" I said with alarm.

"I didn't hear anything," Devon assured me. "Besides, Cindy would be barking if our parents were home. Load another bowl."

Just then my door burst open and my dad walked in past the smoke screen that filled the room. Through the cloud he looked pissed. I looked at the bong, then to him, with what I can only assume was a deer-in-headlights expression. I immediately threw the bong, still filled with dirty water, into my closet. I watched in horror as water drained out and seeped into the carpet. That was going to stain, and the smell would not come out for months. My dad never hit me, but I was truly expecting him to do that on this occasion. In fact, I believe hitting me may have been a more effective way of handling the situation. Instead, he looked at me and said, "Son, I'm so disappointed in you."

With that said, he turned around and left the house. Cathy, my stepmother, took Devon on a car ride and gave her a long talk. It was not until the following week that I would discover my punishment. My dad had enrolled me in a group session for other teenagers whose parents had caught them doing drugs. Over the next eight weeks I would spend an hour and a half every Thursday with seven other kids my age who were all in the same boat. This was not as effective as you would think.

School on Alcoholism and Other Drug Dependencies in July 2008.

"My name is Mike, and I'm here because my dad caught me smoking pot with my stepsister and my dog." That's how I would start every meeting.

TALKING HELPS BUT ONLY WHEN PROPERLY MOTIVATED

Over the course of the next six years, I would eventually find myself drinking or doing drugs with the kids I had met in the exact same group. We would always laugh about how the only thing this group did was made us feel ashamed of ourselves. I felt like my dad was trying to tell me that I was a degenerate with a huge incurable problem, when all he had to do was explain the pros and cons of what I was doing. I wish that he could have told me that he had experimented with pot himself and it is quite common for people to try. I might have been more prone to open up to him and be honest about how often I was using, which was something that he never asked. Instead, I was forced into an embarrassment and shame that I did not yet know how to handle in a healthy way. That might have been due to an inexperienced group counselor or improper upbringing. Regardless, I would not learn how to handle shame effectively until I was in my late twenties. Naturally, I am still struggling with it, but it is a learning process. Talking does help, and the group would have been effective had I gone into it with the right attitude, but being forced into the group at such a young age was not going to help. If you have someone using drugs in your family they have to be ready to stop before they will stop. More importantly, they have to be willing to stop for themselves, not for anyone else. Next I want to introduce you to some of the challenges of "legal" drugs, a topic first mentioned in the last chapter. This topic generated considerable attention with the death of Michael Jackson on June 25, 2009.

Shopaholics

It was early February, the year after I had graduated from pharmacy school and I had been working in a retail pharmacy since that September. I had just logged into my email account when something caught my attention. I had been forwarded an email from a friend and fellow pharmacist and it read as follows:

> The Department of Regulatory Agencies (DORA), Division of Registrations, announces the availability of its Electronic

> Prescription Drug Monitoring Program (PDMP), a secure da-
> tabase of controlled substance prescriptions dispensed by state
> pharmacies and from non-resident pharmacies that ship pre-
> scriptions into the state. The purpose of the database is to provide
> a tool for practitioners and pharmacists to identify abuse and
> receive objective information to provide appropriate treatment
> for their patients.

I had heard about programs similar to this being used in other states. It enabled doctors and pharmacists to work together more closely to flag potential abusers, hopefully before the abuse became too extreme. As I read this email I wondered how people who frequently doctor shop to obtain drugs of abuse felt about this. I read on to discover just how this information could be used against them.

> Information collected by the PDMP is only accessible electroni-
> cally to prescribers of controlled substances and pharmacists.
> Patients may access their own personal data by contacting the
> program. Law enforcement officials may only obtain information
> specific to an individual and upon presentation of a subpoena or
> court order.

I closed my web browser and pondered this for a moment. Personally, I did not like the idea of this information being used to incarcerate a human being. I liked the fact that it is more readily accessible to healthcare professionals than law enforcement individuals. Healthcare professionals, as a group, tend to be more empathetic to the drug abuser and more willing to help them improve. As I briefly explained in chapter 1, doctor shopping is the act of requesting the care of multiple physicians simultaneously without informing any of them that you are seeing multiple caregivers. Prescription drug abuse is no doubt a huge problem in America. Doctor shopping is one of the more common methods in which people obtain drugs. From 2003 to 2007 the records in the state of Colorado indicate that felony charges had been filed 2,245 times against people who had been accused of obtaining a controlled substance by fraud or deceit. This averages out to around 450 charges per year.[9] Regardless of the problem, I could not help but feel a little flustered by this. Was this system another way for our government to obtain information about citizens? And if so, how would this be used

---

9. Cardona, "New database spots," lines 38–41.

against us? I had to think about this system and more importantly, orient myself with it, in order to completely understand how I felt about it.

It was not until late spring of that same year that I finally got around to registering myself with the PDMP. It was mostly because I was working overnight shifts and filling a surplus of narcotic prescriptions from an abundance of people. Two weeks earlier I had received a forged prescription and the patient was arrested. I had to fill out a police report and felt uneasy about that whole situation. I knew that it was much more effective to treat an individual with a drug problem rather than to have them incarcerated, and this conflicted me. I went home that night and registered for the PDMP. Since then, I have been able to check on the amount of narcotics taken by my customers, whether it is from my pharmacy or another pharmacy halfway across the state.

I quickly became accustomed to using this website to check all patients presenting narcotic prescriptions, regardless of age, race, or creed. Within two weeks of registering with the PDMP I reached a moment of clarity. I started to see how many people really were seeing multiple doctors and using multiple pharmacies. I would get an average of fifteen narcotic prescriptions per night. There seemed to be at least two prescriptions each night that I would have to refuse to fill because I was not comfortable dispensing. Now, you may be thinking, "You're the pharmacist! It's your job to fill the prescription and not ask questions!" Actually, the board of pharmacy in the state where I was working would say:

1. Prescription drug abuse occurs in this country to an extent that exceeds or rivals the abuse of illicit drugs.

2. Prescription drug abuse occurs at times due to the deception of the authorized prescribers where patients seek controlled substances for treatment and the prescriber is without knowledge of the patient's other medical providers and treatments.

3. Electronic monitoring of prescriptions for controlled substances would provide a mechanism whereby prescribers could discover the extent of each patient's requests for drugs, and whether other providers have prescribed similar substances during a similar period of time.

This basically translates to the state board advocating that I use the Electronic Prescription Drug Monitoring Program. The state board of pharmacy expects pharmacists to not only fill prescriptions; we are to ensure that each prescription filled is issued in the usual course of professional treatment. This entails ensuring that the drugs dispensed by the pharmacist are not intended by the patient to be abused. We live in what can arguably be called the most litigious country in the world. It is no debate that Americans tend to sue each other, often unnecessarily. If pharmacists or doctors are acting negligent they can be sued for enabling a patient to become addicted. We can also be subject to federal penalties under the Federal Controlled Substance Act. With that said, a pharmacist has the right to refuse to fill any prescription.

So when Armando came to my pharmacy around 11:30 p.m. on a typical busy night, I was ready to do my job properly. He waited patiently at the drop-off window. I glanced over at him as I was finishing up helping Suzie Q over the phone and said, "Hey. Thanks for waiting, I'm almost done." He only smiled and nodded. He did not look the slightest bit annoyed. I have had patients scream at me for taking too long to wait on them. I have also had prescription bottles thrown at me because I could not refill them too soon without first consulting the patient's doctor. Pharmacy is a profession, but we are not always treated professionally. I walked up to Armando, smiled and greeted him, "Hi, how ya doing?"

"Not good," he apprehensively replied. "Can I fill this?"

I scanned the prescription over. It was written for Percocet 5mg/325mg. One to two tablets to be taken every six hours as needed for pain. The doctor, a local emergency room physician, wrote the prescription for a quantity of sixty tablets. According to the directions this should last him around seven and one-half days if he took the maximum amount prescribed. Everything was legitimate. I looked into the dilated pupils that overwhelmed his eyes, and then I noticed that the whites of them were tinted yellow. I slowly said, "Have you been to this pharmacy before?"

He started to fidget, as he replied, "No, I usually go to the one up the road."

A vague answer, as there were several pharmacies to choose from on that particular street and due to his ambiguity I was not sure which one he was talking about. Despite this, I decided not to pry any further. I asked the usual questions that I ask when someone is dropping off a prescription for the first time as I created a profile for Armando in our computer. What is your date of birth, address, and phone number? Do you have any medication allergies? He quickly answered all of these questions without a pause.

"Do you have an insurance card?" I asked.

"No insurance. I don't have insurance." He started to stutter and fidget more. "I was in a car accident a month ago and this back pain is killing me. Will these help?"

"You've never taken Percocet before?" I inquired.

"Is that what this is written for?" He replied. This was starting to get silly and very seriously fraudulent. He was wasting time telling me his story, most likely because he was nervous. "No, I've never had them, but my brother took them once. He said they were great."

Percocet is the brand name for a combination of two drugs: Oxycodone and acetaminophen. The former is classified as an opiod narcotic and the latter is a pain reliever, which you have most likely heard of in its brand name form, Tylenol. Acetaminophen acts primarily in the central nervous system increasing the pain threshold. The drug achieves this effect by centrally inhibiting an enzyme called cyclooxygenase. Cyclooxygenase is actively involved in the production of prostaglandins. Prostaglandins are involved in the sensation of pain. Since acetaminophen acts centrally, not peripherally, it lacks the anti-inflammatory effects of drugs like Motrin (ibuprofen) or Aleve (naproxen). Oxycodone is a very potent mu-opiate receptor agonist. Scientists have identified four different types of opiate receptors: mu, kappa, and delta. All narcotic painkillers are opiod drugs and all opiod drugs exert their effects via activation of one or more of the opiate receptors. Pain relief is experienced by activation of the μ_1 receptor and respiratory depression (slower rate of breathing) is due to μ_2 activation. Oxycodone activates both μ receptors, therefore causing both effects. Opiod drugs alter the way an individual emotionally responds to pain, via changes in pain perception at the spinal cord and higher levels in the central nervous system. The user experiences a sense of euphoria since the drug blocks the release of specific inhibitory neurotransmitters, including GABA and acetylcholine.

"They're very effective pain killers," I replied to Armando. "Is the generic drug alright with you?" I asked. He quickly nodded. "Alright, Armando, it's going to take me about five to ten minutes to fill this, assuming that I have no more interruptions from the phone or other customers."

WARNING SIGNS

Armando was forty-five years old, but appeared to be in his fifties. His clothing hung off of his skinny body in a way that made him look unhealthy. His hair and nails were unkempt and his posture was slouched. He stood a little over six feet tall despite his slouching. His skin was pale with a hint of yellow, which I also noticed in the whites of his eyes; perhaps due to the effect that too much acetaminophen has on the liver. Perhaps the most disturbing and prominent thing about Armando's appearance was the blue tint to his fingernails and lips. Opiod narcotics slow the heart rate and the respiratory rate and this effect is obviously heightened when the drug is being used in higher doses. The end result is something called hypoxia, inadequate oxygen in the blood. A telltale sign of hypoxia is cyanosis, bluish discoloration of the skin and mucous membranes. Hemoglobin is responsible for the red pigment of blood. Hemoglobin picks up oxygen from the lungs and transports it through the arteries to the body, releasing it to the cells via capillaries. Once the hemoglobin has given up its oxygen molecules, the blood appears blue and is transported back to the lungs via the veins. Arteries carry oxygenated blood and veins carry deoxygenated blood. This is why arteries in our bodies appear red and veins appear blue. The bluish discoloration of cyanosis most often appears in the finger and toenail beds, in addition to the skin of the lips and tongue. Armando's smurf-like lips and nails showed me that he was not getting enough oxygen delivered to his extremities.

I alluded to Armando's skin appearing yellow, due to too much acetaminophen. This is called jaundice. Acetaminophen is absorbed from the stomach and small intestine and metabolized in the liver to nontoxic compounds. When taken in excessive doses for prolonged periods of time the normal metabolism pathways become saturated and the excess acetaminophen is metabolized via different pathways, resulting in toxic metabolites. Without boring you too much more with science, I will cut to the chase. The end result is these toxic metabolites causing inflammatory damage and death to the cells of the liver. One hallmark sign of a malfunctioning liver is jaundice, which is why Armando's eyes and skin appeared yellowish. He did not look healthy at all.

Before filling his prescription, I would have to check his history on the PDMP. Once that was done I would have to open the narcotic vault, count out sixty generic Percocet, take an inventory of the remaining

Percocet, and finally document all of this in the pharmacy's Schedule II narcotic inventory book. I would never get to the narcotic vault.

In 1970 the United States Congress enacted a federal drug policy entitled the Controlled Substance Act (CSA). This regulated the manufacture, importation, distribution, and possession of certain drugs. The CSA closed the distribution of drugs with a potential for abuse or addiction in order to protect the public from these potentially harmful drugs. The CSA achieved this by placing drugs into appropriate schedules according to their potential for abuse and accepted medical use in the U.S. Schedule I drugs (C-I) have a high potential for abuse and no accepted medical use in the U.S. Examples of C-I drugs include: heroin, LSD, marijuana, and ecstasy. Schedule II drugs (C-II) have a high potential for abuse but have some accepted medical use. Some examples include: Percocet, methamphetamine, and cocaine. Schedule III drugs (C-III) have moderate to low physical dependence or high psychological dependence potential, but less than that of C-I or C-II drugs. Examples of C-III drugs include: Vicodin or testosterone. Schedule IV drugs (C-IV) have low or limited physical or psychological dependence potential. Examples of C-IV drugs include: Valium, Darvocet, or Xanax. Schedule V drugs (C-V) have a low potential for abuse and examples include: Tylenol with codeine elixir or Lomotil.Intervening

I pulled Armando's name up on the PDMP and was amazed by the number of times his name appeared on the website. Even more disturbing was how clever Armando had been. By sheer accident, I had inputted his last name as his first and his first name as his last. So when I had properly inputted his name I had noticed that he had been giving some pharmacies his name backwards (Armando as his last name and his last name as his first), possibly because he already knew about this program. He had been using a total of eleven different pharmacies, between his real and reversed names, in the last two months. Some of the eleven pharmacies had been used multiple times. He had received a total of twenty-one C-II and C-III narcotics in the past two months. Six of those twenty-one were written for was what intended to be a thirty-day supply. The others ranged from three- to fifteen-day supplies. Many of his prescriptions were being filled on the same day at various different locations and most of the prescriptions were for opiod narcotics, including Percocet or Oxycontin. I quickly gathered this information together and generated a report itemizing all of this information by date. I then printed the report detailing his activity in the last two months and began the part of my job that I loathed the most.

"Armando," I said in a firm voice. He approached the counter while looking wildly around. "What's wrong?" He knew something was up.

"I want to show this to you," I said, as I placed the pages of information on the counter. Three pages containing the date of each prescription, the drug dispensed, the amount, the intended days supply, the method of payment (insurance or cash), the prescriber, and finally the pharmacy in which each prescription was filled. I went over all of this with him. "You're taking too much of this drug far too often. I'm concerned."

"I'm not doing anything illegal. These are all prescribed by doctors," he quickly retorted.

"Do you tell these physicians that you're seeing all of the other physicians?" I asked.

"I don't have to do that." He was getting very defensive.

"Look," I said finally, raising my voice a bit. "I can understand a person seeing a few different physicians to get multiple opinions on a problem. But when you're seeing . . . I had already counted, but glanced over the sheet, pausing momentarily for effect, " . . . sixteen different physicians in a little over two months, that's called doctor shopping. That's illegal if you aren't telling each doctor about the others."

"Can I get arrested for this?" He asked.

"Yes, but I'd prefer that you'd face the problem rather than be incarcerated." I was referring to his addiction as "the problem." "I understand that you're in a great deal of pain, but you have to draw a line somewhere between treatment and abuse. I'm not going to call the police or report this to anyone. Think of this as someone on the highway flashing their lights at you as they pass, to alert you of a highway patrolman up ahead. Drug addiction only leads to jail, death, or recovery. I'd prefer to see you find your way to recovery." I had overstepped my boundaries. I try to never use the word addiction with my customers, unless they mention it.

Luckily, he seemed to understand. "Thank you," he said, and abruptly walked away, leaving his prescription. I checked his profile a few months later and noticed that he had only filled two more prescriptions over the next few days. After that I would like to hope he found his way to a Narcotic's Anonymous meeting, but there is no way to be certain.

PRESCRIPTION DRUGS AND ABUSE

Prescription drug abuse has become a major problem in our country. Gil Kerlikowske, Director of the Office of National Drug Control Policy (ONDCP), said that swift action is needed to address the problem:

> Several recent studies show the startling increase in prescription drug abuse. The 2008 National Survey on Drug Use and Health reported that in recent years the number of individuals who, for the first time, consumed prescription drugs for nonmedical purposes exceeded the number of first-time marijuana users. Monitoring the Future, a study of youth attitudes and drug use, shows that seven of the top 10 drugs commonly reported abused by 12th graders are prescription drugs. And another study, the 2007 Treatment Episode Data Set (TEDS), showed that from 1997 to 2007, there was a 400 percent increase in treatment admissions for individuals abusing prescription pain killers. . . . One factor contributing to the problem is easy access to pharmaceutical products."[10]

I am lucky to have never gotten caught up in the prescription drug abuse wave when I was using. I see people like Armando every day and it is a shame because these drugs are wonderful painkillers when they are used in the way in which they are intended. If you or anyone that you know is falling victim to prescription drug abuse, be careful, there is a thin line between recreational use and addiction. Do not be afraid to ask someone for help. There are many resources out there from your doctor, pharmacist, or any recovery-based fellowship. We have listed several resources at the end of this book, complete with websites, addresses, and phone numbers.

10. Office of National Drug Control Policy, "Director Outlines Plan," lines 14–23, 27–28.

Walking the Beat

Dean Jones

"Hear, O God, have mercy and be gracious to me!
O God, be my helper!"

—PSALM 30:10

There are a number of different ways to approach the topic of addiction. Some authors give lots of explanations, information, and "facts." In the pages of this chapter, Mike gives himself. It is not easy to bare one's soul, to invite everyone into the very personal space of your world. But this view, although it comes with some pain, is paramount to the understanding of addiction. The most obvious target for Mike's comments is men and women in their teens and early twenties as well as their parents. The content, however, has value for everyone with some interest in drug and alcohol addiction. All of us are involved in some way in the processes that either sustain addiction or serve to build a truly wholesome, healthy lifestyle. This may be in the form of supporting a culture of addiction or more directly as we relate to our own addiction, to members of our family, and/or friendship networks. Our level of understanding, our attitudes do make a difference.

I need to begin my reflections for this chapter by admitting that I have never used illegal drugs and I am not an alcoholic. Therefore, my story does not have the immediate attraction of Mike's as he describes experiences like doing drugs in a doghouse. I graduated from high school in 1950. I never heard of or witnessed any form of drug use while I was in my teens. In my family, and church, there were strong behavioral norms around using alcohol in any form. Smoking and drinking were considered "sins." But, as I will share, I have had considerable contact with people who have been addicted. I represent a host of people who view the problem from a distance, but nevertheless are truly involved, trying to help someone, trying to understand a behavior with which he or she has no personal experience. As I mentioned previously, all of us

are involved in one way or another. Perhaps you can relate to my journey, most of it over a twenty-year period in the work of night ministry.
As I walked the streets in the worst part of town late at night I always
wore the standard, white clergy collar as I served others in a "ministry of
presence," not a preaching ministry.

My work with people at night was primarily with adults, in taverns
and on the downtown streets. I do know that alcoholism can be found
in every sector of society. While I was going to Bible school I worked in
a machine shop at night. A man, who ran the power shears, cutting up
big sheets of steel all night, kept a bottle near his machine and sucked on
this through the night. After graduation I became the pastor of a small
church in the sawmill town of Rainier, Oregon. One of the women in
the church asked me to talk to her husband, telling me that he had a
"drinking problem." I did visit this man. But I did not know what to say
about alcohol use, with no experience in my personal life and no class on
addiction while I was preparing for the ministry. This visit was embarrassing. The couple had a large aquarium, so I ended up spending my
time talking about fish. I also visited an older couple on occasion who
happened to live across the street from the parsonage. The woman was
in bad health. Her husband kept her going with regular doses of "hot
toddy," a drink containing lots of alcohol. Again, I said nothing about
alcohol use. As it turned out, I was visiting when she died. The local
mortician was called. He ran a low-cost operation, making the call by
himself. I helped him carry the body out to the waiting hearse, glad that
I was present so that the husband did not need to go through this.

When I returned to the Seattle area to continue my education, I
worked as a social worker for the State of Washington for three years.
A woman in my department held a position calling for liaison work
with other agencies. She kept a bottle at her side all day and turned to
it regularly, resulting in less than a steady walk at the end of the day.
When I held positions as a sociologist I attended several professional
meetings. At one of these meetings in a grand hotel in New Orleans I
was coming down the escalator one morning around 9 a.m. to attend a
morning conference. A friend, Walt, was riding the up escalator. He said
that he was just coming in after an all-night drinking binge on Bourbon
Street. In Seattle one minister with a large congregation became a regular volunteer in the ministry of Operation Nightwatch. This was after he
could claim recovery, but not cure as an alcoholic. His wife left him during

his career as an active alcoholic, but his church stayed with him, pushing for his recovery. He then continued in that church for a number of years, starting twelve-step programs for a variety of problems from alcoholism to addiction to sex and food. Recently, a friend shared her problems about the management of an eighth-grade daughter who may be getting caught up in a drug culture at her school. This school is in a "good neighborhood," not a place normally associated with illegal drug activity.

The school districts that include the town where I live now recently published a booklet titled "Voices and Views: Middle School Youth Speak Out." In reading this booklet, I was surprised by the top ranked concerns of school children at this age today. The middle school students ranked "Drugs/Alcohol/Huffing" third in a list of top concerns. The comments of some of these students are revealing:

- There is peer pressure to smoke, do drugs, and shoplift. It is hard to say no because friends are so important, but you don't want to say no.

- Pot is not bad for you; it only screws up your short-term memory.

- Parents don't care as much about pot—they do care about alcohol and meth.

- Music videos are all about drugs and alcohol. If they do it, I can too and I will be cool.

Although the study did not allow for a discussion of the newer, super-caffeinated energy drinks such as Red Bull, Monster, Full Throttle, and Amp, these drinks have become very popular with the twelve- to twenty-four-year-old age group. And, according to a recent article in *The Journal of American College Health*, there is a link between energy drinks and risky behavior including substance abuse.[11]

In my work downtown at night I saw men and women who were at the low ebb in their strong pull to alcohol and/or illegal drugs. The addiction ruled most every waking moment. Many times I took men to a local detox late at night. One night I transported a couple, Georgia and Jerry, from Tacoma to Wenatchee, Washington, to a detox and treatment center. I invite you to walk with me into their situation for some understanding of the many complications of serious addiction. I will let this story speak for itself. If you are now living with an addiction, the story

11. Parker-Pope, "Taste for Quick Boost," lines 29–36.

should give you encouragement in knowing that there are people who may be willing to become part of your recovery process. This may be a man or woman who is doing twelve-step work in AA or NA, a pastor, or a member of your family. The story also supports the reality that there are windows of opportunity for change. Unfortunately, Georgia and Jerry did not take advantage of a window opened for them. They were living together when I met them. She was from the tri-cities area of Washington State; he was in the states illegally from Mexico. Georgia was into heroin and Jerry was addicted to cocaine. The all-night drive over the mountains to eastern Washington started after a meeting in a motel during which I gave the option of entering a treatment center. At that time no such facility was available for indigent drug addicts in Tacoma.

I first met Georgia while looking for someone to help me learn Spanish. A mutual friend introduced her to me as a person fluent in both English and Spanish. Months later she told me that she had, in fact, run into me on the street a year earlier. That time there was no conversation and I had no memory of the meeting. She remembered the night as the time when one of her friends shot and killed another friend. She was in shock on the street when she turned and saw me, a stranger, wearing the clergy collar. She wanted to talk but was afraid. Later that night she went to the apartment of the fellow who had pulled the fatal trigger. He was lying on top of the blankets in his bed, the pistol on his stomach, crying his eyes out. Georgia tried to comfort him.

That traumatic shooting event months ago was not the most immediate pain for Georgia when we were formally introduced. She was concerned about Jerry. He had been picked up by the police on a charge of possession of drugs and was in jail. I offered to visit him, seeing him at intervals over the forty days he was in jail. These visits were always difficult because Jerry spoke almost no English. On my first visit, I noticed that his arms were marked by skin sores from the use of needles. During the jail time he appeared for our talks with white medication on the sores. These sores healed up. He seemed to improve physically in other ways over the weeks. But he fell into periods of deep depression when he became aware of how hard it was for me to keep in touch with Georgia. She was on the street at night and living in a cheap hotel. Sometimes I could find her and at other times I did not know where she was.

While Jerry was in jail he was escorted into court for a hearing. I attended this hearing with Georgia. An interpreter was available. The defense attorney assigned by the court was bilingual. But the judge did not understand Spanish. It was interesting to observe his actions and to hear him talk about Jerry. During his verbal dialogue about the case he defined Jerry as "someone with a third-grade education." Georgia later told me how hostile she felt at that time. It appeared to her and also to me that the judge was making a hasty evaluation based upon his inability to understand Spanish. Jerry was, in fact, fairly well educated. He could read very well. But he could not speak or read English. The judge also expressed the conviction that Jerry would never pay any fines, therefore, the only way to get anything out of him was to keep him in jail. His sentence was set based on the fact that he had a prior offense on the books. It turned out that this information was false since Jerry was working at the time of the alleged former offense.

As I have indicated, during Jerry's jail time I kept in touch with Georgia on the streets downtown. She informed me that she was on heroin and expressed her deep feelings about Jerry and his general welfare. She seemed willing to do almost anything to raise money to get him out of jail. And she talked about her own drug problem. When I pressured her about going into treatment, she said that she had some "legal things" to take care of and that she needed to raise money for Jerry.

There were times when she appeared haggard and threadbare. At other times there seemed to be a little hope. One night she asked me to take her to McDonald's for some food. She had money. She ordered and paid for a large amount of chicken McNuggets for herself and a cup of hot chocolate for me. I had learned that such a display of money meant only one thing: she was again into drug dealing. A few weeks after the McDonald's visit, Georgia told me that she had reached the point where she was shooting up a gram of heroin at a time and going through several hundreds of dollars a day in the process to maintain her habit. She deliberately selected drug dealing as the way to raise this money. As she explained to me, there were other things she could do to get the money, but she felt that selling drugs was "the least damaging to others."

Two days before Jerry was released from jail, the police picked up Georgia. It took me two days to find her in jail because she had used a different name when picked up. On my first visit with Georgia in jail she was in the middle of withdrawal. She was very sick. She sat across from me in the interview room, arms covered with bruises and scars. She was barefooted. She shook all over. During the next visit, she was over most of the chilling but had moved into a time of deep depression. She expressed strong doubt that she would ever see Jerry again. She just knew that she would be taken to prison again. As she informed me, she had done some three years in prison before and "could not stand going back." In her description of her prison time she claimed that they had "burned her out." For her, this meant that she was totally stripped of any sense of value, of worth to anyone. As she saw things, her only out was to end it all. She talked of suicide. Another pain that pushed her in this direction was the knowledge that her mother was dying or near death and that she had not, could not see her. During this visit with Georgia, I took off my black suit coat and placed it around her shoulders when I saw that she was cold and shaking from the cold. I talked openly with her about the suicide issue. I set up a contract with her that she would not do anything until I had the chance to see her again in three days.

Two days after this jail visit Georgia was transported to a city some two hundred miles away in eastern Washington. This city had a warrant out for her over an unpaid fine of some three hundred dollars. Given her condition the last time I saw her, I felt obligated to visit her in the new jail. I found Jerry on the street, invited him to make the trip with me and we drove four hours to see her, arriving only minutes before the visiting time was over. She was very happy to see Jerry. We were told that she would be going to court that very night. She felt that she would be released on the spot because Jerry had some one hundred seventy-five dollars and she had forty dollars, a total of over half of the money needed. Jerry and I waited around in the small town for the late-night court session.

As it turned out, she was brought into court as the only woman with eight other inmates. They were all led into the court in lockstep, handcuffed with a strong rope strung between each pair of hands. She later confided to me that this was a very dehumanizing experience. When she was called to stand before the judge, Georgia did very poorly. She appeared very bitter and challenged the judge about her fine and days in jail. The judge took a very negative approach to the case, insisting that Georgia remain in jail to do the fifteen days as sentenced. Georgia was crushed at these words. We watched as she was led back to jail. After this scene, we drove through the night, getting back to Tacoma at 3:30 a.m. the next day.

After that long night I lost track of Jerry on the downtown streets. Five days later I got a call from Georgia. She had been able to talk friends or family members into paying the total fine and also giving her bus fare out of town as far as Seattle. I drove up and gave her a ride the rest of the way back to Tacoma. At first I tried to locate a temporary place for her to stay. It seemed impossible to find Jerry. She was now determined to get off heroin. We asked around on the street and were told by one of her friends that he was staying in an old hotel in town. I went with her to the place. She stayed in the hotel lobby while I went up to his room. In my limited Spanish I told him that "una amiga" (a friend) was down in the lobby and wanted to see him. This was the way she wanted me to announce her presence. He dressed quickly and followed me down the steps of the hotel. I watched as they embraced and walked out of the hotel lobby arm in arm, together again after two months of separation.

A week passed before I heard from Georgia again. She finally invited me out to dinner. She and Jerry were staying in a cheap motel near the downtown drug strip. I drove them to a Chinese restaurant and they paid for an expensive family-style dinner. Back in the motel room I became aware that Georgia did not have basic items of clothing when two friends of hers came by the room to give her and Jerry some clothes. The irrational spending of money is one of the characteristics of addiction.

When Georgia stepped outside to talk with friends, Jerry went into the bathroom. After his trip to the bathroom his behavior changed. He locked the door and pulled a chair up under the doorknob. Then he pulled the window shades closed and yanked a metal covering off a heat thermostat so that he could stare at the exposed wires. This paranoid and irrational behavior can be one of the immediate results of using crystal meth, a process sometimes referred to as "tweaking." Jerry was most likely seeing something like bugs crawling out of the thermostat when in fact nothing like this was happening. When Georgia returned to the room her first question was whether or not Jerry had been to the bathroom. When I told her that he had she immediately cussed him out for "shooting up" while a "priest" was around. During this heated exchange I noticed the point of a needle, part of the "works" (hypodermic syringe) sticking out of his back pocket.

Georgia was thrown into a fit of despair, crying as she said that she just could not stay with him through the night when he was acting like this. She said that he had an ounce of cocaine in the room and that he would just keep shooting up until it killed him. During these tense minutes, Jerry expressed a desire to talk with me. Georgia interpreted for him as he spoke in Spanish. He said that he wanted help in getting off drugs and then added that Georgia was also "sick."

I called a detox facility located some one hundred eighty miles away in Wenatchee, Washington. As I mentioned, no such facility was available at that time in western Washington. I told the facility to hold two beds and offered this as an option to the couple. Georgia served again as an interpreter in discussing this with Jerry. After some delay they agreed to go with me. Her words at the time implied that she was at the end of her rope.

It was now 1:30 a.m. I had been going all day. But they loaded up their few personal effects and we started off on a four-hour drive through the darkness over a mountain pass to eastern Washington. There was opportunity for a lot of talk during this trip. At one point, Georgia said that she was very thankful for what I had done for both of them but that she just did not understand why I was doing it. In one city along the route we stopped at a twenty-four-hour restaurant. Georgia went into a restroom. I became anxious when it seemed like she would never come out. When she finally returned to the car she said that she had done something that was "very hard to do." Then she asked me if I had any idea what it was like to flush eight hundred dollars worth of drugs down the toilet.

At 6 a.m. we parked in front of the drug treatment place. There was an emotional parting. I was very tired after driving through the night. Georgia said that she would not be able to make it without God's help. We talked about total surrender of life, giving all to the Lord. I prayed with her, tears in my eyes. They gathered up three plastic bags of personal effects and I walked with them into the facility where I left them after a final round of hugs. I drove back to Tacoma, watching the early morning light signal the dawn of a new day. I wish that I could say that this was a successful ending but it was not. Georgia and Jerry walked away from the treatment facility because they were not allowed to share the same room. They again became involved in drugs. My last contacts with them included visits to the Purdy prison for women not far from Tacoma to see Georgia and a long drive to the prison in Walla Walla, Washington, to visit with Jerry.

Georgia was taken to a hospital in Tacoma from the women's prison. I visited her in the hospital, a guard standing near. Her problems were related to a heart condition, not directly tied to her heroin use. For others addicted to heroin, the physical toll can be very high. One example is the 2006 death from heroin overdose of Austin Meyers, a University of Colorado art student with strong talent in graphic design. His promising career was ended when he was only twenty-one years old, a victim of illegal drugs.

Today it is easy to read about what seems to be a growing international trafficking in drugs. It is now generally acknowledged that the annual value of drugs trafficked through Mexico into the United States has risen substantially. It is a multibillion-dollar business. This trafficking has become a popular item in the news along with word of the drug cartels in Mexico, the killing and violence, and controversy over immigration policies. In the midst of media attention and the tendency to make drugs an anonymous problem, touching people we never see, it is very important to take a close look at real people like Georgia and Jerry, and Mike as he shares his personal story. Or the problem may be closer to you, demonstrated by the behavior of a teenager sleeping in a bedroom in your house, or a friend or other family member trying to climb up the downward spiral of drugs in the context of a country facing major financial problems and heavily involved in a costly war far from our borders.

If you are now preoccupied with where and when the next drink or drug fix will be coming, or if someone you love is in this condition, you know that addiction comes in a surround of strong feelings. Love and hate struggle to the surface in relationships where addiction runs its course. It is easy to grieve over what could have been. It has been some fifteen years since I last saw Harlan, a Native American who lived in Tacoma. Harlan was an alcoholic. With greasy black hair hanging down from a baseball cap and pockmarks on his face, he was not a handsome man. But there was something about him that drew me to him. When I saw him in one of the downtown taverns catering to Native Americans, I often walked with him over to a booth where we shared together. When a family member died over in Montana I was able to help Harlan with funds to attend the funeral. While in Montana he tried to jump over a fence and broke his leg in the process. My goal was to get Harlan into a treatment facility near his tribal home in Montana. But before I could do this I was met one night inside the door of the tavern by several of his friends. They told me that Harlan had died. He had been sleeping outside. He did not change the bandages on his leg. He died of gangrene at the age of twenty-nine. I cried when I heard the news and I vowed to get out of night ministry because it was too hard to take the loss of people I really cared about. But I continued in the work for another eight years. And I continued to feel pain, as when Karen, a Native American princess was found dead in the women's restroom off the cocktail lounge of a night spot on Puyallup Avenue in Tacoma. She died of an overdose of drugs. I had worked with her about the drugs. Her life should not have ended this way.

As I look back on my contacts late at night, I think about how my reactions changed over time. I did complete a certificate program for counseling in alcoholism at Seattle University. After this year-long program, I began to take a clinical approach to folks I met at night, asking questions about how often they drank, how they felt when not drinking, etc. But over time I dropped this approach. I became more interested in simply conveying a feeling of worth, of value to the man or woman I encountered on a dark street late at night. I recognized that my role was more to help the person get on the first step toward recovery. I can still remember a beautiful young woman who stood on a downtown street corner in Tacoma. Heavily into drugs, she tried to convince me that she was "trash," that she was not worth the time of any treatment place. On another night a man sat on the sidewalk outside a tavern. I had seen him before when we talked about his addiction to the bottle. This night I asked him to stand, which he did. Then I gave him a hug with the words, "I love you and God loves you." This man of the bottle was at first startled by my reaction to him. Then he affirmed my attention, giving me the impression that, at least for the moment, he could see some value in himself.

Work with addicts at night is not always a losing battle. Sometimes people do manage to climb up the "downward spiral." Jim was a professional musician before his slide to the mean part of town because of drugs. At one time he owned a view home in Gig Harbor, Washington, had a wife, and all the perks of a good income. He was once featured in a national music magazine. When I saw him he shuffled around in tattered jeans. One night when I met him I encouraged him to let me drive him to his mom's home, not far from downtown Tacoma, and then to admit himself into a treatment place. He hesitated, fingering some loose change in his pocket but finally walked with me to my car. As we pulled away from the curb he pleaded that he needed "at least a beer," but I told him that he did not need this. We talked about treatment. He did get his life turned around. I was happy for him when I met him some months later to learn about his new direction in life.

Then there was the time I battled with a young woman over her drug use. One night I offered to take her to a local hospital where I knew detox was available. But they wanted fifteen hundred dollars, completely out of my budget. So I took her to an emergency room of another hospital. Here they informed me that they did not take drug patients. I pleaded with them to at least exam her, hoping that they might find something worthy of hospitalization. Late at night she fell asleep on a gurney parked in one of the corridors of the hospital. I went home after asking them to call me when she awoke. Very early in the morning I drove back to the hospital, took her to breakfast and then to an office where people were screened for a new state program for addicts. Here I helped her fill out the forms. She was told that she was accepted and to come back in four months. My only option was to drop her off on the street of lost dreams downtown. She went back to drugs but eventually did get free from her addiction. A key message from this work is that recovery, wholeness is possible. I worked with people at the bottom of the downward spiral, and some did climb up against odds. If you or someone you know is somewhere on the downgrade, it is very important to know that change is possible. It is not necessary to slide down into a loss of everything of value.

FAMILY TIES

When doing my work downtown at night I often faced the challenge of working with a spouse or friend of an alcoholic. One of the strong lessons coming from the writing of Mike in the major part of this chapter is the significance of family reactions. In his case, if his Dad had handled the situation differently perhaps his story would have been different. There is considerable variance in the combination of people making up a "family." This chapter invites inquiry into how such family forms as a single mom working two jobs with teenage sons influences possible drug use, as well as the situation where parents have divorced, one has remarried and a teenaged son must adjust to a new parent as well as a new sister who is near his age. I have seen many different arrangements of "family." At the extreme, I have seen old men and women who live alone, but hold dearly to a memory of a wife or husband. For them the person, now dead, remains part of their present life space. One example is the senior citizen I first met in a tavern in Tacoma. He lived in a cheap room near this tavern. A few years before our meeting, his wife of thirty-eight years had died. He showed me a picture of her that he carried carefully in his wallet. It was not a professional photo, only a picture on a food-handler permit. I visited him in his room. He had his checks mailed directly to the tavern, where most of the money was spent. Tom was an alcoholic, with fond and strong memories of his wife. One day his only picture of her was stolen when someone broke into his room, taking everything that might have some value. I helped console him after this loss. For him, it was like losing his wife a second time.

I know that there are many different family forms today. When people live together they have a strong influence on each other. This is most apparent in the case of two people who share life's ups and downs. One night in St. Louis, Missouri, I met a middle-aged man in the Greyhound Bus Depot. He was alone and wanted to talk. His major concern was his wife's excessive drinking. She often became abusive when drunk. One of his coping strategies was to take long walks. I suggested that he get involved with Alanon. I was surprised when he said that he had never heard of the organization, an AA resource for family and friends of alcoholics.

If you are now involved in a family situation where addiction is a major problem you have most likely identified the situation as a problem before the one who is addicted. In the literature about alcoholism it is suggested that the spouse and children of the alcoholic have a longer time "to become sick themselves." You may need special help, including a support network such as Alanon. This does not mean that you are neurotic, which in turn has driven your significant other to drink. The alcoholic drinks, engages in alcoholic behavior, and everyone in the family is affected in the process. It is the drinking that causes the sickness of all concerned. One of the first steps toward wholeness for the person who is sometimes called a "co-alcoholic" is acceptance of the fact that he or she is not "at fault" for causing the alcoholism. My words to you mirror what I have often said to a late-stage alcoholic downtown late at night: "I love you and God loves you."

It may be helpful to consider briefly the sociological dynamics of interaction and the family as a social system. The alcoholic's need for treatment may be obvious. Sometimes it is more difficult to see the hurt in other members of the family. The alcoholic family, like all families, is a social system composed of individuals each with many interrelated needs. Every member of the family has physical, psychosocial, and spiritual needs. In the total experiences of individuals the judgments coming from important others are very important. We are social beings and respond quickly to feedback concerning self-worth. Sometimes we are in situations that encourage an open expression of feelings and experiences. At other times, there are few opportunities for openness. Although past events have made major contributions to our feelings of self-worth, it is the present that must be given primary attention when trying to understand problems. How does one regard him or herself at the moment? What is the habitual pattern in relating to people who are close? How does one express negative and positive feelings? These simple questions are important for everyone.

It is easy to imagine how the alcoholism of one family member might influence other family members if we regard the family as a social system. People in a social system like the family relate to each other through processes of communication that are both verbal and nonverbal. The communication may involve the delivery of factual information as well as many other messages including critical messages about self-worth. Some messages are evasive. People struggle to read clues about themselves as they watch and listen to others in the family. In the alcoholic family, communication processes are not working properly. Basic psychosocial needs are often frustrated.

In normal exchanges there is a reciprocal sharing of verbal and nonverbal clues during which all parties to the exchange participate freely. If a spouse is drunk or irritable because of extensive drinking, the exchange is distorted. The co-alcoholic is placed in the awkward situation of being forced to focus on the alcoholism since it dictates all family events while at the same time he or she is unable to get the normal self-evaluation from the alcoholic spouse. The co-alcoholic can fall into the dysfunctional pattern of looking at the alcoholic for signs of personal worth. If the alcoholic is not drinking on a given day, for example, the spouse may "allow" himself or herself to have a good day.

In the case of the co-alcoholic as well as the alcoholic, it is imperative to understand that trauma and pain can flourish beneath a facade that is used to maintain some resemblance of control. The spouse often struggles in ways that only serve to increase anxiety. Over involvement in church work may be part of this struggle. The co-alcoholic can be very lonely while giving time to church projects. As conditions become increasingly desperate, the spouse of the alcoholic is usually the first to experience some of the sensations of total loss. He or she begins to fear that the entire family is falling apart. This fear may come with a considerable loss of self-esteem when thinking about the loss of the affections of the spouse because of the first love for the bottle. The spouse's feelings for the alcoholic often shift back and forth between sympathy and complete disgust. This amount of stress can contribute to any number of "stress diseases," including migraine headaches and gastro-intestinal disorders. The children in the family suffer in their own ways. They may need professional help to disentangle the conflicting messages coming from an alcoholic parent. They may also need assistance in working through dysfunctional adaptations that they have made to the situation. This includes, for example, the assumption of a "hero role" as a child to "redeem" the family in the eyes of the community.

Changes in the immediate family are only one part of the changes in social relationships coming with addiction. One of the hallmarks of addiction is that the total network of relationships will change over time. With sufficient resources an addiction can be hidden from close friends and family, but sooner or later major changes will unfold in relationships. Some time ago a very wealthy man in Seattle simply booked a flight to Hawaii every weekend where he proceeded to go on a drunken binge. The folks I saw at night did not have this kind of money. In Tacoma I often saw Mary on the streets at night and struggled with her over her drug addiction. As one indication of the major shift in her social contacts, one night in February she asked me if I could first take her to a 7-Eleven store to get a Christmas card and then go with her to her mother's home where her daughter lived. I helped her in these chores and was sad that this woman had been so high on drugs all through the holidays that she had not visited her daughter. For her the circle of "friends" around drugs occupied all of her time.

Chemical dependency, like other major problems such as mental illness and suicide, is best approached from a holistic perspective. Family and peers are important as well as habitual patterns in coping with stress, but neurological forces are also central to the process. Mike's discussion of some basic brain processes in the first part of this chapter is very helpful. All addictions come with significant neurological components. In a recent article in *The American Journal of Medicine,* Dr. Neal L. Benowitz of the University of California, San Francisco, highlighted some of the relevant factors in nicotine addiction, pointing again to the role of the neurotransmitter dopamine, as mentioned by Mike.[12] Nicotine easily crosses the blood-brain barrier, where it binds to nicotine-specific receptors in the brain. This results in the release of neurotransmitters, primarily dopamine, which signals a pleasurable experience and is critical to the reinforcing effects of nicotine and other drugs of abuse. I have a great deal of affinity for such an approach because of a time when I taught medical sociology. To prepare myself for an understanding of the interface between sociological and neurological factors, I audited first a medical school course on neuroanatomy and then a course with medical students in Gross Anatomy. I will refer again to this experience in the next chapter.

GROWING AWARENESS OF THE SPIRIT

One night I was called to the emergency room area of Tacoma General Hospital. When I walked into the hospital that night I was told that a young man was refusing to leave the ER area until a minister was called. He came in by ambulance after taking a near fatal amount of illegal drugs. As I talked to him he said that he could remember being hooked up to a series of machines that monitored his vital life signs. He saw one of the lines on a machine settle into a long, straight line. Then he had the sensation that he was floating up above his body, looking down at it. Next he told me that he "saw Jesus." I discussed with him some practical steps he needed to take and said enough so that he was comfortable in leaving the ER area for a regular hospital bed. He was not kept long in the hospital. I had no contact for some three weeks after his near-death experience. Then he called to let me know that he was going on a mission with an uncle and that he was "off drugs." In my role as a minister on the night scene I witnessed both dramatic and less-than-dramatic ways in which spiritual issues became the primary concern. On another level, the sustaining of an outreach program at night was in itself a demonstration of the "spiritual," a work of faith. One of the best ways to tap into "spiritual issues" is to learn from someone "who has been there."

12. Benowitz, "Smoking Less," 3–10.

"My name is Jim and I am an alcoholic." This self-introduction is not new in a meeting of AA. Jim is just another recovering alcoholic, strongly committed to Alcoholics Anonymous. He is also James B. Nelson, Professor Emeritus of Christian Ethics at United Theological Seminary in the Twin Cities and author of many books on sexual theology, bioethics, and Christian ethical theory. In 2004 he wrote about his personal journey with alcoholism in a book titled *Thirst: God and the Alcohol Experience.*[13] This is a very positive review of the changes he and others have experienced. He feels that he has received the wonder of life "once more." As a professional in theology and ethics, Nelson uses many of the writings in the Bible as personal messages for his joyous return to life. He sees a portion of Psalm 30, for example, as his own song of praise:

> Sing praises to God, O you saints of God,
> and give thanks to God's holy name.
> For God's anger is but for a moment;
> and God's favor is for a lifetime.
> Weeping may tarry for the night,
> but joy comes with the morning.
> As for me, I said in my prosperity,
> "I shall never be moved."
> By your favor, O God,
> you had established me as a strong mountain,
> you hid your face,
> I was dismayed,
> "To you, O God, I cried…
> What profit is there in death,
> If I go down to the Pit?"
> Will the dust praise you?
> Will it tell of your faithfulness?
> Hear, O God, and be gracious to me!
> O God, be my helper!
> You have turned my mourning into dancing;
> you have loosed my sackcloth
> and girded me with gladness,
> that my soul may praise you and not be silent.
> O Sovereign, my God, I will give thanks to you for ever.
> Psalm 30:4–12, Inclusive Language Bible

13. Nelson, *Thirst.*

As Professor Nelson and others over the years see the experience, a spiritual transformation is essential to recovery. In his view we need to "stop playing God" in our efforts to control our own destiny. The divine sovereignty of God is important but God is best seen as not God the transcendent, but God enfleshed in all human life.

> How then do I discern God in the midst of my alcoholism? First, it is clear to me that God neither willed nor desired my disease. I became alcoholic through a combination of factors I have named earlier. But now I want to respond to this addiction faithfully, trusting that the Holy One is present in the midst of it with divine creativity, yearning for my healing and the healing of all those whom my disease has wounded. I want to discern how—by God's grace—this alcoholism can become the occasion for good. Can it actually be used for the reordering of life, for empowerment, for transformation, even for blessing?[14]

Nelson continues to talk, in his book, about a growing awareness of the sacred presence in life. He refers to a letter written in 1953 by Bill Wilson, cofounder of Alcoholics Anonymous, in which Wilson mentions experiencing something like a second conversion after praying to God for release from everything that would be in the way of his recovery. Nelson takes AA's eleventh step very seriously with what he sees as amazing results:

> So also, when I take A.A.'s Eleventh Step seriously—"praying only for knowledge of (God's) will for us and the power to carry that out"—the net result is not that I give up my own will by focusing on God's. It is more paradoxical than this. Once again, it is losing and finding life. In willingness to pray only for God's will and not my own, I receive myself back as a gift. I am grasped by Reality, for the harmony of our wills is what is finally real.[15]

As final words of praise for the power of recovery, Nelson offers the following:

> We know that authentic recovery is more than abstinence. It is more than simply not drinking. It is not wanting to drink. The obsession and the craving thirst have all but disappeared, and we have experienced a wondrous sense of freedom. No matter how much we wanted it, we could not have willed that freedom. We

14. Ibid., 156.
15. Ibid., 160.

could not have created it, no matter how strongly we desired it. It just came as a gift, and we know it is real. Perhaps self-love is something like that.

That appears true of our relation to God. When we have given up trying to climb the heights to the Eternal One, we might sink into the holy arms more deeply than we had imagined possible. In fact, now—for today—that we are free from the desperate escapism of alcohol intoxication, we might even know moments of God intoxication.[16]

NEARING THE END

Alcoholics and drug addicts can recover. The disease need not necessarily lead to death. But sometimes the addiction has so completely claimed the body that death will come. It is most unfortunate that those in professional positions in a faith community are sometimes not as helpful as they could be around "end of life" issues. I was present, for example, when a clergy person made a home visit to a family living with the official designation of "hospice care." This person never talked about death, talking instead of the politics of the church. One month later this clergy person officiated at the funeral mass of the loved one in the family. Sometimes in the journey with cancer and with serious drug addiction or alcoholism death is an appropriate topic to consider and talking can be very helpful for all concerned.

The most striking example of my own inadequacy in honestly sharing around death came for me one night when I was making my rounds on the streets of downtown Tacoma. I had seen "Uncle Albert" (his street name) before, an older man with a flowing white beard and an easy smile. One night he was sitting on a bench on the sidewalk, not far from the Tacoma Rescue Mission. He pulled an official looking sheet of paper from a pocket and held it out for me to see. This document was given to him on his recent release from the hospital. Uncle Albert was an alcoholic. Before his travels to the bottom, he had owned seventeen different businesses. Three of his sons had earned PhDs and were teaching in different colleges. But when I saw him, Uncle Albert was among the faceless crowds of men dependent on their next drink. Not far from where he was sitting, a young man proceeded to tie off his upper left arm with a plastic cord and then plunged a needle into one of his veins, self-

16. Ibid., 167.

medicating on illegal drugs. The paper I glanced at on that last meeting with Uncle Albert was grim. It listed major damage in all major body organs, truly a harbinger of death. Uncle Albert made a simple plea to me. He said that he wanted to talk about "peace," adding that he assumed I knew what he meant. I did talk with him but I really did not see him as someone who was dying. Two weeks after that meeting on the street, Uncle Albert died in a public detox facility. His prior status in life would have given him a room with a mountain view up in one of the modern hospitals in town. Those of us who claim some identification with the faith community must do a better job of talking about "peace," for the addict as well as for family members.

There are many indications that people are now more willing, even thankful to talk about death. One of my good friends, Harold Simonson (introduced in the last chapter), sent me a letter while I was completing my comments for this chapter. At the time he was eighty-two and had successfully completed forty-three radiation treatments for prostate cancer. Then he was given the word that he had developed a "lesion" on his right kidney. He wrote about life and death and how words can become so irrelevant at times. A retired professor of literature, Hal then shared the following with me, words he had written on the backside of his wife's grocery list. The year after he wrote these words he saw the publication of two more of his books, one a second edition with a new forward, and the other a new book, *Through the Church Door*.[17]

Life

I will live
I am living
I lived[18]

CONVERSATION

Now it is time for us to again turn to a conversation as we conclude this chapter on drug and alcohol addiction. On first glance, it would seem that Mike and I have little to share in terms of personal experience. For me, the contacts were with others. I was never involved in anything like an experience of doing cocaine in an oversized doghouse. But as you will

17. Simonson, *Through the Church Door*.
18. As a personal friend, Hal shared these words with author Dean Jones in 2009.

see in the pages to follow, we do have concerns and interests that tran-
scend our age difference. Our conversation took place in a classroom
at a local Lutheran church. We selected the church because we knew
that we would not have distractions; it was a place of silence, removed
from the normal sounds and sights of city life. This, of course, begs the
question of how much the church should be involved in the messy side
of life including problems like drug or alcohol addiction. Individual pa-
rishioners cannot avoid the untidy, sometimes painful aspects of life. Is
the church only a safe haven, away from real life? Or should it include
direct references to help for those going through a major trial? We have
strong feelings that spirituality must not be divorced from everyday life,
no matter how messy life becomes.

Mike: How have things changed over the years as you have been
involved with people in their journey with drugs or alcohol?

Dean: Since I have now been retired for six years, given twenty
years of full-time service to night ministry, and served as a volunteer in
Seattle's Operation Nightwatch before then, my first contacts with serious addiction issues came before you were born. While I was a volunteer
in Seattle, I was on the faculty at the School of Nursing at the University
of Washington, involved with a graduate program for nursing students.
Going back that far in time is not like visiting downtown Seattle when
the sawmills were running and some men eagerly made their way at
night to places where cheap wine and cheap women were easily available.
Murray Morgan wrote about early Seattle, including the rise of "places
of ill repute" near the skid road used by a sawmill to skid logs down to
the mill. This part of town became known as "Skid Row."[19] When I first
walked the downtown streets there were still some of the relics of the
old Skid Row. Back then the problems were primarily around alcohol.
A good reference book for the time when I first helped folks at night is
James Spradley's *You Owe Yourself a Drunk.*[20] Open drug use was rare to
observe. This would change over the next thirty years.

Another way downtown has changed is that the formerly "cheap"
housing and/or places to camp out as one of the homeless have been re-
placed by upscale housing. I can recall, for example, homeless men talking
about life on the hill just north of Seattle's Pike Place Market. According
to them, fights sometimes broke out on the hill. If a man was killed in

19. Morgan, *Skid Road.*
20. Spradley, *You Owe Yourself A Drunk.*

the process they simply rolled his body down the hill to the railroad tracks and shoved him up into an empty railroad box car. Today, that same hill is covered with condominiums and lofts selling for over one million dollars with impressive views of Puget Sound. In Tacoma the old taverns I visited on my rounds along Pacific Avenue are only a part of history, long demolished in the thirst for a "new" business sector. The old Tacoma Rescue Mission was relocated out of downtown. Now a new convention center, hotel, and the growing campus for the University of Washington in Tacoma dominate the scene.

During my time in night ministry I saw the shift from alcohol to more involvement with drugs. Late in my work downtown I was asked by the staff in the Emergency Room of Tacoma General Hospital to visit a family to inform them about the death of a young man. I drove out to one of the better suburbs south of downtown where I parked in front of an impressive, large house and rang the front doorbell. When a man came to the door dressed in a house coat I told him that he should go back upstairs to awaken his wife. I then sat with them in their front room to tell them that their son had been killed in a drug related shooting. This type of encounter would have been very rare back when I first started my work on the downtown streets.

There were many implications of a shift into more illegal drug activity as I continued my work late at night. Some nights I would sit in a tavern up on the Hilltop area in Tacoma, at a place called "Smiley's." Here it was not unusual to see a man holding white powder in his hand and another man holding a roll of bills. Sometimes the police would drive by and shine their spotlight through the front window. I wonder what they thought when they saw a man wearing a clergy collar in such a place. The drug related gangs including the Crips and the Bloods came up to the Seattle area from California. There was a lot more violence on the street at night. One night, for example, I tried to comfort a mother who was working as a bartender. Her daughter was shot and killed in a drive-by shooting. In my early years of night ministry men often carried knives and sometimes used them to cut another man in a fight. One Christmas a stranger gave me a knife as a gift. When I questioned the use of this weapon he said that I could use it to "cut up apples." Then the weapon of choice changed to guns and the whole scene became more violent. Sometimes at night I would drive to a part of the interracial Hilltop area where I could find folks in one of the local taverns. Often before I parked my car men would come over to try to push drugs. When I turned toward them and they saw my collar they immediately backed away.

Mike: How has this writing project changed your understanding?

Dean: For the first time I have a better sense of what it must be like for a teenager to be using illegal drugs with friends. I never saw this part of the problem during my work with adults at night. As you may imagine, it has been a true blessing to hear your story and to know you as you are today. I see you as a very talented man; I only wish that some of the folks I saw through the years could have had the opportunity to read what you have written. On another issue, what suggestions do you have for me as I relate to my two grandsons who are now thirteen and ten years old? The thirteen-year-old will soon be in high school.

Mike: I learned more from my friends than from family. Maybe this is the way it is going to be for kids. I would suggest that you be as involved with your grandsons and their friends as much as possible. There is also a lot of written material available about how to address the issues of alcohol and drugs with children. If I ever have kids I will be brutally honest about my past. This has the danger that they may say that Dad did it, so I can do it. But it might, on the other hand, let them know where experimenting with drugs can lead and make them more likely to come to me, although I do not have all of the answers. It is a tough problem. I cannot advocate complete abstinence for someone who rarely or has never used, only someone who has proven they cannot function as a social user. If they are going to experiment we can't simply say, "don't do it." I always wonder how much more I could have achieved if I had not used drugs, at the same time I often wonder how many of the cherished memories, friends, and fun times I would've missed had I not been there. I've had a lot of "pipe dreams" that I followed through to the end, leaving me with a sense of satisfaction and accomplishment when these goals were completed. As I will say in chapter 3, drugs helped balance out my moods, but the depressions were much lower, when my friends saw this they would urge me to stop; sometimes the words from peers are a lot more powerful than what parents say.

Dean: As we have been talking, I have been reflecting on where we are sitting, in a church. I have been thinking of the spiritual correlates of addiction. As I see it, the touchstone of religion is that we are not alone. We are embraced by the heartbeat of the universe, the heartbeat of eternity. I think that this can be a powerful resource for an addict. It implies that we are not the ultimate captain of our destiny. We must "let go" and let others become involved with us in the journey of life.

Mike: I have heard several addicts say that they have a huge ego but at the same time express the feeling that they are nothing, a true "piece of garbage." We need to step outside our ego, to stop thinking of ourselves too highly. We need new outlets, healthier ways to deal with problems.

Dean: I like to carry the idea of being embraced by the power of the universe a little further by saying that we truly walk with a host of others. This includes the editor and publisher of this book. It is a cooperative venture. Most importantly, this includes you, the reader. The work can only be relevant if you become part of the process. We have been honest with our journey. We invite you to be honest with yourself and others. It is unlikely that we will ever meet you personally. But you have become part of us as together we reach for wholeness in life.

Taking the notion of being involved in all, I am now impressed by the fact that people I walked with in night ministry remain with me. Most have now died, folks like Harlan and Karen. But in some special way they are and will be part of me and who I am. I am thankful for these memories.

3

Mental Illness

Michael Joseph

"Let yourself go with disease, be with it,
keep company with it—this is the way to be rid of it"

—BRUCE LEE

A WORD OF CAUTION is in order as we begin this chapter. The title can be very misleading. The topic is best seen in perspective by the following comments of Dr. Trevor Graham with the University of Colorado at Boulder:

> *As a society, we tend to adopt an "us-them" attitude towards those that may suffer from any number of psychological symptoms. One of the mechanisms by which we distance ourselves from psychological suffering is through labeling people who are suffering as being "mentally ill." This implies that the rest of us are psychologically "healthy" and that we have little in common with the "mentally ill." Although this may feel psychologically comforting to us, it obscures the reality that the majority of us will suffer from some diagnosable psychological disorder at some point in our lifetime. Given this reality, the attitude towards understanding psychological disorders should be shifted from an "us-them" attitude to simply an "us" attitude to reflect that psychological symptoms are a common part of the human experience.[1]*

1. Dr. Graham contributed these words in October 2009 when asked by author Dean Jones to comment on the subject of mental illness.

A MIND CAN BE A TERRIBLE THING

Nerve cells fire electrical signals traveling at speeds of up to two hundred miles per hour, transmitted down the nerve fiber to arrive at the point of stimulation where the electrochemical signal is conducted. This is your brain. Imagine chemicals jumping across synapses to be taken up by receptors at the end of neighboring cells. Each of the billions of nerve cells are connected to up to several thousand others, setting up a wave of perplex electrical activity. The functions of the brain include: coordinating all of our abilities; containing all memories and beliefs; controlling behavior and moods; enabling communication, recognition, understanding, planning, and imagining. What we know about the brain is mesmerizing. Weighing roughly three pounds, this grayish-pink, jelly-like mound of flesh takes up only 2 percent of our body weight but uses 20 percent of our body's oxygen when at rest. No computer has yet come close to matching the awesomeness of the human brain.

Three hundred million Americans walk around everyday with anatomically similar brains, but while the function may be similar in all humans, the thought processes, belief systems, and mood patterns can differ drastically. Of these 300 million American brains, roughly one in four (57 million) suffer from some sort of diagnosable mental disorder in any given year.[2] Mental disorders are the leading cause of disability in the United States and Canada for people ages fifteen to forty-four,[3] but despite the number of people suffering from mental illness, it is still surrounded by stigma. Genetic studies have given us a better understanding of the premise of mental illness but society is no more tolerant of the mentally ill than it was ten years ago.

I had already accepted that something was wrong with my mind by the time I had heard the diagnosis. I remember the day clearly. "My professional diagnosis," the psychiatrist stated, "is that you're bipolar, type II. The majority of the time your mood appears to be hypomanic, but you tend to cycle into very severe, often long lasting depressive episodes." He was from South Africa and spoke with an accent that reminded me of a mix between Australian and British. He was very professional, emphatic, and most importantly, willing to listen. He gave me feedback and expert opinions on the topics that I discussed with him in a nonjudgmental

2. National Institute of Mental Health, "Statistics," lines 1–3.
3. Ibid., lines 4–5.

way. It took me almost thirteen years to find a psychiatrist who made the proper diagnosis and by the time I had heard him say the words "you're bipolar," I had already realized and accepted it as my disease.

I knew enough about bipolar illness to understand that I would never be rid of it, it is part of my personality and it helps define me. I had been struggling with this disease since childhood and had only just started to understand and realize that I was indeed a very irrational, overly dramatic, extra sensitive, extremely moody person because of it. Telling myself that someday I would be free of this mental illness or one day I would be "normal" is not the proper way to approach this disease; accepting it, understanding it, learning how to cope and control it are the methods to living a "normal" life as a bipolar individual. I have learned this, although I would be lying if I told you I do not still struggle with the disease. It is a constant learning process and during this journey I have discovered ways to help and better myself by simply learning to understand myself through introspection as well as discussions with those who know me best.

LISTEN TO THE CHILD

I was only eleven years old when I first felt the results of my bipolar disorder. My mother often questioned me about what was happening at school. One day she was alarmed at the sight of my eye . . . "What the hell happened to your eye? Did you get into another fight at school?" I faced this interrogation as I walked in the door. I had gotten into a fight and had a black eye from the same kid for the second time in three weeks. The questions continued, "Why do these kids keep picking on you? Who was it?" I didn't answer anything and walked straight to my room. It is normal for eleven-year-olds to tease each other and bicker, but for reasons I did not understand until I was much older, I seemed to be extra sensitive to the taunting. The other kids seemed to notice my sensitivity and, in turn, teased me more brutally than most other kids in my class. My dad would always tell me to ignore them and walk away, but this advice was just too hard to follow when the class bully was telling me the perverted things he had in store for my mom.

Eleven-year-old children are not as innocent as they act around adults. Although my dad had good intentions and was giving me the correct advice, he did not realize how much more vulnerable my emotions were compared to his. It is well known that when depressed, manic, or psychotic, people will respond to stress in very different ways when compared to those who are not suffering from mental illness. During a manic or depressive episode a person is very vulnerable to events in their lives and people surrounding them. Keeping this in mind, their behavior also has a strong reciprocal effect on the environment and people around them. Their behavior will often disaffect others due to anger, withdrawal, or violence, which often leads to divorce or separation, job loss, or some other major life-changing event.[4] On the surface, these negative events may appear to be a cause of the mental illness, when in fact they may be brought on by the mental illness itself. It is a fierce cycle since the same events that may have been brought on by the mental illness contribute to the negative emotions that the individual is feeling.

Research has shown that, for the most part, people with mood disorders seem to be impacted more by stressful life events that those suffering from schizophrenia, which is not a mood disorder. This makes sense logically since those people who are extra sensitive seem to overreact to the little things (as well as the big things) that can spoil the day. These are the people to whom I am referring. It is not my place to say that everyone who dramatically overreacts to situations has a mood disorder, but this is one way to help you to understand the personality type that I am describing. Sheri Johnson, assistant clinical professor at Brown University and a staff psychologist at Butler Hospital in Providence, Rhode Island, found that negative life events increase both the rate of disease relapse in people with bipolar disorder as well as the length of time it takes for patients to recover from each episode.[5] Without significant factors leading to stress, patients take an average of just over three months (103 days) to recover from each episode. On the other end of the spectrum, if significant negative events occur before the episode, it takes on average one year (365 days) before the patient is well and healthy again. "In other words," Johnson explains, "Subjects with a stressor took more than three times as long to recover as subjects without a stressor."[6]

By the age of eight I was well accustomed to playground fights as well as giving and receiving verbal taunting. I was shorter and skinnier than most kids my age and not at all athletic, and to make the situation even worse, my parents heavily encouraged me to be actively involved

4. Psychology Information, "Bipolar Depression," lines 15–18.

5. Johnson, "Life Events," lines 102–8.

6. Ibid., lines 79–83.

in sports. My clumsiness often led to other kids harassing me, and with my over-sensitive feelings, I would react inappropriately and sometimes violently.

"It was Robert who hit you, wasn't it? I'm calling his mother," my mom screamed as she barged into my room. I wasn't exactly a little angel and Robert's mom knew it, she never punished him for fighting and she may have even felt her son was justified in giving me a black eye. There were many times that I deserved my bruises from fighting, but this was not one of them. Robert had gone out of his way to make a spectacle of me in front of the other kids at school for the past year. Aggravated by my repeated attempts to ignore him, he finally started hitting me to get my attention. This was the third fight he had provoked in three weeks. He was friends with a few of my friends, but I never considered him one of my friends because of the way he treated me. The first thing that he had ever said to me was a comment about my clothes being "hand-me-downs." Despite his critiquing, Robert was not an eleven-year-old fashion guru, but simply a kid who was taller, more popular, and more athletic than me. This bothered me and he knew it and exploited it. Robert was a soccer fanatic who wore his hair in a bowl cut with a part to the right side. His smile revealed a huge pair of bucked teeth and pointing them out was my only means of defense when he started making fun of me.

"No, please don't call anyone, just stay out of it. You only made things worse when you talked to his mom last time," I pleaded. I had thought my mother's conversation with his mom would put an end to my daily doses of playground torture, but it only exacerbated things; Robert bragged to everyone else about how he lied to his mom and she believed I was the one who started the fight. Kids are not evil; they just lack empathy most of the time. Empathy is the capacity to recognize and understand another individual's emotions. It is encouraged by attempting to put yourself in someone else's shoes, or to somehow experience another individual's outlook or emotions within yourself. How could the other kids at school have been expected to understand that I was a bipolar kid with extra sensitive emotions when I did not even understand why I was overreacting? On the contrary, I did not understand why they picked on me more than the others because I could not empathize. Looking at the situation in retrospect, I can understand that I was an easy target because I would get worked up so much easier than the other kids and, in turn, respond with violence. I was a bipolar kid.

Empathy is necessary if an attempt to live with mental illness is going to be made. Empathy is needed from friends and family to understand or at least recognize what the mental illness may be doing to the person's emotions and how it is impacting their life. Empathy is necessary on the part of the mentally ill individual as well. They must understand that the rest of the world does not feel or experience things in the same way. Empathy, coupled with knowledge of the disease, present two of the best tools for living with mental illness. Society has placed a stigma on mental illness. I admit that I did not have the capacity to empathize with the mentally ill until I understood my own bipolar disorder. One of my intentions in coauthoring this book is to help people empathize with tough issues such as financial loss, drug addiction, mental illness, and suicide and, in the process, help to eliminate the stigma surrounding these topics.

With substantial amounts of research being done today, along with the ease of communication throughout various medical and educational institutions, it is no wonder there seems to be a diagnosis for everything. We are often noticing that we are not alone in experiencing problems in life and doctors are becoming quicker to label patients with a particular disorder. So it is no wonder I discovered a diagnosis that may have fit Robert and many other bullies in my life. It is called aggressive conduct disorder. It is a mental disorder affecting children and adolescents characterized by a longstanding pattern of misbehaving and breaking rules.[7] The symptoms include behaviors such as lying, physical aggression, bullying, or destroying property. This disorder is of major public health concern due to the obvious reasons that these children often eventually inflict serious physical and psychological harm on others. Furthermore, the bullies are at risk for injury, depression, substance abuse, and death by suicide or homicide.[8]

We were running laps in soccer practice and I was trying to keep my head down to hide the new black eye that Robert proudly bragged about giving me. Why did he have to be on my soccer team? I was trying to avoid him because I knew my mom had called his mom despite my attempts to stop her. It was only a matter of time before he would confront me.

---

7. Mental Health America, "Factsheet," lines 1–2.
8. Ibid., lines 21–23.

"Your bitch mom called my mom yelling and screaming about me picking on you," he said, squinting his eyes and showing his bucked teeth.

"You gave me a black eye, what did you expect her to do? And she's not a bitch. Look, just leave me alone," I panted. As we continued running laps around the field he slowed down to get behind me.

"I just told my mom you always make fun of me and hit me and I finally fought back." He said this loudly so the other kids could hear. He was bragging and it was starting to get to me which made him smile, revealing those evil beaver teeth. I felt so enraged by his continuous taunting over the years and often felt powerless, my brain suffered from a mental illness which amplified my emotions making these feelings even more extreme. If I was asked when I was eleven how I felt about Robert I would have said that I hated him, a feeling that I now consider too extreme. Now I realize that he had his own problems; he was a child with an alcoholic father, and I cannot fathom how that affected him. He was clearly exhibiting many symptoms associated with a conduct disorder, which means his brain may also have been affected by a mental illness as well.

A study conducted at the University of Chicago used brain imaging to study the brain activity of aggressive males with conduct disorder versus those of normal adolescent males. The children were shown images in a video of people inflicting pain on others or people being hurt by accident. Both groups of children showed activity in the brain's pain centers, however, the conduct disorder group showed activity in the brain's pleasure centers as well, while the normal group showed no such brain activity.[9] These findings suggest that aggressive children or bullies enjoy inflicting harm on others, which seems obvious to anyone who has had experience with a bully.

"Hey, get back here!" Robert screamed as he hurried after me. I was doing my best to outrun him on my way home after soccer practice, but despite my efforts he was faster. He finally tackled me and immediately hit me a few times. I started fighting back and his two friends jumped on me. I was struggling to defend against the three of them when Robert said, "Stop, just hold him down."

His friends pinned me down on my face in the gravel as I struggled. Even with all of my strength I could not get an arm free and then they

9. Decety, et al, "Atypical empathic responses."

started laughing. That is when I felt the warm, wet joke that Robert was playing on me. I could not believe that he had stooped this low. I started struggling with all my strength and pulled one of his friends into the golden stream. "Awe, you got it on my arm, asshole!" he scolded Robert as he let go of me. I took the opportunity to push Robert over with his pants down and quickly kicked him. I ran away with a urine-tainted shirt and left my pride in the gravel.

Robert's brain may have been wired differently than mine with regards to pain, he could have been feeling some sort of positive reinforcement from seeing other people hurt or upset. Regardless of his behavior, I dealt with it and survived, but my emotions became even more sensitive as I got older. On average, a bipolar person will experience four episodes a year in the first ten years of the illness.[10] It is hard to determine when the "illness" started in my life, but an honest reflection of my childhood clearly points to various episodes of both ends of the bipolar spectrum. All human beings have the capacity to feel emotions that range from not only extreme happiness or sadness, but also bliss, apathy, and highly motivated energetic states, hostility, curiosity, and monotony.

Mania can cause an individual's emotions to be in a volatile state and aggression can escalate into rage more readily. I can recall specific situations when this had happened to me. A few stand out. Perhaps the most noteworthy was during the early winter of my eighth-grade year in gym class. I was twelve years old and a mere few months away from beginning my teenage years. The effects of the life of a teenager were already starting to take hold of my life. I was noticing girls, making new friends, trying to grow up and "act more mature" as the school teachers would often encourage. My mom finally listened to my begging and pleading to change schools after the urine incident. She agreed to transfer me to another school the following year. I was having a hard time settling into the new school while jointly dealing with the pressure that comes along with graduating from junior high school into high school.

My dad and mom were quickly starting to drift apart, a trend that would continue and ultimately end in a bitter divorce within a year. I did not fully understand what was developing in front of my eyes at the time. My mood for the entire year was generally depressed. I was not experienced enough to handle these feelings and depression would sometimes quickly cycle into aggression which, as I alluded to earlier,

10. 4.therapy.com Network, "What is bipolar disorder," lines 135–37.

was expressed as rage. My new school was not a private school like the previous one and had a class four times bigger than my old one. This resulted in me making more friends, but also dealing with a few more aggressive kids than before. I had experience with being picked on and I was dealing with it better than before, at least I thought so. I would react more aggressively when taunted and this often led to the situation dissolving before things got out of hand. I was becoming the angry kid. Being the angry kid is not the best way to handle the taunting of your classmates and I would quickly learn this lesson.

"You're out!" Mr. Dewey screamed after blowing his whistle. "Go sit down until the next game."

I stared at him in disbelief for a moment while the other kids continued to play dodge ball. He was sitting in his chair and had thrown the ball at me when I was not looking. He was our gym teacher. He was not supposed to be knocking kids out of the game. He started blowing his whistle again in an annoying way as he stood up from his chair, a husky, rosy-cheeked, cherub-faced man with dark, unruly hair. "Get off the court, you're out," he screamed between annoying whistles. There was no doubt his blood pressure was raising as his face turned an even brighter shade of red.

I put my head down and walked toward the side of the gymnasium as the other kids started reacting to what had just happened. "Aah haha, Mike! You suck; you just got knocked out of the game by the teacher!" One particular pimple-faced classmate teased me. I quickly looked at Mr. Dewey and he started laughing. My mood went from disappointed to depressed to aggressive in a matter of seconds.

"Go to hell!" I screamed, holding my middle finger up to my taunting classmate.

"That's it! You're sitting out the rest of the class and you are staying after for detention!" Mr. Dewey exploded. Gym class was the last class of the day and Mr. Dewey was well known for handing out detention without hesitation. I was not standing for it at this particular moment though. I had reached my boiling point and I was not mature enough to handle the emotions that I was feeling. I should have just sat down against the wall, kept quiet, and served my detention. Instead, I kicked the solid concrete wall of the gymnasium. I kicked it hard. I can say with the wisdom of experience that a concrete wall will not budge from the impact of the small, flailing foot of an eighth grader. I broke my foot and then dealt with the embarrassment of being the kid who broke his foot by kicking a wall. It was not a smart idea and I spent the next couple of months with a cast on my right foot. This only caused my depressive episode to worsen.

I spent that winter and early spring feeling depressed and worthless most days. I stopped playing sports, stopped reading for fun, and I didn't even enjoy playing video games like I had in the past. Even if I had been interested in my old hobbies, I would not have invested the same amount of energy in them that I had before. I moped around the house and felt void of motivation or energy. Using the foot cast as my excuse for being sluggish, my parents never became wise to what was really happening inside my head. I was spiraling down into the bowels of depression. Homework became a routine; some days I would spend hours sitting at my desk in my room working on math problems, my attention drifting in and out. My mom had long since stopped helping me with my homework because I could not even focus long enough to finish each problem and she would spend more time telling me to pay attention than teaching me. The symptom that most helps me recognize this period as a depressive episode is the direction that my thoughts took; for the first time in my life I thought about suicide. I had not yet gone so far as to devise a plan or make a real attempt, but I started to entertain the thought, a seed was planted that would eventually grow into a huge problem. This, I believe, was my first major depressive episode and it lasted until the end of the school year, a total of eight months.

Over the course of the next year I was becoming increasingly more irritable and moody, however, on the outside I seemed withdrawn, walking by myself whenever possible and avoiding other kids at school. Once I started high school, I kept company with a few other kids who seemed to share my miserable view of life; this only made things worse. My mom, responding to my recent choice of friends and new life philosophy, finally took some initiative and found a psychiatrist for me to start seeing every week. My mood started to shift to a productive and perhaps hypomanic mind frame within a few weeks. A hypomanic mood is a milder form of mania. I was very suggestive, started reading several books at the same time, and started finding new hobbies and appreciating different types of music. In effect, I did not focus on talking about my recent symptoms of depression with my psychiatrist, instead I talked about the amount of energy I had and wrote the depression off as a "phase in adolescence."

This enabled me and my psychiatrist to not fully recognize the disease that I was suffering from as bipolar disorder since he could only make an assessment from the information that I gave him. I remember when he would bring up my depressed mood I quickly disregarded it and talked about something else, sometimes becoming irritated that he would mention the topic. It is difficult for people in mania to be insightful and they may angrily lash out at anyone trying to point out the problem.

Hypomanic episodes rarely persist and often eventually cycle into full-blown mania or depression. By the middle of my freshman year in high school I cycled back into a depressive state of mind, but this time tried my best to keep my thoughts and feelings to myself. I started avoiding people again and my relationship with my mother was deteriorating. She and my father were now in the middle of a divorce and I would be moving to Colorado by the end of my freshman year. I managed to keep my depressed feelings a secret from my psychiatrist and my mother who both told me that I simply had a problem with my behavior and controlling my temper. In retrospect, I had been hiding these feelings as a coping mechanism and it is no wonder I was able to keep them from others. It was not that simple. I was a bipolar kid but I would not officially find this out for another ten years.

DIAGNOSING BIPOLAR DISORDER

Bipolar illness is diagnosed and classified according to the types and frequency of episodes. Some people experience mainly depressive episodes while others can cycle often or even continuously throughout the year. Others may follow a seasonal pattern, being depressed during one season while hypomanic for another. Without treatment hypomanic and manic episodes will last, on average, a few months, while depressive episodes seem to last over six months, although in some extreme cases they can persist for several years. Some people recover completely after an episode and may not experience another for several years. Others, like myself, will continue to have mildly impairing symptoms of depression coupled with up and down mood swings. Speaking from experience, these symptoms will get increasingly worse over time if they are not addressed and treated. Unfortunately, seeking treatment is one of the biggest obstacles people with bipolar illness have to overcome. Since the hypomanic episode can serve as periods of high productivity and the depressive episode may often be spread out over time, many people will not seek treatment until they have been living with the disease for years. A typical bipolar patient may spend years in therapy before a correct diagnosis is made.

It is imperative that bipolar patients receive the proper diagnosis and treatment as early as possible because this illness, among other complications, puts the individual at risk for alcohol and substance abuse, relationship problems,[11] poor job or school performance, and suicide.[12] Furthermore, an improper diagnosis may result in a patient being treated for depression alone. When thought about logically, this seems like a good start; depression is part of bipolar illness so at least part of the problem is treated. It is well known in the medical field that caution should be taken when using antidepressants. Initiating therapy in a bipolar patient with antidepressants alone may actually induce mania in the person, resulting in a switch from a depressive episode to a manic episode. As with many theories in the medical field, much controversy exists as to whether certain individuals are more prone to antidepressant induced mania and some medical experts even suggest that, due to the complexity of the illness, there is no clear link between antidepressant use and manic episodes. Regardless, much caution and care should be taken on the part of the doctor when prescribing these medicines and when a patient initiates therapy with them he or she should be aware of his or her moods.

POCKETS ON FIRE

I really did not want to open the envelope. I felt guilty because I knew what the pages inside would show me, but I opened it anyway. I stared in astonishment at my account statement detailing my activity from the previous month and I remembered why I never opened my bank statements. There are people who balance their checkbooks and those who don't; I have always been the latter. Balancing my checkbook and being fiscally responsible are just not things I do. I have always been accustomed to making more money when I run out, even if this meant working a job I loathed. Of course, this boils down to being irresponsible and impulsive. My lack of accountability with finances led to me holding an

11. National Institute of Mental Health, "What are the symptoms?" lines 39–40.
12. National Institute of Mental Health, "What is bipolar disorder?" lines 3.

account statement that showed I had spent an amount of money meant to last five months in a little less than a month, a manic month.

I started at the beginning of the month and scanned the bank statement that contained several pages detailing my spending spree. The first week looked like a normal college student's bank statement; five dollars at Starbucks to keep me awake through Pharmacoeconomics, seven dollars most days for lunch, drinks at the bar on weekends, a tank of gas here and there, these were expenditures that my bank statements had in common with many of my classmates. But going down the list there were a few things that just did not fit, like the Sesame Street song, "One of these things is not like the other, one of these things just doesn't belong." In my case, it looked as though that first week did not belong on my statement, that week of responsible spending where I was keeping track of the five-dollar coffees and seven-dollar lunches. The three weeks that followed all started with a night at a local bar where I decided to buy a round of drinks for some new friends. One round turned into three and then I lost count until the bartender cut me off with a $130 tab. But it did not matter because I had close to three grand in the bank, aside from the money I had set aside for the next three months rent. The following Monday showed a bill for $180 from Barnes and Noble. I remembered purchasing thirteen books and how excited I was about reading all of them. That was close to four years ago and I have read only five of them. It would have been a better idea to let them collect dust on the bookshelf of the store rather than my room. Over one hundred dollars spent on sushi several times along with nearly a dozen other expensive dinners. As I scanned this list, I thought of my dad's advice when he heard that I was getting a big award in federal loan money: "Don't let it burn a hole in your pocket." That's just want it did.

I saw a few episodes of HBO's The Sopranos and I had to buy each season individually on DVD. Kevin Smith made some good movies so I felt the need to buy them all; plus every comic book that he had ever written. The music I enjoyed had the same effect. If I heard a band that I liked I could not settle for just one CD, I obsessed and bought them all. I had to do everything to the extreme. I had to buy the snowboarding equipment that I would need: board, boots, pants, jacket, goggles, waterproof underwear and shirts, and special socks. I would realistically only go snowboarding a half dozen times that year. This extreme behavior would drive me to succeed also; it was a double-edged sword. The same energy that would push me to thoroughly delve into obsessing over material possessions would push me to obsess over learning and reading. I found the time to read several books over the course of the next month while still focusing on school and exercising daily. I did well to make it appear that I was very active and driven, but I was just winding myself up to plummet into a deep depression.

I eventually solved the money problem by working extra hours and borrowing more money, sinking myself deeper into debt, but that was not the last time I would set my pockets on fire. I would later read that this financial impulsiveness was common among bipolar people.[13] To me, this meant that it was something that could be managed or even corrected. The way we feel about money can be tied to our upbringing and certain preconceived notions we have about money. My father warned me about overspending because we often lived from paycheck to paycheck when I was growing up; at least that is how my mother explained it to me. Realistically, we survived quite well. My father was a firefighter for a major city in South Jersey and he worked overtime whenever we needed more money. As a child, I thought money was hard to come by and would never last long; therefore, as a young adult I would spend it quickly on things I thought would hold value, since "it wouldn't last anyway." I had to eventually realize that I was the one who held value and I did not need to burn holes in my pockets every time I had money. Realizing this was a form of therapy for me and it has been financially enlightening to understand that I can control my finances and even save money, even while paying off the debt I have accrued from my previous years of misguided money management. This theory of our past playing a role in our present view of money and realizing our net worth and self-worth is discussed in detail in the book The Financial Wisdom of Ebenezer Scrooge: 5 Principles to Transform Your Relationship with Money.[14] I recommend this book to anyone who would like a better outlook on money management.

HYPOMANIA

Most of my manic or hypomanic episodes are mirrored in the example that I illustrated in my story. I would carelessly spend money, quickly

13. National Institute of Mental Health, "What are the symptoms?" lines 20–21.
14. T. Klontz, et al, *Financial Wisdom*.

draining my bank account or maxing out credit cards, and enjoying myself in the process. During this time I would be in a very high energy state, which resulted in both positive and negative outcomes. The outcome would depend on how I used this energy, it was either channeled into doing constructive things with my life, like constructive hobbies, community service, education, and work or it was expelled into living in the moment as a party animal. I spent much time at both ends of the spectrum and have found that I require a good balance between work and play to keep my mood stable. I just have to be careful that the playtime is constructive, like exercise, reading, outdoor activities, and keeping the company of positive, like-minded friends. Sadly, overindulgence in drugs and alcohol has attracted much of the energy in my life over the years.

I found myself frequently using marijuana at the end of the day to help calm my mind and stabilize my mood. I went through several long periods of using over the past ten years with very few breaks. I can safely say that I have noticed a definite trend in my use of marijuana. I would start and feel like it was helping to calm me down and keep my thoughts in order. It very well could have been helping at first. But the amount I used would always increase over time and I would spend more time and money with marijuana and less time and money would be focused on other, more important things. Eventually, through a combination of excessive use and slowly realizing I had ignored responsibilities and let other aspects of my live become unbearable, I would spiral into a major depressive episode. These episodes would typically last one to three months, although my longest episode went on for almost a year. I would always have to either completely stop or severely cut down on my use of marijuana to alleviate the depression. I knew from the very first episode that my mood would be better had I just completely abandoned the drug, but it was a habit that I could not stop for longer than a few months at a time.

SEEING IN THE DARKNESS

Tears trickled down my cheeks as I tried to articulate my feelings to this woman I had met less than ten minutes before. I sat in a comfortable leather chair, the typical kind that I had found in the offices of the many therapists that I had seen throughout my life. This time was different though, this time I had voluntarily gone, instead of being forced by my parents. This time I knew I had problems and I wanted to fix them. Despite my ambition and previous experience with therapists, I had no idea where to begin with therapy. I had no idea what I was currently going through and I had no idea why I was crying. I was twenty-six years old and crying like a baby to this woman. Crying just seemed like the right thing to do and she stared at me with empathy in her eyes, tiny wrinkles underneath of them complete with crows feet, she was old enough to be my grandmother. Her name was Robin and I just hoped that she was wise enough to help me figure out a way to untangle the mess that I had made of my mind.

One week before I had been sitting in my car at the bottom of the spiral, ready to die. I had fully gone through with a plan to peacefully kill myself by running a hose from the tailpipe of my car through a crack in the window. I would have seen this plan through to completion had it not been for an invaluable friend intervening and a spiritual-like awakening. I had almost destroyed myself, but I later realized that this moment in life helped me to truly discover myself. However, at this particular moment in time, in the comfortable leather chair, with tears streaming down my dismal face, I was just embarking on my trip to self-discovery. It would be through this self-discovery that I would gain the tools necessary to put the broken pieces of my life back together.

Cognitive behavioral therapy is what it is called. It emphasizes the belief that our thoughts are responsible for the way we feel and behave, and therefore we can change our mode of thought to cause us to act and behave differently.[15] I was introduced to this form of therapy by Robin, who genuinely cared about my emotional well-being. Seeing her provided me with a nonjudgmental, professional opinion; she was not trying to control me or shrink my head. She was simply pushing me to change my life by giving me the tools needed to do it myself. Over the next eight months I would regularly see her and so began my quest to get my emotions under control.

I was in a very long depressive episode and this prompted her to suggest antidepressant medication. It was a reasonable start for therapy, however not the right choice. The antidepressant medication did nothing to stabilize my mood and eventually I would start seeing another therapist who saw the real problem with me.

15. National Association of Cognitive-Behavioral Therapists, "Cognitive-Behavioral Therapy," lines 10–14.

"Yes, I believe that you're bipolar," he reiterated. He was a small, quaint man from South Africa and his diagnosis was right on with my behavior. He was drawing a chart on the dry erase board showing me how my mood fluctuates over time. He drew a baseline in the middle labeled "normal" and then a line representing my mood elevating to mania and then plummeting into depression. He compared this to a normal mood that did not hit the extreme highs or lows.

"Many people suffer from this and many people learn to live and deal with it," he explained in a calm, genuine tone. "We don't necessarily have to put you on medication, you can try to change things like diet, exercise, and proper sleep combined with other ways to stabilize your mood like meditation. I do worry about your drinking and drug use, however. This can have an impact on your mood and I believe it is responsible for your extreme fluctuations. The trend, from what you tell me, is for your mood to accelerate during periods of marijuana use and eventually sink into depression when the mania subsides."

I had been collecting information about my mood for the previous nine months since I had been seeing Robin and this enabled me to give this small man from South Africa, Gerald, enough data to sift through my past and make a proper diagnosis. I would eventually climb out of the depression without medication and learn to understand myself better in the process.

In order for a behavior to be modified, a person must believe the modification will benefit their life and the new behavior must be consistent with the person's values and beliefs. Modification of behavior is easier to attain than eliminating a behavior. Learning to control my moods was a process that did not happen overnight. I had to become cognizant of my behavior and try very hard not to be a "decorator." This meant controlling my emotions and not exploding verbally when someone did something to upset me. I had to learn that when I had problems, I did not need to decorate my surroundings with them. This is a challenge for me everyday, but it takes small changes like that over a long period of time to create major change. This is goal setting; this requires visualizing how I would like to act and behave and constantly striving to behave in this manner. When I slip up, I cannot afford to let this discourage me, it is not like building a house of cards; I do not have to start again from the beginning when things fall apart. I simply analyze my mistakes, learn from them, and move on from the beginning; rebuilding the foundation is important.

I had to talk over my problems from the beginning and learn where I was mentally hung up in order to get rid of my own problems. Once the problems were removed, I was able to rebuild the foundations and move on. Being mentally healthy requires a person to constantly take inventory of and be honest with him or herself.

SUZIE Q

While I consider my own situation, I am now also very aware of the problems of others, especially those I see in my work as a Pharmacist. One night recently I did not want to look at the clock, I knew it was late and I had a lot of work to do. Filling prescriptions can be very mundane and I had spent a good forty-five minutes avoiding it by talking with Sam and his wife and then Armando, the doctor shopper, to help pass the time. I was getting ready to get back to work but something was pulling me away. I felt like I was forgetting something or rather someone. Then it hit me, Suzie Q had called expressing concern about early Alzheimer's due to something she had seen on TV. I worried that she would not go to bed until I called to reassure her that she was not suffering from Alzheimer's disease. I sat down and looked at the clock, quarter after midnight; she would still be awake. I picked up the phone and dialed her number which had been committed to memory from doing this many nights previously.

"Hello?" a groggy voice answered. She sounded sleepy; I was hoping that she had forgotten about the Alzheimer's test Dr. Oz had given her while she was watching Oprah.

"Hi, Suzie, did I wake you?" I nervously bit my lip.

"No, I just took my, um, night time meds . . . and now I'm lying on the couch." She whimpered in a drunken voice. Suzie had a tendency to take more of her medication than she was supposed to, sometimes because she had taken a dose, forgotten, and then simply took another. Other times she purposefully takes more than prescribed to help her sleep.

"What did you take?" I prodded.

"My Seroquel, Darvocet, and a glass of milk," she replied. Darvocet is a combination pain medication containing acetaminophen and mild painkiller that acts as a weak opiod agonist called propoxyphene. This drug will bind to the opiod receptors in a weak way, producing a small amount of pain relief compared to a drug like Percocet, hence propoxy-phene is classified as a mild painkiller.

Seroquel was the med that concerned me, since she would often take two to three times what she was prescribed. Seroquel is indicated in patients with schizophrenia, depression, mania, and bipolar disorder. Suzie was taking it as maintenance treatment for bipolar depression. Seroquel works by blocking specific serotonin and dopamine receptors resulting in blockade of dopamine and glutamate hyperactivity in the brain. The end result is a reduction in the psychotic and manic symptoms.

Somnolence is a side effect of this drug and Suzie would often call me in a half awake state, slurring her speech. She would usually tell me that she took an extra dose of Seroquel; this was something that I admired about her, honesty.

"How much Seroquel did you take?" I asked.

"I took two extra pills," she slurred, "so I could sleep."

"You have to stop doing that, I've spoken to your doctor about that and he doesn't approve, and you know I don't either," I sounded like a parent and she was old enough to be my grandmother. "Look," I sighed, "Suzie, I can tell that you're really tired so why don't you go to sleep and I'll talk to you tomorrow night?" I knew there was a good chance that she wouldn't remember this conversation.

"Okay, I'll talk to you tomorrow." And she hung up.

I was relieved that she had forgotten about the Alzheimer's test from the Oprah show, but now I knew why she failed it. She was overloaded on Seroquel.

When Suzie was more awake and alert she would show a side of her that helped me to appreciate those of us struggling with mental illness. She had suffered with bipolar illness all of her life and it severely impacted her functioning. Despite this, she would present as a pleasant woman who still loved life. Her secret was that she simply accepted the disease as part of her personality and learned to live with it. This is probably the hardest part of having a diagnosed mental illness.

WE ARE THE ANSWER

Even if we are made in the image and likeness of a perfect God, none of us is a perfect replica of an infallible being; we become good or evil, sane or insane when the world tells us so. So you can let the world tell you that you are evil or crazy if you behave in a certain way, but we all have the ability to decide for ourselves. We are responsible for our own behavior despite what type of disorder we have. We all have to learn to live with ourselves and more importantly control ourselves. Some of us can let ourselves get so far out of control that it is seemingly impossible to put the pieces back together. This is where you must find courage inside of you, no matter how much you have convinced yourself it is not there, and you have to grab that first broken piece and start rebuilding. This takes time and hard work to get to where you would like to be, but the end result will be a person who has gone to the edge and come back stronger and wiser for the experience. No matter how bad you think your situation is, there is always something that you can do to get things under control and there are always resources available to help you get there. Some of us have to make the best with what we have and find the best no matter how unfortunate things may seem. Take Lance Armstrong or Steven Hawking, for example, both have suffered illnesses that most people would consider completely disabling, but despite this they have achieved more than the average person. I am certain that they both had moments where they were doubtful and discouraged but they overcame those feelings and shifted their mindsets to a more positive role. Look at what they achieved. I am not asking anyone to win the Tour de France or discover secrets of the universe, although it would be nice if we were all that driven. I am simply asking that we discover our full potential and constantly push ourselves to live to it.

Life's Unexpected Twists

Dean Jones

"If you think mental illness looks bad from the outside you should try imagining what it is like from the inside of yourself. You can be on the ragged edge"

—ANONYMOUS

At this point in this chapter I feel that anything would simply be an anti climax. Mike has shared his story in a very compelling way in the previous pages. He talks about empathy and the account really calls for empathy toward him and others who live daily with the challenge of bipolar disorder. But of course, there are many other forms of psychological abnormality; some, like eating or sleeping disorders, are fought on a very personal level while others find their way into our daily news. There are many ways to approach the topic of mental illness. My comments in this chapter are not intended to be a primer on the topic. I do a lot of sharing from personal experiences and interviews. Volumes on the general topic and specific problems/issues within this topic can be found in any library or bookstore. You may want to turn to other resources for more information on some aspect of mental illness of particular interest to you. A limited list of resources is included at the back of this book.

In January of 2008, Britney Spears was admitted to the UCLA Medical Center's psychiatric hospital on an involuntary seventy-two-hour hold, judged to be a danger to herself and/or others resulting from a "mental disorder." On Valentine's Day, February 14, 2008, Steven Kazmierczak stepped out onto an auditorium stage in a lecture hall at Northern Illinois University and opened fire with two handguns and a shotgun, killing five students and wounding sixteen others before turning one of the guns on himself. After the killing spree, authorities determined that Steven's parents had first placed him in a psychiatric treatment center after high school. He used to cut himself and resisted taking his medications. His shooting rampage came after a spell of not taking his medications. Mental illness has become front-page news. What can be said that might be helpful for family members and other swith this illness? One important part of the picture is that it is important not to stereotype all those with mental illness as "dangerous" people. I have walked downtown streets alone late at night in ministry for some twenty years, seeing many folks with mental illness in the process. I was never confronted by any of these strangers, was never afraid for my personal safety. The only time I was in danger of personal harm was when three men who were heavily into drugs challenged me on a dark sidewalk in downtown Denver.

When we turn to physical or mental processes we automatically shift into some kind of scientific model, looking for explanations and "solutions." We want to consider events in a cause-effect model. This can be very helpful and has, in fact, given us many breakthroughs in our understanding of mental illness. But much remains unexplained by available approaches. We cannot truly "see" the cascading whirlpools of neuronal activity in the human brain. Words on paper, glimpses under a microscope, watching brain activity during deep probes of a living brain, looking at brain activity with the assistance of advanced brain scanning technology, and study of the brain at autopsy all add to our knowledge but the actual event of an affective and/or cognitive earthquake remains beyond the net of our containment mechanisms. Perhaps this is a good place to begin when considering mental illness. It calls for a certain amount of awe and sacred regard for the too-often-taken-for-granted, powerful, pulsating forces of the human brain.

While teaching medical sociology years ago I decided to work on the interface between neurology and sociology. In the process, I audited a Neuro Anatomy class and also worked on a cadaver in a Gross Anatomy class with medical students. In the Gross Anatomy class I was handed a small electric saw to perform the task of cutting open the skull so that the brain could be removed. I came to appreciate the structures and chemical processes inherent in the central nervous system. As part of my work, I obtained funding for a study of the impact of the neurotransmitter dopamine on behavior. This research called for the injection of 6-hydroxydopamine into the blood stream of newborn rats and then measuring the result of this insult to the brain when the animals reached maturity. We know a great deal about which portions of the brain and which neurotransmitters are significant for specific behaviors and mental states. However, all of this knowledge will be of little value if, one day, you are stretched out on the floor of a lecture hall at some university looking up into the dazed eyes of a man holding a rifle pointed at your head. Books on neuronal processes would also not be helpful for the man or woman holding the gun to understand his or her immediate situation. The existential, ephemeral, happening is beyond encapsulation.

For many men and women with some form of chronic mental illness the days and nights flow into each other with a stark emptiness of felt sensory surround. I am thinking, for example, of my brother, Norman. He had a major breakdown when in his mid teens. Now he lives in a nursing home as a senior citizen with schizophrenia. He has spent all of his adult life in various special living arrangements. He has never held a job, never married, never felt the run of normal experiences in high school or college or even having a special boy or girlfriend. When I visit him I am always struck by the tunnel-like environment he experiences every hour of every day. A long, white hall offers little variety. In one place the staff posted a large sign giving the day and a comment about the weather outside, "it is warm today" or "it is raining." I am sure that for many of the residents this sign is beyond their range of effective vision. The wheels on a walker, the steps down a well-trod path, and lots of time spent during the day curled up in a fetal position on a bed that becomes a "world" for the occupant, these are the limited environment of my brother Norman and others like him. On his sixtieth birthday I gave him what he wanted, a Lincoln Log kit packaged for a ten-year-old. I love my brother and only wish that I had lived a little closer to Seattle over the years so that I could have visited him more often. As I write this, he is recovering from a second transient ischemic attack (TIA) during which his blood pressure dropped to seventy over forty.

Another of my brothers, Arthur (Art), lives in the Seattle area and keeps me informed of Norman's condition. Most recently, he was moved into a rehabilitation center from the hospital. He is "not doing very well." He cannot sit upright on the side of his bed or in a chair, so he remains in bed where he is partially "cranked up." He eats in this position. Norman does recognize people and speaks in a very soft, barely audible voice. Art is thankful that he seems not to be in pain, is not anxious, or agitated. On one of my last visits, Norman was living in a different nursing facility. At the time of the visit, he was very agitated. I sat with him for a cup of tea. As I stroked his back and repeated softly the words, "It's okay, Norman," he relaxed. When our mother died the nursing staff carefully prepared him for the trip to the cemetery. I picked him up and was impressed by the way they had brushed his hair, given him a haircut, and even managed to get the loan of a dress jacket from one of the staff members for the occasion. Their feeling was that Norman needed "closure" around Mom's death. Three years later when Dad died he was not up to the trip out of the nursing home.

As I was doing a final edit of this chapter, Norman slipped into Hospice Care. Art wrote to me, giving me some of the details of one of his last visits with our brother. By speaking close into his ear, Art could get Norman to hear him. Art reminded him of the time he swam across Lake Washington to Mercer Island. Norman's response was a big smile and the words, "I sure did!" In a voice that was so faint it could barely be heard. It is hard for me to imagine that Norman could remember a big event form his early teens given the way he has lived for the last fifty years. In his visit, Art sang hymns into Norman's ear. Norman began to sing along, and seemed to know the words better than Art. In the letter to me, Art went on to talk about possible arrangements for a proper memorial service when this becomes necessary. I am very thankful that Art has been around to share with Norman. As the publisher prepares this book for publication Norman is better, eating and gaining some weight. I am planning a trip to Seattle and hope to see my brother again.

There are many issues in every situation involving mental illness, for the person with illness as well as family members. It is best to acknowledge and appreciate the range of issues, from the use of psychotropic medication to approaches such as cognitive behavioral therapy and spiritual issues. We are truly one: body, mind, and spirit. The focus may best be on one part of the whole at one point in time and then another at another time. It is not helpful when someone with a strong interest in one part of the whole is extremely negative about other aspects of the person. This can become a problem, for example, when a clergy person does not acknowledge the appropriate role of psychotropic medication. Or when a person trained in the biomedical model fails to see the role of hope, even faith for the person who is ill as well as for family members.

As you may know, there is often some confusion over the term "schizophrenia." It is sometimes used inappropriately to refer to "split personality." An informational, downloadable brochure distributed by the International Schizophrenia Foundation located in Toronto, Canada, gives some helpful detail including the following:

> Schizophrenia refers to a group of biochemical diseases which can affect a person physically, mentally and emotionally. Schizophrenia can change the way a person hears, sees, tastes, thinks and feels. Some studies show that the predisposition to schizophrenia is inherited. It affects one to three percent of the population and strikes mainly young people in all walks of life.[16]

Danger signals include the following:

- Extreme fatigue and feeling of weakness
- Difficulty in concentrating and getting organized
- Loss of interest, withdrawal
- Depression unrelated to life circumstances
- Vague fears and anxieties

16. International Schizophrenia Foundation, "About Schizophrenia," lines 1–4.

- Changes in sight, hearing, touch, taste or smell
- Change in character or behavior
- Headaches
- Insomnia[17]

Schizophrenia can affect society in many ways:

Schizophrenia is a frightening disease which can bring about a great deal of suffering to the patients and the family and severe problems to society. Schizophrenia is an important factor in social aid and welfare costs, health care costs, employment inefficiency, impaired learning ability, alcoholism, broken homes and suicide. The average person with schizophrenia will cost one to two million dollars to society, directly and indirectly, in his/her lifetime.[18]

When mental illness becomes a major media event as in the case of the recent coverage of Britney Spears one result is the dissemination of information valuable for all who face the problem, including family members of the one who is ill. Janet Kornblum wrote a very informative article titled "Families Often Lost in Trauma of Mental Illness" for USA Today.[19] In this article she includes a list of facts about the illness and recovery drawn from the National Alliance on Mental Illness (NAMI). Key pieces of this list are shared below:

1. Mental illnesses are biologically based brain disorders. Contrary to popular myth, they cannot simply overcome.

2. Mental illnesses are not related to a person's character or intelligence.

3. Mental disorders are widespread. About 1 in 17 Americans have some form of serious mental illness; mental illness affects 1 of 5 families.

4. Four of the 10 leading causes of disability are mental disorders, according to the World Health Organization.

---

17. Ibid., lines 12–20.
18. Ibid., lines 39–42.
19. Kornblum, "Families Often Lost," 10D.

5. Younger and older adults are particularly susceptible to mental illness. But mental illness can strike anyone.

6. Untreated mental illness can lead to disability, unemployment, substance abuse, homelessness and suicide. The cost of untreated mental illnesses to the United States is more than $100 billion a year.

7. Treatments—a combination of pharmacological and psychosocial care and support – improve symptoms and quality of life for 70 percent to 90 percent of people with serious mental illness.

8. The sooner a mentally ill person can be treated, the faster he or she can recover, minimizing the effects of his or her illness.

9. Stigma erodes confidence that mental disorders are real, treatable health conditions.[20]

Those who are part of the over 57 million Americans who experience a mental health disorder in any given year or approximately one in four adults and one in five children,[21] help us to understand the condition as they talk about the journey. We are invited to consider or "imagine" some very specific dimensions of life "on the edge" in the following lines coming from a source "unknown" as shared in a recent article from NAMI of Greater Chicago:

- Imagine . . . that nothing seems enjoyable or fun anymore. Even your favorite activities, spending time with friends, listening to music, or going to the theater, no longer give any satisfaction of pleasure. What would it be like to be unable to enjoy yourself?

- Imagine . . . that you suddenly find it difficult or impossible for remember anything you read. You read a page in a book, but when you set the book down, you can't remember what you read. How would you deal with your work or your studies?

- Imagine . . . that you can't remember anything your boss or techer says. You sit through class or a meeting really trying to pay attention, but when it is over you can't remember what was discussed. How would you feel about going to class or work every day? How would you explain your difficulties to your boss, teachers and parents?

20. National Alliance on Mental Illness, "What is Mental Illness?" lines 14–40.
21. Ibid., lines 17–18.

- Imagine . . . that you live in a black and white and gray world, because all the color has faded away. Someone "pulls the plug" on the energy in your body, and all but 20 percent of your energy drains out. You feel full of hot, dry sand, too tired to start even the simplest task. How easy would it be to do your normal activities?

- Imagine . . . that simple things you used to do automatically, like deciding what to wear or which radio station to listen to, take enormous effort. Even after deciding, you aren't sure you made the right decision. How would this complicate your daily routine? What if you had to handle major decisions like where to go to college or big changes like moving to another state?

- Imagine . . . that you wake up every morning for weeks and can't think of one good reason to get up. You think the world would be better off without you. How much hope would you have fore the future?[22]

Through the dedicated efforts of people working with NAMI and a host of local, community-based volunteer groups, nonprofit organizations, and informed churches new hope is possible. One of the messages of these various groups is that we need to gain a better understanding of persons with mental illness. It is helpful to know that the illness may leave the affected person in a situation where personal hygiene is neglected. Perhaps we need to ask the questions suggested by NAMI: "How would you feel? How would you look? What would you do?" And we must all be advocates for the potential change possible with effective treatment including medication and involvement by qualified mental health professionals.

One of the other national groups in addition to NAMI is Depression and Bipolar Support Alliance (DBSA) with over one thousand support groups around the country.[23] Very helpful information such as the following is circulated by DBSA in brochures and through other mechanisms:

> As with other chronic illnesses such as diabetes, heart disease or asthma, people with mood disorders should see themselves as managers of their illness. Depression and bipolar disorder are

22. National Alliance on Mental Illness of Chicago, "Imagine What It's Like," lines 1–12.

23. This alliance has main offices in Chicago (1536 W. Chicago Ave.) and can be reached through its website: www.DBSAlliance.org.

treatable, but they are not yet curable. For many people, depression and bipolar disorder are chronic illnesses. If severe depression and/or manic episodes reappear at some point in your life, don't panic. Your experience with previous episodes puts you one giant step ahead in the process of recognizing symptoms and getting help. By continuing your treatment plan, you can greatly reduce your chances of having symptoms recur.[24]

Today helpful information is available from a variety of sources. These include the considerable amount of free information from the National Institute of Mental Health (NIMH).[25] In a small booklet on depression the following advice is given about how to help a friend or relative:

Offer emotional support, understanding, patience and encouragement.

Engage your friend or relative in conversation, and listen carefully.

Never disparage feelings your friend or relative expresses, but point out realities and offer hope.

Never ignore comments about suicide, and report them to your friend's or relative's therapist or doctor.

Invite your friend or relative out for walks, outings and other activities. Keep trying if he or she declines, but don't push him or her to take on too much too soon. Although diversions and company are needed too many demands may increase feelings of failure. Remind your friend or relative that with time and treatment, the depression will lift.[26]

This same booklet gives the following advice for the person caught up in depression:

- Engage in mild activity or exercise. Go to a movie, a ballgame, or another event or activity that you once enjoyed. Participate in religious, social or other activities.

- Set realistic goals for yourself.

- Break up large tasks into small ones, set some priorities and do what you can as you can.

---

24. Depression and Bipolar Support Alliance, "Introduction to Depression and Bipolar Disorder," lines 1–8.

25. National Institute of Mental Health, www.nimh.nih.gov.

26. National Institute of Mental Health, "How can I help a friend?" lines 1–7.

- Try to spend time with other people and confide in a trusted friend or relative. Try not to isolate yourself and let others help you.

- Expect your mood to improve gradually, not immediately. Do not expect to suddenly "snap out of" your depression. Often during treatment for depressions, sleep and appetite will begin to improve before your depressed mood lifts.

- Postpone important decisions, such as getting married or divorced or changing jobs, until you feel better. Discuss decisions with other who know you well and have a more objective view of your situation.

- Remember that positive thinking will replace negative thoughts as your depression responds to treatment.[27]

A lot of information and helpful agencies and organizations as well as trained professionals in our country make it much easier to access help when it is needed. In other countries, such critical help is much more difficult to obtain. Reports on the mental trauma after the recent devastating earthquake in China revealed the harsh reality of heavy need balanced with few resources. One source, for example, reported some 16 million mental health patients in the country but only 19,000 psychiatrists or assistant psychiatrists.[28] More recently, news sources have reported a shocking shortage of mental health services following the earthquake disaster in Haiti. Unfortunately, in our country local mental health services are strained to the limit with cuts in budgets and the increase in demand related in part to the economic downturn. Writing in a guest commentary for the *Daily Camera* on November 5, 2009, Dr. Barbara Ryan, the Executive Director of the Mental Health Center serving Boulder and Broomfield Counties spoke about the problems confronting her center. She pointed to increasing rates of problems such as depression, anxiety, and suicidal thinking. Her Mental Health Center served some 10,000 people in 2004. In 2008 this number increased to 15,000 and was expected to rise even higher in future years.

27. National Institute of Mental Health, "How can I help myself?" lines 5–14.
28. MSNBC, "Trauma rampant," lines 31–34.

INSIGHT FROM A CLINICAL PSYCHOLOGIST

Dr. Jan Hittelman, Licensed Psychologist with Boulder Psychological Services in Boulder, offers some very helpful insights on the general topic of mental illness.[29] As he sees the situation, it is far too easy to make general statements about "mental illness" which, in fact, covers a wide range of behaviors. There is a very marked difference, for example, between a condition such as schizophrenia and depression. Perhaps it would be best to make a distinction between those disorders that are truly triggered by brain disorders compared to those conditions where environmental factors are most important. Most of the people Dr. Hittelman sees do not need psychotropic medication. Talk therapy is their primary need. In those cases where medication is indicated, Dr. Hittelman can make the proper referral to a psychiatrist to start this process just like any other therapist. Dr. Hittelman warns that the distinction between brain disorders and environmentally caused conditions is not that "black and white." Depression, for example certainly has biochemical components. The differentiation is a function of the unique individual and there is always a significant interplay between the biochemical and environmental factors.

Like many working in counseling today, Dr. Hittelman uses cognitive behavioral therapy, a term used before in this book. The intent is to change thinking, but not to simply change behavior. It is more of a widespread impact primarily aimed at changing thought patterns to impact emotions. It is natural to have emotional reactions when things happen to us. Rethinking the matter can change the situation. To illustrate this process, Dr. Hittelman shares his own reaction to a situation while he was living in New York. It was not unusual for him to face a daily onslaught of heavy traffic and sometimes road rage. He found himself becoming very angry, yelling at other drivers and fighting the urge to tailgate them as they turned off the freeway. Then he learned in a college class that half of the people in the country have an IQ of less than one hundred, half over one hundred. He then transferred this bit of information to the freeway, telling himself that the road rage warriors were in reality part of the 50 percent of the population with low IQs. This took the sting out of the offensive behavior and he calmed down. His change in thinking affected his behavioral reaction and his stress level dropped.

29. Comments credited to Dr. Jan Hittelman in this section are from a personal interview with author Dean Jones in March of 2009 in Boulder, Colorado.

"The majority of my clients do not need meds . . . they are able to work through their problems," says Dr. Hittelman.[30] He does, however, acknowledge that sometimes meds are important. A case in point is the college student who recently came to his office. This young man did not talk about a long history of underlying issues in his life. It was like the depression came suddenly, with no apparent reason. The approach in this case was to steer him to a psychiatrist, since the problem was most likely one of an imbalance in brain chemistry. People are complex. A lot of things are at work. It is helpful to consider the interplay between "nature and nurture." Like other clinicians today, Dr. Hittelman would not be comfortable with the easy turn to medication for military personnel in Iraq. As told in the lead article in Time magazine for June 16, 2008, people like Christopher Lejeune, an Army sergeant, are routinely given medications to reduce stress. In his case, a visit to a military doctor gave him the diagnosis of depression and a quick trip back to the fighting armed with Zoloft and the antianxiety drug clonazepam.

Based on considerable clinical experience, Dr. Hittelman highly recommends that more attention be given to stress and how we manage it. Today, we have a stressful environment that is unique in many ways. As adults, for example, we can process an event like the 9/11 disaster with over three thousand people dead from the crash of a plane into the World Trade Center, but an eight-year-old child has a hard time handling this kind of an event. "Stress is at the heart of everything, we all experience stress, there is good and bad stress."[31] When kids come for help around problems like depression or addiction they will always talk about stress. And there are very powerful techniques for stress reduction that can be taught in a limited period of time.

Taking our queues from professionals in the field, all of us can become more alert to stress factors and coping techniques in our daily life. Switzerland and other European countries are ahead of us in seeing the importance of stress reduction. Health insurance policies in those countries, for example, often cover the cost of going to a spa. Knowing that this kind of experience is beneficial, we can prescribe it for ourselves. In Colorado, natural hot water pools in places like Glenwood Springs and Steamboat Springs attract people from around the country. If such an outing is beyond the reach of someone's budget, other, less costly

30. Ibid.
31. Ibid.

or no-cost uses of time can be purposefully planned. I see meditation as another option for stress reduction with the added attraction that no financial cost is involved. Research has shown the powerful role of stress reduction. According to a new study conducted by the American Association for Cancer Research, stress-reducing psychological intervention increases the quality of life and survival rate among women with recurrent breast cancer. Data from a previous study, "The Stress and Immunity Breast Cancer Project," demonstrated that women who received psychological intervention had a 45 percent reduced risk of breast cancer recurrence.[32] In the current study focusing on mortality rates, those women who experienced recurrence of the disease and who had earlier received psychological intervention had a 59 percent reduction in the risk of dying of breast cancer. In other words, women who were taught stress reduction techniques experienced a lower mortality rate compared to a matched sample.[33] It would save us a lot of money if we focused more directly on stress. Medications do not solve underlying problems. They often only treat the symptoms. With severe depression, a person may need medication, but then work can be done to wean this person from the need for daily medications. This is not to say that the major, chronic forms of "mental illness" such as bipolar disorder and schizophrenia do not require continuing medication.

Dr. Jan Hittelman summarizes his approach in a column he wrote for the Daily Camera newspaper on July 29, 2008.

> When we experience feelings like anger, depression, and anxiety in response to situations in our lives, we typically assume that those feelings are the result of those situations. Furthermore, we blame those external events for our resulting mood. Most people don't realize, however, is that there's an intervening variable that actually results in our emotional response. That variable is our evaluation of situations that we encounter. It's not the situation itself but the way we think about it that determines our emotional response.[34]

It is not difficult to find echoes of cognitive behavioral therapy in many different places. The following quote from the book titled The

32. Willingham, "Less stress helps," lines 10–13.

33. Ibid., lines 23–25.

34. Hittelman, "Internal Evaluation," Fit 9. Printed with permission of the *Daily Camera*.

Daily Reader for Contemplative Living with excerpts from the works of Father Thomas Keating is one example:

> The contemplative journey, because it involves the purification of the unconscious, is not a magic carpet to bliss. It is an exercise of letting go of the false self, a humbling process, because it is the only self we know. God approaches us from many different perspectives: illness, misfortune, bankruptcy, divorce proceedings, rejection, and inner trials. God has not promised to take away our trials, but to help us to change our attitudes toward them. That is what holiness really is. In this life, happiness is rooted in our basic attitude toward reality. Sometimes a sense of failure is a great means to true humility, which is what God most looks for in us.[35]

THE MENTALLY ILL OFFENDER

Margaret, a middle-aged woman, lives in the greater Seattle area. She volunteers to help others as she is able and she walks on her own personal journey with mental illness. I talked with Margaret in 1996 while I was writing a book that I titled The Other Chamber: A Portrait of the Mentally Ill Offender.[36] This book looks inside a state mental hospital and travels with men and women who have had personal experience with various law enforcement agencies. What is it like to be mentally ill and to be confined in jail? Consideration of this part of the population is very timely, since in the United States more than 756 people per 100,000 residents are in the criminal justice system, a rate five times the average for countries in the world.[37] One of Margaret's comments merits special mention: "If you think mental illness looks bad from the outside you should try imagining what it is like from the inside of yourself. You can be on the ragged edge."

During one of those "ragged edge" experiences, Margaret cried for six days and nights. She has vivid memories of different episodes during which she was out of control. Once during a time when she was having hallucinations she took off down a major freeway, driving on the wrong side of the highway. As she recalled the drive for me, she said that she thought at the time that the other cars coming toward her were in the

35. Keating, *Daily Reader*, 165.
36. Jones, *The Other Chamber*.
37. Webb, "What's Wrong?" cover story.

wrong, while she was driving correctly. She said, " . . . to me it looked like my vehicle was on the right side of the yellow line."

If you have never had the opportunity to talk with someone who has experienced some form of major mental illness and who has spent some time in jail or prison, you may find it interesting to consider the range of people who know this experience firsthand. People like Melissa. Her story is also shared in my book on the mentally ill offender. Looking at her in the community, you would never know that she has spent time in a county jail. Melissa is an attractive single mother. She gives her time as a volunteer in a center for the mentally ill. With a degree from a prestigious university, Melissa wants to work as an administrator in an agency serving the mentally ill.

A few years before I spoke to her, this talented young lady had a serious psychotic episode after going without her prescription medications for six months. Her days were filled with voices and cascading emotions. She walked into a department store at a major shopping mall and started grabbing merchandise off the racks and out of display cases. With her body draped in stolen merchandise she started to walk out of the store when she was apprehended by a half-dozen security guards. From the shopping mall Melissa was escorted to the local jail where she was placed in a holding cell. She will never forget the hard concrete floor, the hole in the floor for a toilet, and the lack of human contact. In her own words, she says, "Three days and three long nights, a nightmare. Fortunately, my family got to an attorney. I went to court and was then signed over to the state's mental hospital."

When I talked with him, Ralph was thirty-eight. His blond hair was cut short and he wore a brown mustache. His jail record stretched back to his teens. Ralph described life in a "crisis cell" where he was shackled to the floor, chained to metal rings. Here he was totally naked, after tearing off all of his clothes, bare skin against the cold floor. No blankets. No furnishings of any kind. Only the writhing of hands caught in metal cuffs, wrists bloodied in the useless struggle. Screams and threats came from his mouth for hours on end. Ralph, someone who is proud of his ability to order food and to eat properly in a decent restaurant, Ralph, a man who once went to public school, now he is Ralph, the naked, writhing body in a jail crisis cell. He urinates and the warm liquid dribbles down between his legs. Then he defecates and lies in this putrid mess for hours.

This book focuses on "how to survive" in difficult times, including times of recession or drug and alcohol abuse or addiction as detailed in the last two chapters. Looking at the situation of mental illness, the focal person at the time of an acute psychotic episode does not hold the power to determine the outcome. Survival for him or her and the well being of the larger community is dependent on the responses of officials representing the city or the state. It is the responsibility of all of us to know something about the official management of the mentally ill person and to become involved in some way to make sure that policies and funding are truly doing what is best both for the one who has mental problems and for the larger community. It becomes very easy to point to some given individual as the source of "problems." A law enforcement person or someone else responding to the mentally ill individual may, in fact, be at fault. But other times it is the system as a whole that needs revision. I am thinking, for example, of the time I worked for the State of Washington as a social caseworker in Child Welfare Services. At that time it was the policy to place a child who was innocent, who had committed no legal offense into a juvenile detention facility along with children and teenagers who were seriously delinquent. There was no special place for those children who became wards of the state simply because of something like abusive parents. The innocent or "dependent" were placed together with the delinquent. After a few months of residence in detention with delinquents it was not unusual to return a child to a parent who had abused him or her. This was done at the direction of the court. At that time our Department of Child Welfare Services did not give special education or counseling to the parent. One wonders what kind of education this child had in such a place. As an individual caseworker I had no choice in this matter. The system was at fault. In a similar way, serious miscarriages of justice can occur at the system level in law enforcement.

In a jail or prison the monitoring of inmate behavior must give special consideration to the particular situation of the man or woman who has some form of mental illness. Steven shared with me some of his behavior while in jail. He told me that he regularly passed his psychotropic medications on to someone else instead of taking them himself. Some of the other inmates appreciated the "laid back" effect that this special kind of drug triggered. On at least one occasion Steven was given LSD through the bars from the hands of a jail trustee.

In the case of Margaret, the woman mentioned in connection with driving the wrong direction on the freeway, her contact with police officers was very beneficial to her survival. She had known seven years of crying, of ups and downs. The two officers who arrested her were kind. They told her that they did not want to hurt her. She was taken to court and then admitted to a county hospital. In this hospital she was given medication and in four days she felt like she was "born anew." Unfortunately, contact with law enforcement is not always this positive in terms of outcome.

Warren, a sheriff's deputy in Pierce County, Washington, shared the story of Mike with me. It was Warren's opinion that law enforcement only made Mike's problems worse. Standing six foot nine and weighing over three hundred pounds, Mike was a gentle giant. He was most comfortable when in custody. Warren called him a "system failure." He robbed repeatedly just to get back into jail or prison. His underlying mental illness was never addressed. One time when Warren picked him up after he had thrown a rock through a window, he was told that his action could have harmed a small boy who was inside the building at the time. Mike's response to this information was to cry, as he thought of the ten-year-old boy. He cried in the back of the patrol car all of the way to the jail.

Frank, a County Designated Mental Health professional, is very negative about the behavior of law enforcement officers. When I interviewed him, he volunteered the following comment: "When I am on the street I always feel more danger from the police than from the mentally ill . . . the officer is heavy on control . . . he or she responds to the mentally ill person in the same fashion as someone who lives within the normal range of emotions and behavior." Frank then went on to tell me about times when officers "inside and outside the jail beat people senseless for nothing more than making verbal insults." One inmate was taken into a holding cell and beaten until he could not move. Frank has seen mentally ill inmates strapped to the floor between two eye bolts on a thin pad with feet shackled to one eye bolt and hands to another. Sometimes they are left in their feces and urine for hours.

One critical area in the community management of the mentally ill is the need for better cooperation and communication between different segments of the response team. It was not unusual for Frank to put himself between a client and a law enforcement officer. Unfortunately,

Frank was not called to the scene when a man he had known in the State Hospital was confronted by the police when he set up a temporary camp in a city park. When neighbors saw him holding a gun they called police. At the time this man was under the delusion that he was in charge of all of the police forces in the western part of the country. He fired shots over the heads of the officers. When asked to put down his gun, he told the officers that he would do this if they first put their guns down. Shots were fired directly at the mentally ill and delusional man. He died on the scene. Frank is convinced that if he had been called the man would not have been killed.

John, an Institutional Counselor with the Department of Social and Health Services for the State of Washington, told me that, in his opinion, political decisions are often made with little regard for either the welfare of the client or the long-range community consequences. Although jail is expensive, it is cheaper than the State Hospital. At the time of my contact, the per-day cost in the nearest city jail was only fifty dollars compared to over three hundred dollars per day at the State Mental Hospital. Although cheaper, jail is not the best place for someone with mental illness. Wendy, a jail supervisor, laments the sad plight of these people, saying, "They are brought to a place that gives them little help, little treatment, and little hope." In jail they are either placed with others who have no understanding of mental illness or housed alone in isolation, away from all human contact, save that of a busy, overworked corrections officer. Here they are left, with their voices, their demons, and their illness.

It would be inappropriate to generalize from the above comments taken from my book to all times and places with respect to the relationships between mental health professionals, law enforcement personnel, and the mentally ill offender. I know that today, programs like Windhorse Community Services in Boulder sustain very good daily cooperation between mental health professionals, local police, and sheriff's deputies. At Windhorse it is not unusual for a counselor to call law enforcement when necessary during a contact with a client or family member.

HOMELESS AND MENTALLY ILL

The mentally ill are part of the homeless in every city in America. The faces of some of these people remain with me although I have now been retired for some four years from my work in night ministry. In Portland,

Oregon, a middle-aged man was desperate as he approached me on the east end of the Burnside Bridge. He was profoundly paranoid. This made it impossible for him to remain in a temporary shelter where men were given bunks, one on top of the other. In these close quarters he was overwhelmed by feelings of being attacked. The FBI was "after" him, he saw snakes coming up out of a coffee cup. For some reason he trusted me. I walked him back across the Burnside Bridge and then hailed a cab. I gave the driver all of the money I had, asking him to take the stranger up the hill to the University of Oregon medical center, knowing that they maintained a very good emergency mental health outreach. Back then what I offered was normal cab fare for that distance and the driver obliged.

The encounters with folks who struggled with mental illness continued for me. One night a woman in downtown Tacoma approached me with her problem. She felt that she needed to again be admitted into Western State Hospital, not too far from Tacoma's downtown business district. She had hitchhiked down from Seattle, thinking that she could simply admit herself, not knowing that the system does not work like that. I learned that she did have a medical record at one of the hospitals in north Seattle where she could get emergency care. I drove her back to Seattle and to the hospital she mentioned where they did know her and they welcomed her. Another night in St. Louis, Missouri, I met a man who said that he was a member of a group for bipolar disorder and that at one time he had been a college professor. He had taken a bus to St. Louis in a fit of mania, heading for the West Coast. When I saw him he was in the Greyhound Bus Depot and very agitated. He needed medical attention. I drove him to a local hospital where the psychiatry intern who saw him did a very good job, which included contacting his primary care physician back in New Jersey.

Some of my most memorable encounters late at night came in St. Louis as I tried to be helpful to a ninety-two-year-old homeless, "bag lady," carrying with her a collection of plastic bags that held all of her possessions. Martha knew the schedules of the men and women who cleaned the restrooms in the two large bus depots downtown. When they were not around she used these facilities as a place to wash her clothes. She was homeless after being deserted by her children who had managed to get all of the proceeds from the sale of her home. At times Martha was friendly, once offering me some of her chocolate covered raisins as she sat in the eating area of the Greyhound Bus Depot late one night. But later, she was admitted to the city's mental hospital. When I learned of this, I made a visit. Martha did not talk to me. She had taken a tube of lipstick and smeared her face from ear to ear with the bright red lip coloring. When she was released from the hospital to return to the street, this ninety-two-year-old was much worse. My last memory of her is meeting her outside the bus depot. She had been tossed out into the cold, dark night because she had no bus ticket. I gently took her by the arm and led her to my car. I drove her to a shelter where I walked up the stairs with her and then she spoke softly the words, "thank you."

FAMILY AND FRIENDS AND MENTAL ILLNESS

Family members will be impacted in major ways by mental illness, as indicated by Mike's insightful story and in my comments about my brother. One part of the family equation that merits more attention is the reaction of parents when a young child first hears voices or shows other signs of mental illness. Matthew spent time in prison after following through on directions given to him by inner voices. He was given specific instructions about the need to kill his roommate with a large knife. In talking about his life, Matthew was most impressed by the way it was always necessary for him to do something very dramatic in order to get help from the system. As he put it, "I was getting sicker and sicker until I finally committed my felony and then started to get help." Years before his incarceration for murder, Matthew faced a policeman after his mother hit her head in a fall. In a delusional state, he grabbed his mother thinking that he was protecting her, but she fell and was injured. A neighbor called the police. It is unfortunate that his mother did not follow up on Matthew's early childhood experiences of hearing voices.

Matthew shared with me the fact that his first experience with the hearing of voices came when he was only five years old. At the time, his favorite TV show was the Flintstones. One afternoon he heard an announcer say that another program would take the place of the Flintstones. Voices in his head told him to go to downtown Portland, Oregon, and kill the TV people. His mother did ask him what was bothering him. He told her that he was going to kill the TV people but there was no sharing about the voices. When Matthew was seven, he was stretched out on top of his sister's car in the warm sun. A tree was near the car. He heard voices—coming from the tree—there was no person near at the time.

One childhood experience of hearing voices did get response from an adult, however. That came while Matthew was in school. The voices told him to defecate in the urinal in the boy's bathroom. When he did so the janitor told his teacher and he was sent to a school psychologist. At the time, he was given an "ink blot test" but was never told the results.

Sometimes the actions and words of a small child are so alarming that parents are forced to listen. Max, for example, was only seven years old when he first tried to kill himself. After writing a suicide note, he jumped out of his bedroom window. Since the window was only six feet from the ground, the fall netted him some bruises but was not fatal. At the age of ten, Max wrote the following letter to his parents. This was not a suicide note; Max remains alive at the time of this writing. His parents continue to cope with his mood swings and love him dearly:

> Dear Mommy and Daddy:
> I am really feeling sad and depressed and lousy about myself. I love you but I still feel like I want to kill myself. I am really sad but I just want to feel happy again. The reason I feel so bad is because I can't sleep at night. But, I can't control it. It is not me that does control it. I don't know what controls it, but it is not me. I really, really need some help.
> Love Max!!!! I love you Mommy I love you Daddy.[38]

It is significant that the above lines appeared, not in an obscure psychology journal, but in Newsweek, a popular news magazine, on May 26, 2008. The article on bipolar disorder came with a front-page picture and included six pages in the magazine, one indication of the interest in and importance of mental illness at all stages of the life cycle today. Popular attention can be a mixed blessing. As in the case of Attention Deficit Disorder (ADD), there is now an over-diagnosis of bipolar disorder.

The last chapter included references to drugs and alcohol at the middle school age. Mental illness is also an important concern for parents of middle school children. Dr. Jan Hittelman offers the following advice:

> As parents, we must but real effort into creating opportunities to frequently talk with our children about challenges and experiences in their lives and do it in a way that will foster ongoing open communication about a wide range of risk behaviors and topics. This is particularly true during the middle school years

---

38. Carmichael, "Welcome to Max's World," 33.

when children are often more receptive to parental feedback that they will be during high school.

These talks should be a discussion and not a lecture. A simple rule of thumb is to make every effort for your child to do most of the talking: ask questions, encourage and respect your child's opinions, let them know that you appreciate them sharing their points of view even if you don't necessarily agree with them. After they have fully expressed themselves, that's the time to share your feelings, opinions and concerns.[39]

As a father, I know that being a parent is a lifelong commitment. Moving beyond the early years of life and the middle school years, parents continue to face the challenge of understanding their son or daughter's behavior. An insightful article titled "Depressive Disorder in Highly Gifted Adolescents" written by P. Susan Jackson and Jean Peterson appeared in the Journal of Secondary Gifted Education in 2003. In this article a number of case studies help us see the problematic nature of parent/child relationships when the teenager faces major depression. The suggestion is that the disease may have more striking symptoms when the adolescent is above his or her peers in intellectual ability. Some of the issues for Jared, a high school senior, are reflected in the following comments:

> Shockingly, he revealed that no one—his teachers, his friends or his family—was aware of his depressive state. Just the week before, his father, a highly successful entrepreneur, had spoken with him, concerned that Jared might be studying too hard. He advised Jared to pace himself in light of approaching final exams. Jared reported that his father questioned his diminished energy and suggested some exercise, a healthy diet, and "down time." Jared was quick to assure his father that he would attend to pace and explained his fatigue in terms of senior-year pressures: predictable, undesirable, and easily dealt with. He offered nothing more, and his father did not press him further.
>
> As Jared recounted this exchange with his father, he revealed profound shame for his calculated and easy deceit. He was ashamed about the ease with which he could dupe his father and confused by the fear and guilt that fed and accompanied his duplicity.[40]

39. Hittelman, "What's on the Mind?" Fit 9. Printed with permission of the *Daily Camera*.

40. Jackson and Peterson, "Depressive Disorder," 182.

The parents of a child with mental illness live daily with the challenges of the illness and the systems responding to this illness. This challenge continues as the "child" becomes an adult. I felt the pain of Bill's parents, Jim and Betty as they shared their life experiences. Bill attempted suicide on eight different occasions. Betty kept a diary of all these occasions plus the long saga of encounters with the criminal justice and mental health systems. Jim, a very successful businessman, found it very hard to interact with the official systems around mental illness. One time, for example, Bill was confined in jail and Jim was anxious about his possible release time. He wanted to make sure that plans were in place so that his son would not be simply returned to the street. But it became very difficult for the caring father to get accurate information from the system. This was frustrating for Jim because he was accustomed to a smoother flow of information in the world of business. Both Jim and Betty, however, are thankful that their son does get the basics of food and a place to stay while he is incarcerated. This gives them a temporary reprieve from worry about how their son is doing as one of the homeless mentally ill.

Among the street population at night, men who were part of a loose-net gang told me that anyone showing signs of having mental problems was shunned by the group. Such a person was called a "space case," someone who could not be trusted. This does not mean that everyone who is mentally ill ends up isolated totally from others. If you have been living with some form of mental illness, you can most likely point to times of good, positive relationships. One extreme example is the situation of James, a man who has spent time both at Western State Hospital for the mentally ill and in the Pierce County Jail. But when I talked with him in his apartment he was most interested in telling me about the woman he lives with, the love of his life. At the time of my contact, James was in his early forties, a "good looking" man with a strong upper body, but confined to a wheelchair. His ready smile hides the long saga of trauma he has experienced in his tango with mental illness and other problems.

Two years before our meeting, James took a major turn in his life. This came after a two-day spell of intense feelings about taking his life. He jumped into the path of an eighteen-wheel diesel truck passing below him as he stood on an overpass in downtown Seattle. When the truck driver backed away, James was left with the most massive mid-body damage ever seen at a local trauma center. His body cavity was nearly separated. Major organs were displaced. He was unconscious for three months. Now James has 50 percent to 70 percent hearing loss in both ears. He will never again walk normally. His days are spent in a wheelchair. James does manage to attend sessions at a community center for the developmentally disabled and mentally ill. And, best of all, James lives with a woman he loves. Social relationships need not end with the long journey of mental illness.

There is another way to talk about social relationships and mental illness. This points more directly to "strategies for survival." In most cities community mental health centers can become a good resource for information and social support, both for family members and the man or woman with mental illness. At one time I served as the Chairman of the Board of Directors for the Community Mental Health Center located in Pierce County, Washington. This center maintained a drop-in clinic. One of the staff members, a personal friend, Larry Baker, started a support group for family and consumers. The term "consumer" has become increasingly popular to avoid the stigmatization that can come from terms like "patient" or "client." Consumer is now used to refer to a wide range of people who are living with some form of mental illness. In this group, consumers learned about their medications. Family members shared their challenges. A good way to locate possible resources is to contact the National Alliance for the Mentally Ill.

BODY, MIND, AND SPIRIT

One of the most important books about mental illness and "religious" or "spiritual" issues is the 2009 publication of Nancy Kehoe titled Wrestling with Our Inner Angels: Faith, Mental Illness, and the Journey to Wholeness.[41] Dr. Kehoe is a clinical psychologist and a Catholic Sister. Her book is a strong statement about seeing a "patient" as a whole person, not simply someone with psychiatric symptoms. People like Beverly and Russell and Buddy come alive in a new way as they share their stories. Dr. Kehoe takes readers into her life as she directed a Spiritual Beliefs and Values group in a psychiatric day treatment center. This was a safe place where patients could talk about their spiritual life without fear of being seen as more delusional with the possibility of being given

41. Kehoe, *Wrestling with Our Inner Angels.*

higher doses of medication. Most of their caregivers were not sympathetic to the "God talk." In the group, people could discuss issues like their struggle with doubt and belief—and God's goodness against the shadow of a personal sense of evil. The group was simply a place where people were given a chance to talk about their beliefs. The sincere and sometimes profound emotions and ideas coming from this group add a new dimension to traditional discussions of mental illness. It is very moving, for example, to read how the group expressed intense feelings of loss for the family members of those who died in the tragedy of 9/11. As a society we can learn from people who too often are stigmatized or identified only in a very limited way.

Beverly was one of the regulars in Dr. Kehoe's group until her death from cancer. After her death she left all of her extensive written material including diary accounts to her friend, Nancy. The following is her personal advice for those who are going through pain:

> A philosophy for my life, especially if I am in pain (written in pain): When you are in pain, you must 1. Wait for the relief which has always come by God's grace; 2. Function as well as you can with as little self-pity and self-hatred as possible; 3. Still "be kind to all I meet" as much as I can; 4. Take it one day at a time; 5. Treat yourself and others as lovingly as possible. When you have failed, accept God's, others' and your own forgiveness as soon as possible. Then with His help, "Take up your bed and walk."[42]

Another "patient," Jennifer who has spent her adult life in the mental health system offers the following:

> Our true natures are bled out of us by some religious teachings, terrifying family experiences and the pain of mental illness. We are not just pieces of damaged psyches. When you get rid of the toxic material many of us have carried from our early experiences, the majestic spirit can emerge.[43]

Russell found his way through Buddhism, especially the practice of Zen, a new experience for him after his dance with voices in his head and homelessness:

> Buddhist teaching says, "It takes a great question, great faith, and great courage to follow a spiritual path." I see the great courage for me in dealing with all my hospitalizations and several suicide

---

42. Ibid., 32.
43. Ibid., 39.

attempts. For me, the practice keeps clearing out the stuff that gets in my way, the bad karma that takes me off course. I have a real appreciation of my life these days.

Chanting in my Zen practice, playing my guitar, and singing allow me to express my feelings that have been quiet for a long period of time. Music gives voice to parts of me I can't express in any other way. If you talk to someone about your depression, they aren't likely to listen for too long, but if you sing the blues, they will include you in their life, and you can include them in yours. When I sing, I am in touch with my spirit.[44]

A final lesson from the writing of Dr. Kehoe is her valuable insight into how working with the mentally ill changed her. As a religious, she was very familiar with the practice of retreats and the voice of God calling her to service. The term "religious" is used here as the common word for a woman who has given herself to full-time work for the Roman Catholic Church. But it was in her work with people in the psychiatric program that truly put things in perspective for her. She changed in her ideas of God, in the way she prayed, and how she saw herself in terms of spirituality in general. This is a clarion call for all those who work in the field of mental health, as well as those who have a role in the community of faith. We too must evaluate and reevaluate our own spiritual walk.

While working on my book about the mentally ill offender, a man attending the church that I attended in Tacoma volunteered his story for the volume. Although I had seen him often in church, I never placed him in the category of one who is mentally ill. He was not part of the "in" group at church but he was accepted as part of the congregation. Part of his story was about one time when he was picked up by the police and served time in jail. While he was incarcerated he was delusional most of the time. We might be surprised if we knew the mental health issues for some who are part of a community of faith in which we are involved. One of the most promising developments around mental illness is the growing awareness and involvement of faith communities. In the Boulder area a new group called the Interfaith Network on Mental Illness (INMI) is making a significant impact.

Rev. Alan Johnson and Joanne Kelly are cofounders of INMI.[45] Both have adult sons with serious mental illnesses and each had a brother who

44. Ibid., 45.

45. Interfaith Network on Mental Illness can be reached by contacting Rev. Johnson at revalan2004@comcast.net.

died by suicide. INMI is an outreach program of The National Alliance for the Mentally Ill for Boulder County. The group also receives strong guidance, direction, and support from the First Congregational Church of Boulder. The first Interfaith Conference was in the fall of 2007. Since then, this group has formed an Advisory Board, wrote a mission statement, and convened programs in May, which is Mental Health Month, and in October during Mental Illness Awareness Week. Nationally recognized speakers have been brought to Boulder. These have included: Rev. Susan Gregg-Schroeder, Rev. Craig Rennebohm, and Sister/Dr. Nancy Kehoe. Educational programs have also been offered with local support groups. The funds for these programs come from those who make donations, as well as NAMI–Boulder, the Mental Health Center serving Boulder and Broomfield Counties, and the Mental Health Ministry of the First Congregational Church, Boulder. One of the compelling reasons for starting this new group was the awareness that traditional safety nets were beginning to unravel with the state of funding for mental health services in general. In times of need, people do turn to their clergy when mental health issues arise. But frequently clergy feel ill equipped to respond and they may have little knowledge of available resources. They may also be too busy to attend traditional classes and workshops. INMI affirms the significant role of spiritual resources in a person's healing and in providing hope.

The activities planned by INMI merit serious consideration by other communities. From the beginning this group in Boulder has been interfaith. Participation has included people from Protestant and Catholic congregations in town as well as those who are Jewish or Buddhist. Consumers, or those with mental illness, are also taking leadership roles, along with strong lay members from a variety of faith communities. INMI has shown the movie The Soloist to the community with a panel including a Buddhist therapist, a psychiatrist, and a consumer, as well as the film Minds on the Edge: Facing Mental Illness, with reactions from a psychiatrist, a parent, an attorney and a consumer. The movie Lars and the Real Girl was also shared with the community together with a panel including a family therapist, a clergy person, and an art therapist.

INMI has now developed a Mental Health Resource Guide for Faith Communities.[46] This guide includes such details as the following:

---

46. The guide is available by emailing Rev. Johnson at revalan2004@comcast.net.

- Some basic information on mental illness such as the statistic that one in every four families in faith congregations is touched in some way by mental disorder and the reality that mental illness impacts all aspects of a person's life.

- Information from such national organizations as NAMI and NIMH.

- Pamphlets on a variety of different forms of mental illness, from anxiety disorders to schizophrenia to substance abuse.

- Details on how to find the right mental health care provider.

One of the most innovative contributions of INMI is the anticipated development of an interactive, computer-based training package that clergy can download and use at their convenience. The planned modules include general information about mental illness as well as specific, urgent issues that congregants may be facing. Topics to be included are: mental illness basics, pastoral counseling verses long-term therapy, finding resources in your community, and talking to your congregation about mental health issues. Hopefully, this package will also include more urgent issues such as how to help returning vets cope, how to help someone who is psychotic, and how to help a suicidal congregant.

Joanne Kelly is one of many who walk between the world of mental illness and the world of the faith community. As mentioned above, her son lives with a combination of problems stemming from schizoaffective disorder—a mix of schizophrenia and bipolar disorder—and she has been diligent in her reach for a meaningful faith community. Not unlike others in her situation, she has found that ministers are not always sympathetic to people with mental illness. In one church she attended, the pastor, a woman, had a daughter-in-law who had schizophrenia. But the pastor had no sympathy for this young woman. One Sunday Kelly listened as another preacher boldly proclaimed that if people were truly diligent in their spiritual practice, they would have no need for psychotropic medications! Kelly was so thankful that her son was not with her that Sunday. She is very concerned about keeping him on his appropriate medications. With the meds he is able to function fairly well, but has serious problems without them. This young man does not understand that he has mental illness, and as a result, has a hard time taking his medications seriously. This is true for many of those who suffer with serious mental illnesses. The part of the brain that registers things like mental illness is simply not working properly. As a mother who cares, Kelly does not appreciate someone advising from the pulpit that it is okay to ignore your doctor's orders.

From the experiences of Kelly, it is obvious that more must be done to educate church leaders and others about mental illness. It does not help when someone "of the cloth" becomes obnoxiously arrogant in defending his or her position. In the case of the pastor who proclaimed that medications were for spiritual losers, Kelly was so distraught that she confronted the man, telling him that it could be very dangerous for him to say things like that. He put his nose an inch from hers and said, "When I am up there talking I am inspired by God, you cannot tell me what to say!" Thankfully, more ministers today are taking a very different stand, and are becoming supportive of work to help the community become aware of the problems of those who live with mental illness and their families.

What can churches do? Kelly would like to see communities of faith support those with mental illness much like they do in the case of other problems such as a heart attack, cancer, or a stroke. In the church she now attends, the congregation has accepted the challenge to support people with mental illness and to offer education on the condition. They try to show the same compassion for people with mental illness as they do for people with other problems. More specifically, the group has had a series of Sunday afternoon sessions when someone from the community or from the church share their story, perhaps around bipolar disorder or about brain injury.

Kelly is a leader with NAMI and, as mentioned above, she was key in starting the INMI work for Boulder. She is very supportive of the effort to build a community-wide coalition, helping faith communities get support and resources. NAMI offers a lot of resources including literature, support grants, and classes. One issue is the appropriate role of a pastor or other church leader. Kelly was discouraged when she talked to one pastor who informed her that he did not want to "know too much." He saw his role as simply referring congregants to specialists who would help them with the physical aspects of their illnesses. He did not want people to depend on him for answers. Referrals are important, but it is also important for faith community leaders to have a basic understanding of mental illness.

As I have suggested, there is now a growing awareness of mental health issues and the dimension of faith. On the NAMI website recently the following insightful comments were offered:

> Religious communities are in a unique position to combat stigma and provide a message of acceptance and hope. Proclaiming the values of social justice, respect for all persons, and non-discrimination, faith communities can reach out to individuals and families affected by mental illness in many helpful ways. Sharing the message that all persons are worthy in the eyes of God, a faith community may be the only place where a person with a mental illness truly feels accepted, valued and loved.
>
> For people who find no other welcome in the larger community, being welcomed in a house of prayer by a concerned and caring community can make a critical difference for consumers with mental illnesses and their families. Churches, synagogues, and other places of worship can spread the message that serious mental illnesses are "diseases of the brain" and help families understand that "it's not their fault." They can open their doors and their hearts to consumers and be a supportive presence in their on-going recovery.[47]

As one example of the work of NAMI, the national newsletter recently circulated a copy of an article first appearing in Schizophrenia Digest titled "The Power of Higher Powers."[48] This article documents the story of two women, Thelma Gordon and Connie Rakitan and their work as part of the Mental Health Ministries of the Archdiocesan Commission on Mental Illness in Chicago. Some ten to fifteen adults from all faiths meet semiweekly as partners in prayer and socializing. There are equal numbers of members with a mental illness and volunteers. Since this program began, people have found it helpful in their recovery. The process of praying, talking, and doing arts and crafts together in a context of faith seems to add a welcome component to the lives of people with mental illness. The very virtue of hope, that connection with the church, a place to express and explore one's faith and even talk about crisis in faith, in a place that's nonjudgmental and nontherapeutic, helps to make sense out of suffering and becomes very valuable for those who participate.

---

47. National Alliance on Mental Illness, "Ministry, Mental Illness," lines 15–22.
48. Morra, "Power of Higher Powers," 19–23.

One very important contribution of the article from Schizophrenia Digest as reprinted by NAMI is the detailed account of the experience of Chris Summerville in Canada:

> When Chris Summerville was a teenager, he struggled with severe clinical depression that persisted throughout his adult life, often resulting in suicidal ideation. As a Christian, this caused him tremendous guilt. He thought he shouldn't be experiencing such despair if he prayed hard enough. Summerville became an evangelical pastor at age 17 and continued that vocation for the next 25 years. In his last year as a pastor, he "came out of the closet" about his depression during a sermon.

"It was very awkward for the congregation," he recalls. "Even though they were very loving, they were shocked that their spiritual leader would have existential despair." That experience, says Summerville, was the reason he resigned as pastor in 1994.

> Today, at age 55, Summerville continues to minister, but in new ways. He is the executive director of the Manitoba Schizophrenia Society, interim chief executive officer (CEO) of the Canadian Schizophrenia Society, and on the board of directors of the Mental Heath Commission of Canada. Summerville has made it his life's mission to alter the concept that mental illness can be dealt with from a mind-body perspective. "I know it's radical for someone in my position to say this, but the biomedical model is deficient," he says. In Canada, Aboriginal people have taught us that if you want to talk to us about mental health, then talk to us about the mind, body, and spirit connection. The Eurocentric, biomedical model has proven to be deficient because of its exclusive emphasis just on biochemistry.[49]

Summerville and a growing number of his peers believe that faith is the number one missing element, "the forgotten dimension" in mental health services. But others are reluctant to address faith in a professional context, he says, because their issues of counter transference get in the way. If they do not consider themselves spiritual, or do not believe in discussing such issues, they will feel very uncomfortable when a consumer talks about spirituality.

> Several medical publications have discussed the issue in recent years, including the Journal of Ethics in Mental Health and the Psychiatric Rehabilitation Journal, each of which dedicated an

49. Ibid., 20.

entire issue to spirituality and recovery in 2007. Summerville attributes this to the recovery model, which has shifted care for the mentally ill from strictly passive—relying only on medicine and therapy—to a more active model that suggests people can recover meaning and process to their lives despite the effects of their illness." What's fundamental to the recovery model is hope," he says. "Hope that I can move beyond my illness; hope of recovering the things I lost. With the emphasis of hope, people become more interested in the concept of spirituality in mental illness because hope is essentially a spiritual issue."[50]

One of the most powerful resources for looking at the role of faith in mental illness is the written work and videos available at Mental Health Ministries.[51] Rev. Susan Gregg-Schroeder, Coordinator of this program, freely shares her personal story in talks around the country. She was serving one of the largest United Methodist churches in the country as an associate pastor when she developed severe depression, sending her to a psychiatrist and to the hospital. One of the most difficult parts of this experience was the way it affected her family. For a time the "problem" was managed by turning to silence. She feared that she would lose her job if she became open about what she was going through. Fortunately, Rev. Gregg-Schroeder was able to tap the services of both a pastoral counselor as well as a psychiatrist. Now her passion is to encourage communities of faith to do their part in reducing stigma and providing a positive milieu for those who live with mental illness and their families. One of the interesting experiences of Rev. Gregg-Schroeder is that the scriptures, very close to her as a pastor, became both a source of inspiration as well as a place where she found expressions of her own inner dilemma. Portions of Psalm 88, for example, touched some of the low she was experiencing:

> For I am full of troubles, and my life draws near to the place of death. I am counted among those who go down into the pit. I am as a man who has no help or strength—a mere shadow; cast away among the dead, like the slain that lie in a grave, who you remember no more, and they are cut off from Your hand. You have laid me in the depths of the lowest pit, in darkness, in the deeps. (Psalm 88:3–6)

50. Ibid., 21.

51. Information about these powerful resources is available at www .MentalHealthMinistries.net.

Mental Health Ministries outlines a five-step program for congregations that begins with a significant quote from former first-lady Rosalyn Carter:

> People with mental problems are our neighbors. They are members of our congregations, members of our families; they are everywhere in this country. If we ignore their cries for help, we will be continuing to participate in the anguish from which those cries of help come. A problem of this magnitude will not go away. Because it will not go away, and because of our spiritual commitments, we are compelled to take action.[52]

1. *Education.* If ministers, priests, amams and rabbis do not educate themselves, they will not be able to recognize the symptoms and make appropriate referrals to counselors and psychiatrists. This is often made more difficult because many religious leaders are hiding their own struggle with mental illness from the hierarchy of their religious organization. As clergy leave the ministry in record numbers, we can no longer ignore the mental health needs of our clergy and their families.

2. *Commitment.* This means that the church leadership commits to be intentional in seeking ways to become a caring congregation. It is often a concerned lay person who initiates this process because pastors are so overwhelmed with other responsibilities.

3. *Welcome.* Seek ways to integrate persons with a mental illness into the faith community. Welcoming and hospitality require us to reach out to persons in a way that allows for the mutual exchange of joys and concerns. When we take the time to really get to know another person, the barriers between "us" and "them" break down.

4. *Support.* We are brought up to be strong, self-sufficient and independent people. It is hard to ask for help and so often we keep our struggles hidden. But God wants us to care for one another—and allow others to care for us in our time of need.

5. *Advocacy.* Mental illness is a justice issue involving such basic human rights as access to medical care, stable and supportive housing, and job training. Once a congregation has developed a

52. Mental Health Ministries, "Mental Health Illness," line 1.

mental health ministry, a natural next step is to be involved in advocacy.[53]

The topic of mental illness is not to be taken lightly. Mental illness is something that some very talented people must struggle with throughout their life. As Mike was finishing his part of this chapter, the *Daily Camera* featured a story about Steven Thomas, a thirty-six-year-old millionaire. Thomas was the founder of a Boulder-based software company. He was diagnosed with bipolar disorder in April of 2008 but he refused medication. On Sunday, July 13, 2008, his body was found below a high cliff near Honolulu, Hawaii. Thomas had been missing for two weeks. The high possibility is that his death was another tragic taking of life in suicide. Working together as a total community, we can make a difference for individuals and their families.

CONVERSATION

This conversation took place on the lower level of the main hospital building in a large medical complex. As we sat in a booth in the cafeteria on this level, our first impression was that all seemed very neat and orderly in this place. Employees were easily spotted by the color of their uniform—white, black, blue, green—and name tags. Some chatted informally as they shared coffee. We knew that up on other levels of this building the mood in some patient rooms was not this casual and upbeat. The complex also includes a rather somber looking building labeled simply "Building 9." It is for "Behavioral Health." All of the impressive buildings and carefully structured roles reminded us that most of the health issues we face are confronted in less than ideal circumstances of real life where roles and diagnostic labels are sometimes confusing.

Dean: One of the things I have been thinking about is that I feel that I have learned a lot about bipolar disorder during our time together. Would you say that your friends and people you meet have a good understanding of this disease?

Mike: No, I don't think that my friends have a good awareness of bipolar disorder. They tend to think of it as an expression of irrational behavior or erratic moods and may use it as an insult. I generally do not tell people immediately about my mental illness. Many times they are taken off guard. They may have a bit of understanding, but they do

---

53. Ibid., lines 22–24.

not have empathy. But some do, usually those who have had firsthand experience including the patients or "customers" I see in my work. They have a good understanding; they have been there themselves.

Dean: Looking at your interaction with Suzie Q, I can see a lot of professional, caring involvement. This prompts me to ask if you see yourself in some role with people that is different than your major role today since you are now at the early stage of your professional career.

Mike: I am not going to do what I am doing now forever. I would like to deal more directly with drug addiction and/or mental illness. I would also like, at some point, to consider teaching either students or patients.

Dean: Looking back over this chapter, I feel that we could have spent more time on the process of societal labeling. We did consider this in the many references to stigmatization. Societies have labeled "mental illness" in very different ways over the years. There was a time in Colonial America when people were routinely flogged in public simply on the assumption that they were mentally ill. On the other hand, in some third world countries those with a mental illness were seen sometimes as having some kind of super-human power. On the individual level, we have looked at how a person's definition of him or herself is very powerful from judgments about being an abuser verses an addict in the case of drugs or alcohol to the sometimes difficult labeling for someone who is bipolar. Societal labeling and self-labeling are important in all areas of life. In one country, everyone carried a low-grade infection, making them listless and tired all of the time. With no base for comparison, they concluded that this was a normal way to live. In a very different situation, the labeling process can limit options, including counseling, if a person has been involved in a dysfunctional marriage for over thirty years but sees this as "normal" for marriage. I can see where someone with a mental illness could label him or herself in such a way that reaching for wholeness would be very difficult.

Mike: We want to put a name on everything, turning what is really grey in real life to either black or white. I don't know how I feel about this. We can label someone as mentally ill and they do not strive for more. I am labeled as mentally ill but I am happy, even thankful for it. I have achieved a lot. I am just thankful for this disorder; it has made me feel things on a level that others simply can't, both good and bad. I would also like to say that I am also thankful for my experiences in the use of drugs. All of this has helped to define me; it makes me who I am. I would not want to take back either the mental illness or the drug use. I feel that I need to say this.

Dean: Now I am thinking of the differences in our ages. At seventy-eight I know that I sometimes think of an object and then forget its name. My mother had Alzheimer's during the last year of her life. My father, on the other hand, died at the age of ninety-six and never had any form of dementia. I know that I have changed. Back when I was thirty-six I memorized a list of some seventy-five authors and the titles of their books or journal articles while preparing for my written PhD exam. At that time I was also working at least thirty hours a week while taking a full course load at the graduate level. I know that I am different today, but I do not think that I have any kind of dementia. I audit classes at the University now and also get involved with different writing projects.

Mike: The aging process is unstoppable. The body and brain get older. But look at what you are doing. You are doing everything you can. This is your birthright. We are all called to live life to our full potential; to be all we can be.

Dean: Both of us have empathy. We want to help others. We say that we need to reach out to others. What would you say is the best advice we have given in these pages?

Mike: We say that people have options. Medications may or may not work. There are other options. You and I know enough about the brain to know that every experience has a chemical component. When we have good thoughts the brain registers this. We can set goals and create good feelings. Positive feelings are good for combating depression, even better than prescribed drugs.

Dean: I also think that community is important. Today social interaction takes many forms, including the options available on the Internet. This can enhance community or become problematic. It is much more difficult, for example, to understand why someone does not return an email than to evaluate interaction that is face to face. We do not have the nonverbal clues including subtle facial expressions to help us understand the interaction. No matter our emotional state, we are social by nature. We need community. In difficult times others can become so very important. Not necessarily to give us "professional" advice, but simply to give some social support.

Mike: A good support system is very important when dealing with mental illness.

Dean: Maybe one way to end this conversation is to again acknowledge that we are both holistic in our approach to mental illness. People are one: body, mind, and spirit. As we have discussed throughout this book, spiritual inspiration can come in many different ways. There is a basic need to rise above what we can see and feel; there is a spiritual realm to tap into and this can be very valuable.

4

Suicide

Michael Joseph

*"Somehow, like so many people who get depressed,
we felt our depressions were more complicated
and existentially based than they actually were"*

—KAY REDFIELD JAMISON

PARKED AT THE BOTTOM

I HAD JUST GOTTEN the car a month earlier and it was a lot more comfortable than my previous vehicle. I was sitting in the driver's seat smoking a joint by myself, playing with my iPod. I was too depressed to enjoy the music, but I needed some background noise. I decided to set the iPod to shuffle so it would randomly play songs from the hard drive. That decision, I would later decide, was the catalyst to my eyes being ripped opened. At that current moment, however, my eyes were soaked in tears and clouded with a darkness that only someone who has experienced severe depression can understand. This particular depressive episode had lasted over four months now and I knew from previous experiences that it would not get better unless I did something drastic. Admittedly, up until that point in time doing something drastic was the only way for me to get attention from others. The attention, any attention, would help me to feel better for a short time and give me a false sense of value, but any sense of value is better than none. This was my patented method for getting out of a depression. I would tell someone that I was depressed or thinking about suicide and they would focus enough energy on me to make me feel special. Just like a child crying to get attention, I was victimizing myself. This is obviously not a rational way to deal with depression.

This time, however, provided me with the mental break that I needed to realize just how pathetic my stunts for attention were. I had decided to sit in my car and sleep. Forever. This time I had not told anyone my plan and I thought that I would see it through to the end. I chose a rather painless killer, carboxyhemoglobin (CHG). Well, carbon monozide, but CHG is the end result of inhaling copious amounts of carbon monoxide. Hemoglobin is a type of protein in our blood that is responsible for carrying oxygen to the cells. When someone inhales carbon monoxide it binds to the hemoglobin 200 to 250 times greater than oxygen, creating the compound CHG. The problem here is that in the presence of large amounts of carbon monoxide, like car exhaust, the hemoglobin in the body will become saturated with carbon monoxide and will no longer be able to efficiently transport oxygen to the body. The victim will eventually pass out and in time the body will suffocate due to lack of oxygen. I had just extinguished the joint and was listening to the music when I noticed the first symptoms: headache, mild nausea (at first), dizziness, and finally weakness. Before I knew it I was asleep.

THE BEGINNING

When faced with the reality of solving our problems, it always helps to look back to the beginning when the problem first started, so perhaps we had better start from the beginning. Flash back to me at thirteen years old in the middle of my first major depressive episode. I had no idea what to make of all of the feelings I was experiencing and was very confused. I had broken my foot by kicking a wall in gym class and wearing the cast gave me an excuse to mope around the house and not partake of any activity. For the first time in my life I was entertaining the idea of suicide. I had no plan to do so, just random thoughts of taking my own life. I felt like it would be easier for my family and the few friends that I had if I were not around. It was late spring and my cast was due to be taken off soon. I was watching *MTV Unplugged*. The show featured a group I had heard about but had never actually listened to, Nirvana. Their popularity had skyrocketed when the lead singer, Kurt Cobain, had killed himself earlier that spring. The band playing was Nirvana and the lead singer was Kurt Cobain, one of the most influential musicians of his era. I was experiencing this display of raw emotion for the first time and as I sat in front of the TV watching Cobain sing in his melodramatic voice, entranced, I began to appreciate the music. There was a strange look about him, unkempt hair, an old sweater, torn blue jeans, and black Converse Chuck Taylors. He was not the typical rock star. What was strange to me was how sad he looked; a look I can now recognize as depression.

Really enjoying the music, I started to wonder why such a talented person would ever want to take his own life. I was dealing with the emotions of the first years of teenage life along with a broken foot. My feelings of suicide, I thought, were justified, while his life seemed so great. At some time while I was experiencing this epic moment in music for the first time, my father came into the room, looked at the TV, and announced, "Is that Kurt Cobain? What an idiot!" I just slowly turned around and looked at my dad for more insight on this, because I saw someone who was talented and for some reason extremely sad and this puzzled me. "When you kill yourself you go straight to hell," My dad proclaimed as if he had heard this bit of knowledge from Jesus Christ himself. After pondering that thought I decided that day to stop thinking about suicide because I did not want to risk going to hell. That was the extent of my suicide talk with my father and unfortunately, the thoughts of suicide would creep back into my mind, despite my fear of eternal damnation.

On April 8, 1994, a few months before I would see him perform on TV, a suicide note was found near the dead body of Kurt Cobain. Many people do not believe that Kurt Cobain killed himself and I am not here to persuade you either way. I would simply like to point out that Kurt Cobain, a known bipolar patient, had a suicide note written in what was mostly assumed to be his handwriting. The note itself is full of red flags indication that he was indeed bipolar and suicidal. He was also a heroin addict, making him a perfect candidate for discussion in this book. Although he was a man with many talents, he was burdened by a disease that can easily swallow your life if you are not careful to properly educate yourself and accept the disease before it takes over. In his note, Cobain says:

> I haven't felt the excitement of listening to as well as creating music along with reading and writing for too many years now. I feel guilty beyond words about these things.[1]

---

1. Cobain, "Suicide Note," lines 8–10.

Here he admits to experiencing a loss of pleasure from normally pleasurable activities. This feeling is called anhedonia, something I mentioned in chapter 2, that many drug addicts will experience after long-term abuse. Anhedonia is also a common symptom of the depression that comes along with bipolar disorder. The note went on to express more anhedonia as well as feelings of escape:

> I have . . . a daughter who reminds me too much of what I used to be, full of love and joy, kissing every person she meets because everyone is good and will do her no harm. And that terrifies me to the point where I can barely function; I can't stand the thought of Frances becoming the miserable, self-destructive, death-rocker that I've become.[2]

It is clear that feelings of escape are being felt here. This is how I felt before I passed out in the driver's seat of my car with the engine running. I wanted to escape. The note contains a full page of handwritten confessions of Cobain's feelings surrounding his music, his family, fans, and perhaps most important, his personal feelings about himself. It is a tragedy that Kurt Cobain died, however I believe that knowing he was a bipolar suicide helped me to crawl up the spiral out of the bottom that I had found in my car that day.

AWAKENING

A vibration in my pocket startled me from my uncomfortable slumber in the driver's seat of my idling car. All the edges were fuzzy and I felt a bit cartoonish as I looked around and tried to orient myself. How long had I been asleep? I looked at the clock and realized it could not have been more than a few minutes, but it felt like I had just been awoken from an eternal slumber. My pocket was still vibrating and I tried to concentrate on the heavy metal screaming from the speakers. I did not like the song that was playing and thankfully it was just fading out. I immediately recognized the next song but with my brain functioning at a snail's pace, I could not associate the music with the players. The sound was distorted but lyrics were clear in my ears as if I were supposed to be doing more with the words than just hearing them:

> Take a step outside yourself
> And turn around

2. Ibid., lines 33–39.

> Take a look at who you are
> It's pretty scary[3]

I looked around my car and tried to focus on the hose coming through the small opening at the top of the driver's side window. There was a towel stuffed along the opening to keep the poison inside the car and the music was still playing:

> ... So wasteful ... [4]

It seemed like certain words were jumping out of the song into my poisoned head. I had heard this song before and now it was all starting to come back to me. I was slowly orienting myself to what I was doing and how I was feeling and when my pocket started to vibrate again I suddenly realized that I was getting a phone call, but did not care to see who it was. I was more interested in listening to the music.

I looked at the iPod to see who was playing and it was Nirvana. Kurt Cobain was singing a song that the band had covered from the group Devo. I hadn't ever actually noticed the words to this song before and suddenly the lyrics seemed to be the only thing in the world that I could focus on. The song was challenging me to look at who I was, telling me I was amazing. Each individual interprets lyrics in different ways and I was starting to get an idea of what these words currently meant to me. The high hopes and expectations that I had set for myself were not as important as I thought they were; there was a lot more to the world than me and my struggle:

> Take a step outside the planet
> Turn around and around[5]

The poison continued to enter the car as I grabbed my iPod and glanced at the name of this song, "Turnaround." My pocket started to vibrate again and this time I was coherent enough to pull the phone out and look to see who was calling. Amada, my best friend; I had spoken with her earlier in the day and she had told me that she might stop by my apartment. Dread overwhelmed me; I hoped she was not here. I did not want anyone to see me until I was in a casket. I put the phone down, shut off the music, and closed my eyes. The nausea and dizziness started

3. Nirvana, "Turnaround," stanza 1, lines 1–4.
4. Ibid., stanza 2, line 6.
5. Ibid., stanza 5, lines 1–2.

to come back to me now. My thoughts drifted back to the lyrics of that song and I thought, *"What the hell am I doing?"* This whole situation involved many more people than just me. I had a history of depression. Right now I was depressed and had felt that way for several months. At that moment nauseated from the fumes, I took a step outside of myself, turned around to look at who I was and, in fact, it was pretty scary.

I was about to graduate as a doctor of pharmacy after four difficult years of college followed by four even more difficult years of grad school. I had good friends, and I was a good friend to them in return, although I was not acting like it now. I had a flash of clarity and from that moment on I started to view myself differently. I did not need to die. The thoughts that I was having about the world being better without me were a figment of my imagination, brought on by my own self-hate. The world would go on without me, and I would simply be a ripple in the still waters of life. Killing myself would not make things better, it would confuse a lot of people and worse than that, I would not have the opportunity to turnaround and fix my mind and my life. I was no Kurt Cobain, but I did hold value to those around me. I shut the car off and completely rolled down the window, the towel fell onto my lap and the hose landed on the ground outside of my car with a clank. As I sat there, in my car, pathetic, mentally beaten, and slightly poisoned, I accepted for the first time in my life that I was suffering from some sort of mental illness. It was something I had always known but never fully accepted. My pocket started to vibrate again and this time I answered.

"Hello," I said in a low, pathetic voice.

"What the hell are you doing? I've been trying to call you for ten minutes. Where are you? I'm parked in front of your apartment and you're not here."

"I'm sitting in my car in the garage. I'm, uh, I was um, trying to kill myself." I quickly mumbled the last part in a monotone, as if I were talking about the weather.

"What? Really, what are you doing? Let me in, I'm walking around the back to the garage."

"Okay, I'll be right here."

I got out of my car and immediately threw up. Then, nauseated, I stumbled to the garage door, opened it, and there she was, picturesque as always, her eyes the type of icy blue that pierces your soul, contrasted by her vibrant red lips, and all surrounded by her pale, beautiful skin. I was in love of course, but settled on friendship instead because my constant fluctuating moods were too much for her to handle in a romantic relationship. Right now she was not happy and that somehow made her look even more attractive to me; she was beautiful when she was mad. Her skin would flush over a shade of red, her lips were always so full and vibrant, and at that moment all I wanted to do was to kiss them and have her arms around me.

"What are you doing?" She said as she walked into the garage. "What the hell is that?" She screamed as she examined the hose running from my tailpipe to the ground outside of my car. "Are you alright? You look like shit, I'm calling the police. I'm bringing you to a hospital, this has to stop. Why are you doing this?"

"I don't need the police and I don't need a hospital," I said. Although I knew I needed to see a doctor, I did not think the emergency room physician was the right person to help me. "Let's just go upstairs and talk. I'm really confused and depressed right now." Tears poured out of my eyes because I had inadvertently performed another stunt to get attention. I was recreating my cycle again to deal with the depression. I would not do it this time, though.

I would like to say that things got better that day, but that is not exactly how it happened. Superficially, things got worse before they got better; life became harder once people knew that I was depressed and suicidal. Some people treated me differently, and I could not blame them because they probably did not even realize that they were acting differently and making me feel uncomfortable. I did not stop thinking about suicide that day either; however, it became a lot easier to talk about it. Amanda would call me almost daily just to talk and sometimes ask me if I still thought about suicide. I would always lie to her and say no because it made me look sane and life was easier that way. I had a psychiatrist, Robin, to talk to about those things and I had faith in her. Besides, it was embarrassing to talk about suicide and the emotions surrounding it with my friends. Often people will talk negatively about someone who takes their life in suicide and assume that they are weak-minded or stupid, but I had a new understanding for what goes through someone's mind as they take the final action in suicide. I truly felt like I was a burden to those around me, and maybe to some extent I was a burden. What was important was that if I had looked hard enough I could always find a reason to live, a reason to keep going no matter how terrible things actually seemed. This is a feeling that I try to embrace and constantly keep in mind. I am as thankful for this experience as any. It opened my eyes to a world outside of my head. I know that I can control that world to some extent, but I had to learn that there are just some things out of my control and it is my duty to accept those things and move on.

Walking on the Edge

Dean Jones

> *At the grave of a suicide*
> *You sat in judgment of him—you, whose feet*
> *Were set in pleasant places: you who found*
> *The Bitter Cup he dared to break still sweet,*
> *And shut him from your consecrated ground.*
> *Come, if you think the dead man sleeps a whit*
> *Less soundly in his grave—come, look I pray*
> *A violet has consecrated it,*
> *Henceforth you need not fear to walk this way*

—SARAH PLATT, 1886[6]

It is not unusual to read about suicide in the popular press. Pauline Jelinek, a writer for the Associated Press, reported in May of 2008 that the rate of suicide in the Army reached an all-time annual high of 115 soldiers in 2007, another result of the on-going war in Iraq.[7] As this book was being prepared for publication the serious mental health problems related to the fighting in the Middle East continue to increase and become a timely topic of major news sources. This is illustrated, for example, in a *Time* magazine report on July 12, 2008, about the problems women face when coming home from military service.[8] Unfortunately, extensive use of the Internet has given some a new option to make their

6. Bennett, *Palace Burner*, 128.

7. Jelinek, "Soldier Suicides," 6A.

8. Fitzpatrick, "How We Fail," 42–45.

last actions a public event. In November of 2008, Abraham Biggs set his computer to chronicle his own death as he proceeded to take a drug overdose. A live Internet audience saw his body finally lying motionless on his bed, followed by the letters LOL and the one-word message, "hahahah." Some members of his virtual audience encouraged him to do it, while others tried to talk him out of it, and some discussed whether he was taking a dose big enough to kill himself.[9] One of the problems in any suicide event is that it can trigger the same behavior in others who are "on the edge."

Now I want to digress for a minute at this point in this chapter. Throughout the book, we have covered a lot of information that may be helpful in different kinds of struggles to climb up the downward spiral. At this point in our journey together you have shared many very painful scenarios with us. More will follow in the remaining pages of this chapter. Perhaps it is time for you to pull aside from the heavy material, take time to look around, and touch whatever it is that brings you joy or pulls you toward the future. As I write this it is mid-April in Colorado. We are now waiting for the melting of the last major snow of the season. I look outside and am impressed by the mantle of fresh, white snow covering the ground, a special look of beauty. The unevenness, even ugly places on the lawn are not visible. But the snow must melt for me to see the patches of bare or brown grass where special attention is needed. If the snow always covered things I would never see the lovely flowers announcing a new spring. We need the full spectrum of the seasons, in life as well as in the weather. Sometimes it is too hard to truly look at reality. But at other times it is so very important to really look, to really see.

Let me repeat the words you first saw in chapter 1 of this book. As you may recall, I invited you to join me in a walk along the Coal Creek Trail near where I now live. Out on this trail we can see the distant foothills of the Rockies. Free flowing, billowy white clouds add to the beauty of the sky. On a winter morning, attention is pulled to the small world of a new patch of fresh fallen snow. In the distance the snow-covered peaks of the Rocky Mountain range invite trail walkers to pause before hurrying on. It is true that an early morning walk on this trail has become a time of inspiration for me. I delight in the sight of a pair of mallard ducks, swimming in the clear water of the creek. The male holds high a proud head of green and blue hues that shine in the reflection of the sun

9. Madkour, "Florida Teen Abraham Biggs."

like precious gemstones. The female wears her camouflage uniform of different hues of brown in keeping with her role to sit protectively on the new life waiting inside frail shells of egg after mating season. At 6 a.m. on a winter morning, the white outline of the moon hangs high in the western sky while in the east a new day dawns with shades of pink and red held on unique sprays of cloud formation.

Now let us walk together, again, on the rough road sometimes leading to premature death by suicide. We do not have control over who reads these pages. We are with you, wherever you stand with respect to any of the problems covered in this book. If you know someone who is at high risk for suicide our hope is that something in these pages will help. If you, yourself, are in a very difficult situation, please know that help is available. As I share, I know personally that it is possible to walk off a high bridge, not giving in to the urge to end it all. Anyone who has been involved in night ministry for any length of time can share stories of men and women for whom suicide was the major agenda. Back when I was working in Denver a man called me late one night. I met him in an all-night eatery where he immediately went into a scenario that included suicide ideation. He was out of work and felt that he would never be able to find a job again. I told him to search the want ads and made an appointment to meet him again at the same place a week later. At our second meeting I again talked openly with him about suicide. I asked him how he planned to take his life. He said that he had some pills. I instructed him to get in his car, telling him that I would follow him home, and then that I wanted to watch him flush the pills down the garbage disposal. At his apartment I was introduced to his wife. He went into a bedroom, came out with a bottle of pills, and threw these pills down the drain of the kitchen sink before turning on the disposal unit. Two weeks later this couple invited me back to share a lunch. At that time he was proudly wearing a Texaco shirt, announcing his new job. He was working but did not yet have a paycheck. The lunch was simple, primarily soft, white bread, bologna sandwiches, and canned soup. I noticed that his wife was not wearing her wedding ring. Then I discovered that she had hawked the ring to buy the simple fare to thank me for bringing her husband back. The survival suggestion here is that it is okay to talk openly about suicide. Such talk can, in fact, mean the difference between life and death. In an ideal situation concern should also be given to the need for counseling after heavy talk about suicide. Surviving one crisis does not mean that all problems have been solved.

In Tacoma, Washington, I had another similar late-night encounter. A man was sitting alone in a booth at Brown's, a tavern/restaurant in Tacoma's interracial district. I could see that he was in a bucket of depression. Taking a seat in the booth across from him, I first simply sat, nursing a glass of diet cola. Then I slowly began talking, saying something innocuous like "hi" and waiting for silence to have its play in the interaction. Over time this stranger began to offer a few words and then to begin talking at greater length. He had been walking the streets for three days and nights. He had also been doing some drinking. He was out of work and was sure that his boss would not take him back. He had also convinced himself that his wife would no longer want him around. He said that he was seriously considering suicide. I suggested that he call his wife. He said that he could not do that. I offered to make the call, going back to a pay phone hanging in the hallway leading to the restrooms in the tavern. His wife answered immediately and offered warm words of encouragement for her husband. Back in the booth I shared the greeting with John and offered to drive him home. On the way he wanted a cup of coffee that I purchased for him. I climbed the stairs with him up to his apartment where his wife greeted both of us warmly. Two weeks later I made another contact. John had his old job back and at least for that time was over the suicide scenario.

Years ago while I was working late at night in downtown Denver, a Native American man wanted to talk with me in a tavern. The tavern was dark and this man was a stranger to me. He began the conversation by talking about suicide and then informed me that he had a loaded .38 on his person at the time. I was not sure what to do. I was not and am not a mental health professional. Some kind of action was called for. I attempted to put him in touch with his most recent contact, the local VA hospital. I must admit that I was relieved when some of his buddies came along and he drifted away from me. I would not have taken him to a facility in my car, knowing that he was carrying a gun.

In the early years of Operation Nightwatch in Seattle, the founder, Rev. Bud Palmberg, was called to the scene as a young man edged out of a hotel room window, threatening to jump. Bud made his way up to this man's room and talked to him through the open window. When the man said that by jumping to the ground he could get his sister to listen to him, Bud convinced him that in all likelihood the sister would never know about his death. A few minutes after this tense conversation began, the stranger crawled back into his room. When Bud felt comfortable with the emotional state of the man he went down to the hotel coffee shop for a cup of coffee. Before he could finish the coffee a hotel employee came rushing up to him. The young man who had talked of suicide was reported to have locked the door of his room with new shouts of "ending it all." Bud hurried back to the room. The hotel manager unlocked the door. Inside, Bud found the man sprawled out on the floor, blood smeared over his body. He was trying to cut one of his wrists. Bud shoved the knife out of his grasp and used his tie as a bandage and tourniquet to stop the flow of blood before calling 911.

This man did survive the suicide attempt. Bud visited him in the hospital. When he was released Bud invited him to stay with a family in the church. Things seemed to be going along fairly smoothly. But when the family went on vacation the man set the house on fire. Bud and the members of his congregation did not immediately give up on the stranger. He was next invited to sleep in the church. One morning Bud was greeted by shouts through the locked door of his office. The man had locked himself in the room and had again cut his wrists. He collected the blood in a paper cup and was throwing this fresh blood at the books lining the office. After this episode the man was admitted for treatment in a local mental health facility. He never returned to Bud's neighborhood. When last heard from he was in prison on charges of arson.

For me there is a personal sadness in repeating this story. Years ago while teaching a class in a community college I used the story as an illustration of suicide behavior. As I described the scene in the hotel room, a young man in my class asked me not to be so graphic with the details. A woman in the class shared some of her own problems around the chronic health issues of her mother. I tried to be helpful regarding the parent but did not really talk with her about her own anxieties. Several months after the end of that school quarter, I learned that this woman who had completed my class took her own life in suicide.

At one time the Seattle outreach of Operation Nightwatch held a few hotel rooms that were offered to the homeless on a first-come, first-served basis. Men and women used these rooms when they could not find a place in the regular emergency shelters run by the city. Sometimes there was no opportunity to follow up on the very difficult problems facing the folks who used these rooms. It was only after the fact that Rev. Norm Riggins became aware of the trauma a seventeen-year-old girl was going through. When her room was being prepared for the next guest the following lines were found written on a scrap piece of paper and placed on top of the bed. They reflect the deep hopelessness of the young, temporary occupant of the room:

> To my friends I say goodbye
> Hoping they won't ask why.
> The pain is now too hard to take
> So I've chosen not to wake.
> Life is hell, you can't win
> Giving up can't be a sin.
> Now my so-called friends do not weep.
> For my strength I no longer keep.
> I can't bear to think ahead
> Oh, how I wish I were dead.

Many years ago now, Father Don Erickson started a special ministry to reach the children on Seattle's streets. I talked with him early in this process when he was having a real problem getting any kind of financial support for his efforts. I bought him a piece of pie and a cup of coffee as we talked in one of the downtown coffee shops. At one point Father Erickson was in tears as he tried to share how he felt about wanting to help the "throw away kids," while not getting the support to do it. At the time I had no personal experience with the reality that street ministry does not automatically attract financial support. Now that I have been through the difficult times I can better understand his feelings.

I wanted to know more about the work of special ministry to the kids on the street. Father Erickson talked about his experiences. One of the most difficult encounters he recalled came around the suicide attempt of Stan, a thirteen-year-old. This boy was a regular on the streets. He had been in so many foster homes that he had lost count. On the street he fell into a pattern of drugs, hustling people for money, and petty theft. Stan made two serious suicide attempts. Each time the thirteen-year-old took a large quantity of pills. Stan was wanted by the police. Father Erickson talked about his dilemma as he sat one night with Stan in a car parked outside the King County Hospital. The boy was in pain. Father Erickson knew that a lot of pills were involved. He felt that medical attention was needed, but also knew that Stan would be turned over to the police as soon as he was admitted to the hospital.

As Father Erickson recalled the long hours with Stan he mentioned how hard it was for him to watch a thirteen-year-old boy who was out of his mind from drugs and talking only about wanting to die. It is interesting that this journey, like that of Mike, involved the words from a song. As part of this death trip, Stan sat for hours staring off into space while listening to the song, "The Rose." In this song as sung by Bette Midler in the Mark Rydell film, *The Rose* strong symbols of life and death are highlighted. The song tells of a heart that is "afraid of breaking," about the fear of waking and refusing to take chances.

Perhaps the most direct reference to self-destruction is the comment about the soul that is afraid of dying. This type of person is described as "never learning to live."

The images of this song could be interpreted to mean that death is good, that it leads to better things like the seed dying in the winter to become a lovely rose in the spring.

Both the words and the compelling melody could and did capture the imagination of a teenager as in the case of Stan.

Stan did survive the two attempts at suicide. He was placed in detention at the Juvenile Center in Seattle. Father Erickson maintained contact with him. On one visit to the facility, Stan said that he wanted a new pair of tennis shoes. Father Erickson was able to get the shoes for him. Stan explained that he had walked in lots of places that he now felt ashamed about. He wanted to start out with new shoes, walking only where Jesus would be glad to see him walk.

A number of years ago I volunteered for Seattle's Crisis Clinic. Contrary to popular opinion, a crisis line does not only receive urgent calls when something like a suicide is in process. I discovered, for example, that some callers simply wanted information about the location of emergency shelters in the city. The more serious calls remain as strong reminders of the very difficult situations some people get into. One night the caller was holding a knife to her neck as we talked on the phone. I went through the normal routine of advising another volunteer who triggered a trace of the call to the police. My job was to talk to the caller until the police arrived. I recall her surprise when the police arrived. Anne Rule, the noted author who traced serial killers with her pen, was one of the most famous volunteers at the Crisis Center. This was after my time. While she was there Ted Bundy was also a volunteer. One night he walked her to her car after a late-night shift. At that time she had no idea who this man was. After he was executed for his string of murders she wrote his story in a bestseller, *The Stranger Beside Me*.

One of my most difficult memorial services was for a boy of fifteen who had hanged himself in a juvenile detention facility. This teenager was Native American. I was asked to officiate at his service for the community. His mother came to me before the service, bringing a small scrapbook of mementos of his life, offering this to me in preparation for the service. During the service, which was very well attended, I invited those present to share memories of the boy. This became a very emotional time for family, friends, and the staff from the detention facility.

Nancy Smith
Born: 8/9/1956
Died: 6/7/2000

An obituary is not a way to share the colorful hues and passionate flow of emotions that make up a life. A memorial service does a better job, especially when those who speak are elegant in their use of words to capture memories of a loved family member or friend. In the memorial service for Nancy the words resonated both with the passion of life and richness in expression. To say that Nancy's death was one of the many every year listed as "suicide" says very little about her. She was a much-loved mother, wife, and member of a close-knit community of friends.

In memory of her, friends and family members shared story after story of how Nancy was full of life, always ready to help others. She was the one who gave a helping hand to a friend trying to navigate the challenges of the snow-covered Wasatch Mountains during skiing ventures. As a child, Nancy was caught up in the round of childhood mischief and pranks, including one experience when she and a friend drove a VW bug up into the mountains on a lark and then, for some reason, locked themselves outside with the keys inside. After an unsuccessful attempt to break into the car by throwing rocks they gave up and hitchhiked home. At the memorial service one friend described in detail her memory of going with Nancy into a clothing store to try on their very first bras. Nancy, full of life; a person dearly loved by all who came into contact with her.

Much of the service of memorial was directed to the three children of Nancy. Speakers gave lots of assurance that Nancy thought first and foremost of her children. She talked of them when she was with others, always holding them in high regard and deep love. And Nancy was much more than a mother. She was blessed with an exceptional mind, with a special interest in physics and math. One friend described how he had worked for some eight hours trying to solve a math-based riddle. Then he called Nancy and she solved the problem in ninety seconds! Nancy knew many aspects of computer technology, from the workings of video games to high tech issues as explored in Silicon Valley.

In contrast to most memorial services, those speaking in honor of Nancy did not shy away from open discussion of depression and bipolar disorder. One friend mentioned her own walk with depression, referring to days when she simply could not get out of bed, spending up to twenty hours out of twenty-four in bed. And she was always close to Nancy. During one long spell of depression, she simply stayed in bed for hours at a time. At the time Nancy preferred to curl up on her own couch. The mutual experience with serious depression became a bond for these two women. At the memorial service Nancy's oldest brother, John, gave the best portrait of the disease of bipolar disorder. John, like his sister Nancy, is blessed with a keen intellect and also lives with bipolar disorder. He is a law school graduate and now teaches at the college level. In his words, John mentioned long talks with his sister during which they would share the experiences of taking the high road into hypomania and then sinking into depression; the world of someone with bipolar disorder. In an echo of the last chapter, John mentioned the difficulty Nancy had in getting a good professional diagnosis and then treatment. John commented that the family was "surrounded by bipolar disorder like water surrounding an island." Two images sustain John after the death of his beloved sister: one is that she was taken by the disease, it was not something she would have done without the severe depression; and secondly, John has strong faith in a loving Heavenly Father. He feels very deeply about eternal life and the opportunity to see his sister again in the eternal city.

LISTEN TO A MOTHER

Deirdre Parker is one of the mothers who needs to be heard today. Talking with her, I am reminded that all of the main topics of this book are, in fact, related. Suicide, for example, does not stand alone. Deirdre's son ended his life in death by suicide. At the time he was suffering from bipolar disorder, which was diagnosed after the auto accident in which he experienced serious, traumatic brain injury. This injury came as the result of a fatal car accident in which he was the driver. All of the topics mentioned in this book are intertwined: financial loss, drug or alcohol dependency, mental illness, and suicide. One publisher who reviewed the manuscript for this book was critical of the project because he felt that "too much was covered under one umbrella." The truth is that the problems and coping techniques are related. Throughout this book we have been committed to listening closely to those with personal experience. We can learn if we take the time to listen. One of Deirdre's major concerns is the way our medical and criminal justice systems are operated. She has been diligent in her search for resources in her personal journey as she copes with the death of her son. One resource she strongly recommends is the National Alliance for Mental Illness (NAMI). She is also thankful for the support of other parents who have lost a child and for professionals in the field.

As Deirdre sees the system, too much is done only "after the fact." We must be aware that everyone who is mentally ill is at high risk for any number of behaviors that can land him or her in jail. As she says, "We need to look at how we raise our kids." We need to educate people and we need to tell the truth. As others emphasize as well, it is important to take the stigma out of mental illness. Deirdre knows what it is like to be stigmatized as a mom with a son and a daughter with bipolar disorder. Some, even in her own family, let her know that she was a "bad" mom! If those who criticize ever went through the experience they would be far less judgmental, according to Deirdre. She feels strongly that parents need to look closely at the behavior of their children, watching for things like depression, locking a bedroom door regularly, and any signs of drug use. The problems for parents are increased, as Deirdre sees it, by our culture, including most of the major media such as newspapers and TV. In her opinion, graphic portrayals of suicide events are simply not helpful for survivors. When such problems as the parents going through divorce are added to the mix, life becomes very difficult as children try to avoid a personal slide down the spiral into suicide.

Deirdre urges more involvement in the criminal justice system, working for change. She has been appointed to serve on a task force to study the treatment of those with special problems in the justice system.

She sits on a task force with judges and other professionals along with another person with direct interest as a family member. Depending on how the boundary is drawn, if all those with addictions, post-traumatic stress disorder (PTSD), and mental illness of some kind are grouped together they represent a large part of those in jail or prison at any one time. From her personal experience with the system and in reading of statistics, Deirdre is aware that this is especially true in the sate of Colorado. It therefore becomes very important to consider how these people are treated. Whenever suicide occurs in a correctional system it is very upsetting for the inmate population and for the staff.

What went wrong in the case of Kiernan Teague Watson, Deirdre's son? He was driving down Interstate 287 near Boulder, Colorado, one night. There was a frightful crash with another car. The car he was driving was sheared in half. Kiernan and the other boy in the front seat were declared "dead" at the crash site. But Kiernan was airlifted to a hospital where he remained in a coma for twenty-eight days on a ventilator. Although his neck was broken at C2, he was surprisingly not paralyzed. While he was in the hospital with serious brain injury the police came into his room to arrest him for his part in the auto accident. In his confusion, he did not know what he had done to trigger an arrest. His major problem at the time was that he was struggling with the new-to-him diagnosis of having bipolar disorder. He was not unfamiliar with this disorder since both his sister and father had the same problem.

At the time, Kiernan had lost so much weight that he weighed only some one hundred twenty pounds, spread over a six-foot frame. At his trial everyone testified in his behalf. The judge ordered him to jail. Knowing that her son was suicidal at the time, Deirdre kept as close contact as she could given the circumstances. It was always a struggle for her to get others to see his situation. The jailer said he was not suicidal. Her calls to a parole officer where never returned. The major step toward doom came when Jason was transferred from the jail to a halfway house. She hand delivered two life-saving bottles of prescribed medication to the staff, trusting that they would monitor proper taking of these meds. After his suicide, she found to her alarm that those bottles had never been opened. He was in the halfway house for six days without his medication. Again, she had major problems trying to call him. A woman at the scene said she saw him crying and that he was, in fact, suicidal. When he was released from the halfway house she did not know where he was. But she surmised that he would head for his dad's house, her ex-husband because he was out of the country for a month. Deirdre did her best to get the sheriff's department to allow her to enter the place. But they refused. When entrance was eventually gained, her lovely son was found hanging from a balcony. That fateful day was January 28, 2003. The following words of memorial, shared at his funeral, speak of the wonderful blessing that was and is Kiernan:

> Kiernan was a truly sensitive young man known for his love and kindness by anyone he touched. This beautiful boy, with a truly great sense of humor, could lighten up the darkest day. He was about to emerge from adolescence, when he got caught in the wrong space in time. Due to Kiernan's extreme sensitivity, he was not able to escape his dilemma.

> I will always long for the warmth of my brother and best friend.
> You meant the world to me.
> And I will always miss looking back
> And seeing you traipsing along behind.
> With my love always,
> —Marissa

Now, five years after the tragic events around the death of Kiernan, reports continue to surface around the problems in the criminal justice system. In August, 2008, Timothy Thomason, a man with non-Hodgkin's lymphoma, was waiting for a legal settlement that would give him $150,000 after the Denver Jail denied him critical medical treatment when he was incarcerated. Timothy was arrested in connection with the growing of marijuana for medical purposes. He suffers severe pain and anxiety every day. In jail, Timothy told a nurse that he could die if he suddenly stopped taking his medications. She told him that he could only have ibuprofen while he was in jail. Immediately, he began to suffer "extraordinary amounts of pain and anxiety." Commenting later on the experience, Timothy said, "I've experienced excruciating pain in my life with my cancer, but this was one of the most painful and scary experiences I've ever had."

TAKING THE LOW ROAD ON A HIGH BRIDGE

Some fourteen years ago I was in a very difficult situation. My wife of forty-five years surprised me with a divorce. I started attending a divorce recovery group in a local church. We were told not to date within the group, but I started dating one of the women who had also been through divorce. This became a serious relationship, but I had a growing feeling that it was not a good fit for me. In the middle of these troubled days, I traveled to San Diego where I contacted some of the church leaders in an attempt to get a night ministry going for that city, an effort that did not produce results.

One day I was walking up on a high bridge. I was depressed over my personal life and could see only a bleak future. As I started across the bridge, I had a sudden urge to jump down into a line of cars passing several hundred feet below. When I noticed a woman starting to cross at the other end of the bridge I considered asking her if she would walk me across the bridge to help insure that I would not follow through with this impulse. Instead, I turned around and made my way back to the flat, even, and safe surface of a regular sidewalk. Never again have I had this kind of feeling. In subsequent contacts with suicidal men or women at night I was much more sympathetic to their situation. And I am so thankful for the last fourteen years. Life has been good to me. I have been blessed in many ways and I am so grateful for the time. My blessings include: training for the Leadville 100-miler in the Colorado Rockies at an altitude of over 10,000 feet, spending precious time with grandchildren, and auditing seminary classes at the Graduate Theological Union in Berkeley, California, as a Visiting Scholar. And I have found true love with a new wife. I have the opportunity to build a life in these last decades of life.

A personal strategy for survival coming from my own experience is that I must do a better job of facing problems, not running away from them. My first run from issues came when I ran away from home as a teenager. I crawled out of my bedroom window one night and hitch-hiked from Seattle to a town in Texas and back. On my return, I announced that I was going to Bible school to prepare for the ministry. In my family, church was all-important. Unfortunately, there was no talk about why I ran and no comments about the fact that problems must be faced, not avoided. It seems paradoxical that my thoughts of suicide would come after years of work in night ministry. It was more difficult for me to accept the reality of God's love for myself than to help others in their search for hope and faith. Caregivers in general sometimes neglect their own spiritual growth in a preoccupation with the needs of others. There is profound strength in truly touching the ultimate author of life and death. Looking back, I can also see the need to truly talk about major turns in life. I had little background for dealing with divorce, and found dating as a senior citizen to be a challenging affair. Like others my age, I did not really talk about these changes in my life with others. This is always a good thing to do.

TEARS OF SUICIDE

A vibrant university in a lovely setting at the foothills of the Rocky Mountains, the University of Colorado at Boulder would not be a place to expect any significant problems around suicide. But unfortunately, four or five students at this prestigious place of higher learning take their own life every year, twice the national average for universities. Amy Robertson, a Licensed Clinical Social Worker (LCSW), is the Suicide Prevention Coordinator for this campus. She favors a cognitive behavioral approach, saying that people get into negative feedback loops, ending up with patterns of hating themselves. Robertson spends her time both in intervention and in public health education around suicide. As part of her educational work, she offers training on suicide behavior. One of her recent target populations for this training was those at CU who are involved in Continuing Education. She finds that it is not unusual for students to end up in Continuing Education. This option is offered by the university as one way to help students who are getting low grades in the regular college courses. They want to improve their grades, and so turn to this option hoping for a few high marks. At this time in their life, they may become depressed. The classes also attract people from the larger community who may be going through major changes in their life, a time when depression and perhaps thoughts of suicide may be significant. Robertson feels that it is important for the staff at the university to be alert to signs that a student is going through a tough time. With appropriate awareness, a referral can be made and this can become very significant in preventing suicide.

Now school authorities recognize that suicide must be given attention before students reach college age. Recently, the Douglas County School District in Colorado was forced to deal with the suicidal deaths of two sixteen-year-old boys, one fifteen-year-old girl, and one fourteen-year-old girl. Families throughout the district received the following email from the school district:

> We ask that you have conversations with your children that fit your family's values and beliefs. It would be an appropriate time to encourage children to watch out for their friends and seek help from a trusted adult if they or their friends need support during this difficult time.

In an article written for the *Denver Post*, Tom McGee and Kirk Mitchell quote Lanny Berman, Executive Director of the American Association of Suicidology, in relation to the tragic events in Douglas County.[10] Berman reinforces the idea that suicide is more likely when someone is personally aware of such behavior on the part of others. Experience has shown that those at risk of suicide because of depression or other problems sometimes attempt to kill themselves after hearing that someone else has done so. Teenagers, whose lives are filled with stress and confusion, can be particularly vulnerable to suicidal thoughts. As Berman and others tell us, it is important to be aware of the warning signs flashed by those contemplating suicide, to listen, to be observant, and to ask someone knowledgeable to let you know whether to be concerned.

With considerable experience in suicide prevention, Robertson finds the work of Thomas Joiner, in his book *Why People Die By Suicide*, to be helpful. The book comes with a heavy shadow of personal loss. Back in 1990, Joiner's father was one of the some one million people around the world who died of suicide that year. One night he drove the family van to an industrial park, took a sharp knife, and cut his wrists. It is not unusual for people to become depressed at some time in their life. On a typical college campus many students will go through times of depression. The major issue for Robertson and others working in this field is to consider why the depression sometimes turns to hopelessness and eventually to suicide.

Following the insightful work of Thomas Joiner, Robertson sees three major factors paving the road to suicide. First, there is an "acquired ability to enact lethal self-injury."[11] This simply means that the person becomes numb to the thought of pain or any other negative feature of a lethal act. It becomes something that, contrary to normal thinking, is a behavior that is okay. When asked to explain the higher rates of suicide at the University of Colorado at Boulder, Robertson suggests that perhaps the mindset of risk taking is one of many factors contributing to high rates. The campus is close to high mountains. Rock climbing and other fairly risky sports are popular for some students. Perhaps risk taking translates into a pattern where one becomes numb to danger.

10. McGhee and Mitchell, "Spate of teen suicides."
11. Joiner, *Why People Die by Suicide*, 210.

The second factor of high importance to those who work with suicide prevention is "feelings of burdensomeness."[12] Although not a suicide note, the letter written by the boy in the third or fourth grade to Santa Claus as quoted in the first chapter of this book is a classic expression of burdensomeness. As you may recall, the boy felt deeply the pain of his parents trying to get by while his father was unemployed. He said that he wanted God to take him home so that his mom and dad would not need to buy him anything. He felt that he was a burden to them. At an older age, this sense could become part of a very dangerous mindset with potential for lethal self-injury. Robertson sees students who feel that they are a burden, that they have disappointed their parents, and that they really are worth nothing to anyone. This is best confronted directly with such questions as: "I see that you perceive yourself to be a burden on your family, but do they see it that way?" In contacts with patients, Joiner probes further with statements such as: "Let's review the ways you have contributed to people or society, not just right now but in the past too."[13] Sometimes this discussion is committed to an index card and handed to the patient who is also instructed to expand on the list at home.

In the other chapters of this book the topic of "spiritual issues" was given attention in a separate section of the chapter. But the topic can be simply woven into a general discussion of suicide. Proclaiming the importance and reality of individual worth has been one of the most important hallmarks of the general community of faith over the years. It is unfortunate that this message is so seldom linked to the thought processes that accompany suicide behavior. We are told that we are "made in the image of God," a little lower than the angels (Gen 1:27). "Every hair on our head is numbered," we are of so much more value than the birds of the field that the Heavenly Father cares for (Matt 10:30). God, in his mercy, sent his only begotten Son for us according to Christian tradition. We are important. We are not trivial grains of sand on the beach of life. We have value! This is spirituality at the highest level.

Turning to the third factor in suicide analysis, "the sense of belongingness," we can again see the extreme relevance of the faith community.[14] "Church," whatever the word means to someone, is intended to denote a loving and caring community. Unfortunately, this community

---

12. Ibid., 210–11.

13. Ibid., 211.

14. Ibid.

has at times fallen into hurtful patterns of labeling some people as okay while others are cast aside or condemned openly. All faiths proclaim heavily the reality of belongingness. One of the best responses to a person wrapped up in the chains of suicide ideation I have ever read was the final comment of a Buddhist monk to a young woman after an hour-long time of crying and sharing in a Starbuck's coffee shop. The first lines in this quote are those of the monk; the reference to "she" refers to the young woman who was having thoughts of suicide:

> "You are not alone. We are all related. If you kill yourself, it means you kill your friends and your parents and me too, because we are one body." She nods and turns away. That night, she called me and said she had realized that I was right.[15]

Unfortunately, some who become caught up in the mindset of suicide are unable to see that in fact, lots of people are pulling for them; they are not alone. Robertson has attended community debriefing meetings for college students after the death of a student by suicide, only to be surprised to see over three hundred people in attendance. It is so sad that the person, now deceased, could not have truly taken into account these people, these others who did truly care.

If suicide ideation comes knocking on your door or a door close to you, it is important to know that there are local and national resources to draw on. In Boulder, the Hope Coalition is a valuable resource.[16] On February 26, 2009, this coalition sponsored a free conference for "gatekeepers."[17] The statistics on suicide as shared for the state of Colorado at this conference mirror the national situation. Young females ages fifteen to twenty-four have the highest rate of suicide attempt, but no age category is immune from this tragedy. Middle-aged, working males can be at high risk during times of economic uncertainty as well as men who are older and fearful of the erosion of retirement benefits. It becomes important to recognize key symptoms that may indicate depression. For adolescents, the following symptoms are critical as shared at the conference:

15. Loudon, *Blue Jean Buddha*, 146.

16. For information, see info@HOPECoalitionBoulder.org.

17. Participants in "The Gatekeeper's Keys: Compassion, Courage, and Critical Information" conference were given packets and some of the statistical and bulleted information is shared in this section of the book.

- Poor performance in school

- Withdrawal from friends and activities

- Sadness and hopelessness

- Lack of enthusiasm, energy or motivation

- Anger and rage

- Overreaction to criticism

- Feelings of being unable to satisfy ideals

- Poor self-esteem or guilt

Risk Factors for depression in the elderly include the following:

- Certain medicines or combination of medicines

- Other illnesses

- Living alone, social isolation

- Recent bereavement

- Presence of chronic or severe pain

- Damage to body image (from amputation, cancer surgery or heart attack)

- Fear of death

- Previous history of depression

The extent of the problem in any age category is alarming. A national panel of experts shared their information in a public statement labeled "Safeguarding Your Students against Suicide" in 2001. The following statistics came from that pooling of information as shared at the Hope Conference:

- Suicide is the second leading cause of death among 20 to 24 year-olds

- More teenagers and young adults die from suicide than from all medical illnesses combined

- The suicide rate peaks among young adults (20–24)

- One in 12 US college students makes a suicide plan

- Clinical depression often first appears in adolescence

- The vast majority of young adults aged 18 and older who are diagnosed with depression do not receive treatment.

Dr. Jan Hittleman, licensed psychologist who is quoted in chapter 3 of this book, puts statistical detail in more compelling words in an article he contributed to the *Daily Camera* newspaper on October 25, 2005.

> There are few things more devastating for a family than the suicide of one of its members. In the last 45 years suicide rates have increased by 60 percent worldwide. The World Health Organization estimates that in the year 2000 approximately one million people died from suicide. A global mortality rate of 16 per 100,000. One death every 40 seconds.
>
> Approximately 32,000 Americans kill themselves every year. The number of suicide attempts is much greater and often results in serious injury. Nationally, suicide is the third leading cause of death among youth ages 15–24. Approximately 11 youth commit suicide every day. The elderly have the highest rate of death by suicide. Nationally, approximately 15 elderly individuals die from suicide daily. As disturbing as these statistics are, it is widely believed that they are underestimated as many suicides and attempts go unreported. The good news is that suicide is very preventable, if the right resources and information are in place.[18]

We can learn from professionals like Dr. Hittelman who work with suicide issues on a regular basis. Jon Richard, PhD, was the keynote speaker at the Hope Coalition conference in 2009. He first shared personal experiences that powerfully highlight some of the most relevant things to do or not to do in the case of a suicide in the making. While he was a graduate student he worked in a group facility for people with mental illness. During this time he became a good friend for "Mark," a young man in his twenties. For about a year, Dr. Richard and Mark spent a lot of time together, watching TV at night, etc. Mark was a "nice guy who happened to struggle with disordered thinking and delusional ideas." One year after Dr. Richard left the facility he learned that Mark had died, a suicide from an overdose of medications. He had become extremely distressed when the facility moved to a new location. This was a suicide that could have been prevented. Mark sent out a bunch of emails in which he mentioned that he could not tolerate the pain of moving. There were SOS calls and notes. Those who received all of these messages just did not "get it." Dr. Richard sees that as a good lesson in the need to be engaged, to be more aware, and to watch for SOS signals.

18. Hittelman, "Asking the Tough Questions," D1. Printed with permission of the *Daily Camera.*

Another story, also told by Dr. Richard, is even more graphic in its lesson for all of us. This is the story of the young man who recently posted his suicide journey on Facebook. This man, in his early thirties, had suffered some significant risk factors, including the failure of an important relationship and substance abuse problems. Several weeks before his death, he posted dire messages on the Internet, statements such as "What did I do to deserve this life?" On the day he died he was preoccupied with thoughts of "being the first one to hang himself going out of Portland." He would become a "shooting star" over everyone. At least one of his friends saw these words and asked, "Are you dying or just moving out of town." At least three postings showed a specific procession to suicide and yet, no one got it. This was, in fact, an emergency. If 911 had been called perhaps this young man would not have hanged himself on that dark night after he tried to get his message out. There are preventable deaths. It requires thoroughness and attentiveness. It is not necessary to have a degree or to be licensed. It is important to listen and to be the kind of person who is willing to act. This includes being able to help the person link to sources of help. The person in a difficult place can be encouraged to call the National Suicide Hotline: 1–800–273–TALK (8255).

One of the rewards for Dr. Richard and others in the helping professions is that "success" stories can be told and re-told. Richard works in an employee assistance program. He recently worked with a man in his fifties who struggled throughout life with a learning disability. It was always hard for him to deal with the challenges of school or work. He had been abused as a child and lived with bipolar disorder that had never been correctly diagnosed. He spiraled down and up into spells of depression and mania. Anyone is more at risk when they have both misery and agitation. If a person is truly, totally depressed he or she can get to the point where extreme inactivity is the primary reaction, perhaps to the point of not getting out of bed. This condition is not as risky for suicide as the case where there is both depression and also enough energy to be angry or to take actions that can cause death. In the case of the man in his fifties, it was his bosses who not only referred him to the employee assistance program but also offered to take him for his first visit. Properly diagnosed and treated, this man returned to work with a new sense of well-being. He regained his ability to function and was out of the danger zone. As Richard sees it, this kind of involvement does not require a genius, simply someone who is willing to take the time and listen and to help a person link with a source of help.

Perhaps the most important suggestion shared by Dr. Richard is that we need to reevaluate the term "prevention." We are, in fact, not commissioned to solve all problems. We can not restrain a person when they seem to be entering a danger zone. The notion of prevention can, in fact, sometimes result in inactivity because the stakes are so high. Instead of prevention it would be best to focus on risk "reduction." This is something tangible that we can do. One important element is simply being available to someone and making efforts to ensure that they have friends and professionally helpful resources to turn to. In a family where one member is going through a hard time it is best to recommend that all guns be removed from the home, perhaps given to another family member living at a distance. Guns are a most lethal way to ensure death by suicide. We can pull the risk of suicide down. We may not reduce suffering to zero, but we can reduce the risk enough to pull the person back from the edge. We can get them connected to people who will take them a step further toward safety, people who will help them in their climb up the downward spiral. If we reduce any one of the risk factors we can forestall the action. It is best to reduce a number of factors. It is a myth that directly asking someone if they are thinking of taking their life in suicide is increasing the risk of them doing it. This has never occurred. It is directly asking that can help the most.

In a paper on "Preventing Suicide," for the National Association of School Psychologists, Stephen E. Brock, Shane R. Jimerson, Richard Lieberman, and Eric Sharp offer the following suggestions when facing the warning signs of suicide:

- *Remain Calm.* Becoming too excited or distressed will communicate that the potential caregiver is not able to talk about suicide.

- *Listen.* Allow for the discussion of experiences, thoughts and feelings. Be prepared for expression of intense feelings.

- *Do not judge.* Try to understand the reasons for considering suicide without taking a position about whether or not the behavior is justified.

- *Provide constant supervision.* Especially when working with youth, do not leave the individual alone until a caregiver (often a parent) has been contacted and agrees to provide appropriate supervision.

- *Remove means.* As long as it does not put the caregiver in danger, attempt to remove the suicide means.

- *Get help.* For students (and anyone) this means not agreeing to keep the suicidal thinking of a friend secret. Tell an adult or involve school mental health professionals, such as a school psychologist, as soon as possible. For parents and other adult caregivers getting help means taking action immediately. Seek guidance and support from school or community mental health resources.[19]

In March of 2010, Dr. Michael H. Allen, Director at the Depression Center of the University of Colorado in Denver, was the keynote speaker at another Hope Coalition Conference. This conference was focused on men, depression, and suicide. One of the concerns of Dr. Allen is that more must be done in the community for those who carry a small risk as well as those who are at large risk. The public media and other venues need to include more information about mental illness in general as well as depression and suicide. In the Boulder area, Amy Robertson continues to be at the forefront in public education on suicide, giving presentations to business groups, the college community, and local churches. In the 2010 conference, a number of salient factors were considered at length including the following:

- The rate of suicide has been rising since 1999.

- Suicidal thinking is common, with 10 percent thinking about it in their lifetime.

- There is a considerable gap between professional services and their use and those who most urgently need these services. One survey found that 44 percent of those with suicide ideation saw no need for treatment. Some 20 percent of mental health system suicides are preventable with more training for staff, regular assessment and the treatment of co-morbid conditions, continuity of outreach, and the restriction of means such as weapons.

As suggested above, one function of a community action group such as the Hope Coalition is to bring highly regarded specialists to events open to everyone. Another important function is to become a milieu where many people with direct, personal experience can express

19. Brock, et al, "Preventing Suicide," S9–34.

themselves and encourage each other. For example, the Hope Coalition website recently shared a story as told by Angie Michaiski:

> My youngest daughter, Nicole (Colie), from all appearances seemed to have everything going for her. Colie was loving, caring and sweet. She loved spending time with family, friends, and her boyfriend, Nick. Colie was employed as a nanny, caring for two preteen girls and was attending College for Massage Therapy. She enjoyed her many travel experiences with family and friends. Colie was known by all for her love of music and her gifted singing voice. From elementary through high school, she performed in school plays, talent shows and even sang the National Anthem during Homecoming for her senior year. She wrote, recorded and filed a copyright for her song "Living on the Edge."
>
> At the age of 20 on New Year's Eve, 2003, Colie took her life. Marisa, Colie's older sister and I found Colie hanging in her room. That memory will never be forgotten, the pain remains and our lives changed forever.
>
> Colie's spirit lives on through Colie's Closet, a nonprofit organization that will provide financial assistance and educational resources for the professional treatment of depression and suicide prevention. Supporting Colie's Closet will make a difference in helping at risk individuals live on.[20]

Colie's Closet, the Hope Coalition, and Second Wind work together to decrease the risk of suicide in Boulder. Colie's Closest trains high school students to go into classrooms to educate their peers about depression and suicide. The new nonprofit, Second Wind of Boulder County provides financial assistance to purchase counseling for suicidal students.

As I conclude this part of the chapter, I am reminded that the Dalai Lama and leaders of other major religions have made and continue to make strong statements about the dire need for a new, passionate spiritual revolution, changing the way we relate to each other and to our planet earth. Our problems today will not be solved by institutional or political means alone. Each of us must embrace a vision that includes intrinsic connections between our thoughts and actions. And we need to reevaluate the hunger for false securities and exploitation too prevalent in our world today.

---

20. Hope Coalition, "Letter from Colie's Mother."

While this chapter was in the final stages of editing, the body of a forty-two-year-old woman was found on the Coal Creek Trail near our home. In this book I share my times of inspiration when walking on this trail. The coroner confirmed that the woman had died from a single, self-inflicted gunshot wound to the head. Suicide ideation and the final result of a suicide act are not far from where you and I live. There are many things going into the package that makes life joyful, worthwhile. Part of this package is affirmative action in handling our own dark places. Another important part of life for all of us is to become involved in some helpful way with the problems of others. This book gives lots of suggestions that will hopefully complement your journey in life.

I am well aware of the serious nature of any mention of suicide. One compelling image for me is that of people who have second thoughts as soon as they take some action planned to end life. Kevin Hines, one of the very few survivors from a jump off the Golden Gate Bridge, talks about how he changed his mind seconds after leaving the bridge in his free fall into the cold, salty waters of San Francisco Bay. He knew immediately that he could have taken steps to get out of the misery that propelled him into his final attempt. There are more chapters to be written in every life. And there are more life ventures for those family members and close friends of the one who has taken his or her life in suicide.

CONVERSATION

For this last conversation in the book we met at our favorite coffee shop. Most of our meetings in connection with the book were in coffee shops. This seems appropriate, since the major problems discussed in the book are entwined with everyday experiences such as going to a coffee shop.

Mike: What prompted you to include suicide in this book? This is a topic that is hard to talk about.

Dean: It is tough to discuss, but also very important. I guess one of my personal issues is that I did have that brief time on a high bridge. My experience was nothing like your life-changing episode, but it is something I still recall. Suicide has now become timelier to consider with developments including the cases of post-traumatic stress disorder (PTSD) as part of the fallout from the war in Iraq and Afghanistan.

Mike: I agree that it is good to talk about it. But it is not easy. Too many people take the attitude of anger, like I described with my dad's comments regarding suicide when I was a teen. He'd say, "If you kill yourself you go straight to hell," and that was all he'd say about the topic. It is all too easy to ignore underlying issues with quick judgments of the act of suicide.

Dean: Your story is a major part of this chapter. This must have been very hard for you to re-visit.

Mike: It was hard. But after I wrote about it I felt better. It was good to sit back and see how much I have progressed from that dark day.

Dean: As this chapter suggests, gatekeepers are very important. People are much more likely to turn to friends or someone like a pastor than to seek out professional counseling help. For this reason, of course, it is very important to share basic information. I admit that in the past I was not a good "gatekeeper." I am thinking, for example, of the time I was teaching in a university. In one of my large lecture classes I faced over a hundred students. I was interested in publishing, not in students. One day a young man came to my office to apologize for missing the midterm exam. I noticed a fresh scar on his forehead as he told me that he had tried to take his life in suicide. The truth was that I did not know who he was. He was in my class. To be a gatekeeper it is important to have a relationship, to be someone who is accessible. Unfortunately, even in the family, established dysfunctional patterns of relating can make it very difficult for a family member going through a hard time to find a receptive ear.

Mike: A gatekeeper can be very important. In my case I had a friend to talk to every day. I wish that I had something very concrete to share on how to be proactive. What people can do varies considerably. Talking is always important but it can be very hard to do.

Dean: This topic pulls us to think of life in a different way. At my age, I am impressed by the reality that life as we know it does not go on forever. There is something special about every day.

Mike: Yes, there is something about every day. Just waking up and breathing is special. It is really sad when people get into the state of mind where they do not want to experience this anymore. This is hard to acknowledge.

Dean: Life is interesting. We just watched a much incapacitated man struggling along the sidewalk in front of the coffee shop. He seems barely able to walk, even with the aid of a cane. Some folks do not have much to be thankful for, but they keep going on.

Mike: They have accepted their situation. Many times the problems are proceeding faster than their acceptance. If we can just deal with it we can cope.

Dean: I am reminded of my research for my master's thesis. I interviewed people in nursing homes. In one of these care facilities, I saw a woman who was blind. As she reclined on her bed I saw a face that was radiant. She seemed to be full of joy and was a true blessing for all who came into contact with her. Blind and with major health problems calling for residence in a nursing home, this woman was much more positive than students I saw everyday in my classes at graduate school.

Mike: What we have said about acceptance of life in this book has been good. In the first chapter we mentioned the problem of people who are having financial difficulty becoming too pre-occupied with the lifestyle of the extremely wealthy. Sometimes our society is not good in terms of encouraging people to embrace themselves as they are. Of course this does not mean that goals and aspirations are not good. Our media bombard us with ads for pills of all kinds and with images of youth and perfect health. This does not help if someone is dealing with a difficult turn of events in real life. It is very difficult for people with major mental illness to truly accept who they are. This is due in part to the stigma attached to mental illness in our society.

Dean: As a final comment, I want to say that in some places in the community of faith we are seeing more attention to problems like suicide. Some twelve years ago I was invited to share in a sermon at the First Congregational Church in Tacoma. After the service a woman greeted me in the narthex, telling me that she appreciated my sermon. As I recall, she was a social worker and felt that sometimes she did not get encouragement for her work. I had no contact with this woman after that Sunday but some three weeks later I was told that she took her life in suicide. At that time I was not aware of any church in town offering adult forums on suicide or any sermons mentioning the topic. This is in contrast to a recent experience I had in Boulder. The First Congregational Church of Boulder invited Amy Robertson, a major contributor to this chapter, to give a presentation at an adult forum for the congregation. She responded to questions and gave some basic background information about suicide. Hopefully, this will be the normal occurrence, not a rare event in the life of a church.

Resources

CHEMICAL DEPENDENCY PUBLICATIONS

Block, Joyce. *Family Myths: Breaking Free From Family Patterns and Becoming Our True Selves.* New York: Simon & Schuster, 1994.

Cermak, Timmen L., and J. Rutzky. *A Time to Heal Workbook: Stepping-Stones to Recovery for Adult Children of Alcoholics.* New York: Putman, 1994.

From Survival to Recovery: Growing Up in an Alcoholic Home. Virginia Beach, Virginia: Al-Anon Family Group Headquarters, Inc., 1994.

Herzanek, Joe, David Hicks, and Tracey Lawrence. *Why Don't They Just Quit?: What Families and Friends Need to Know About Addiction and Recovery.* Boulder, Colorado: Changing Lives Foundation, 2007.

How Al-Anon Works for Families and Friends of Alcoholism. Virginia Beach, Virginia: Al-Anon Family Group Headquarters, Inc., 1995.

Lemonick, Michael D. "How We Get Addicted." *Time,* July 05, 2007.

Living Sober. Alcoholics Anonymous World Services, Inc., 1998.

Lowinson, Joyce H., Pedro Ruiz, Robert B. Millman, and John G. Langrod. *Substance Abuse: A Comprehensive Textbook.* 4th ed. New York: Lippincott, Williams and Wilkins, 2005.

Lydon, Susan G. *Take the Long Way Home: Memoirs of a Survivor.* San Francisco: Harper Collins, 1994.

Martin, Joseph C. *Chalk Talks on Alcohol.* San Francisco: Harper Collins, 1989.

Narcotics Anonymous, Fifth Edition. Narcotics Anonymous World Services, Inc., 2006.

Paths to Recovery: Al-Anon's Steps, Traditions and Concepts. Virginia Beach, Virginia: Al-Anon Family Groups, 1997.

Peele, Stanton, and Archie Brodsky. *The Truth About Addiction and Recovery.* New York: Fireside, 1992.

Pittman, Bill, and Todd Weber. *Drop the Rock: Removing Character Defects.* Center City, Minnesota: Hazeldon, 1993.

Washton, Arnold, and Donna Boundy. *Willpower's Not Enough: Recovering From Addictions of Every Kind.* New York: Harper Collins, 1990.

CHEMICAL DEPENDENCY WEBSITES

http://alcoholism.about.com/od/about/a/alcoholism.htm

http://alcoholism.about.com/cs/info2/blfam.htm

http://alcoholism.about.com/od/about/u/symptoms.htm#s4

http://Alcoholism.about.com/od/sa/a/blind041129.htm

http://nida.nih.gov/

http://www.niaaa.nih.gov/

http://www.aa.org/?Media=PlayFlash

http://al-anon.alateen.org

http://na.org/

Mood Disorder Publications

Basco, Monica R. *The Bipolar Workbook: Tools for Controlling Your Mood Swings.* New York: Guilford Press, 2006.

Burgess, Wes. *The Bipolar Handbook: Real-Life Questions with Up-to-Date Answers.* London: Penguin Books, 2006.

Fast, Julie A., and John Preston. *Take Charge of Bipolar Disorder: A 4-Step Plan for You and Your Loved Ones To Manage the Illness and Create Lasting Stability.* New York: Warner Wellness, 2006.

Jamison, Kay R. *An Unquiet Mind: A Memoir of Moods and Madness.* New York: First Vintage Books, 1995.

Miklowitz, David J. *The Bipolar Survival Guide.* New York: Guilford, 2002.

Phelbs, Jim. *Why Am I still Depressed?: Recognizing and Managing the Ups and Downs of Bipolar II and Soft Bipolar Disorder.* New York: McGraw-Hill, 2006.

ADVOCACY AND SUPPORT GROUPS
FOR BIPOLAR DISORDER

Depression and Bipolar Support Alliance, (800) 826–3632, www.dbs alliance.org.

Child and Adolescent Bipolar Foundation, www.bpkids.org.

National Alliance for the Mentally Ill, (800) 950–NAMI, www.nami. org.

Step Up for BP Kids, (866) 992-KIDS, http://www.stepup4bpkids.com/.

ADDITIONAL ONLINE RESOURCES
FOR BIPOLAR DISORDER

Yahoo Health, http://health.yahoo.net/.

National Institute of Mental Health Booklet on Bipolar Disorder, http://www.nimh.nih.gov/health/publications/bipolar-disorder /index.shtml.

McMan's Depression and Bipolar Web, http://www.mcmanweb.com/.

Bipolar Significant Others, www.bpso.org.

Mayo Clinic Mental Health Center Information on Bipolar Disorder, www.mayoclinic.com/invoke.cfm?id=ds00356.

Guide to Bipolar Disorder, www.bipolarworld.net.

Bipolar World, www.bipolarworld.net.

Children and Adolescent Bipolar Foundation, www.cabf.org.

Robert D. Sutherland Center For the Evaluation and Treatment of Bipolar Disorder—CU Boulder, (303) 492–5680, http://rdsfounda-tion.org/.

NON-EMERGENCY INFORMATION
ON SUICIDE RISK REDUCTION

American Association of Suicidology (AAS)
4201 Connecticut Avenue, NW, #408
Washington, D.C. 20008
(202) 237–2280

SAVE—Suicide Awareness/Voices of Education
7317 Cahill Rd., #207
Edina, MN 55439
(612) 946–7998

Suicide Prevention and Advocacy Network (SPAN USA)
5034 Marietta, GA 30068
(888) 649–1366

National Mental Health Association
1021 Prince Street
Alexandria, VA 22314
(800) 969–NMHA

American Foundation for Suicide Prevention
(888) 333–2377
www.afsp.org

NATIONAL SUICIDE PREVENTION HOTLINE NUMBERS

800–273–TALK (8255)
800–SUICIDE (784-2433)

Bibliography

4therepy.com Network. "What is bipolar disorder." No Pages. Online: http://www.4therapy .com/professional/research/treatment/item.php?uniqueid=4665&categoryid=323&.

Adcox, Seanna. "Dear Santa: Letters from children take a more serious, selfless tone this year." Associated Press, December 20, 2001. http://nl.newsbank.com/nl -search/we/Archives?p_product=APAB&p_theme=apab&p_action=search&p _maxdocs=200&s_dispstring=Dear%20Santa&p_field_advanced-0=&p_text _advanced-0=(%22Dear%20Santa%22)&xcal_numdocs=20&p_perpage=10&p _sort=YMD_date:D&xcal_useweights=no (accessed July 8, 2010).

American Medical Association. "Alcohol and other drug dependence are treatable diseases." No pages. Online: http://www.ama-assn.org/ama1/pub/upload/mm/388 /alcoholism_treatable.pdf.

Amour, Stephanie. "Foreclosures Take Toll on Mental Health: Crisis hotlines, therapists see a surge in anxiety over housing." *USA Today*, May 15, 2008.

Axling, William. *Kagawa*. New York: Harper and Brothers, 1946.

Bartels, Lynn. "Poll: Coloradans say jobs are nation's primary concern." *Denver Post*, A1, June 21, 2010.

Belluck, Pam. "Recession Anxiety Seeps Into Everyday Lives." *New York Times*, A1, April 9, 2009.

Bennett, Paula, ed. *Palace Burner: The Selected Poetry of Sarah Pitt*. Urbana and Chicago: University of Illinois Press, 2001.

Benowitz, Neal L. "Smoking Less: Neurobiology of Nicotine." *American Journal of Medicine* 121, no. 4:1 (April 2008) 3–10.

Brock, Stephen E., Shane R. Jimerson, Richard Lieberman, and Eric Sharp. "Preventing Suicide: Information for Caregivers and Educators." Bethesda, Maryland: National Association of School Psychologists, 2004.

Cardona, Felisa. "New database spots prescription drug abusers." *Denverpost.com*, September 17, 2007. Online: http://www.denverpost.com/search/ci_6913581.

Carmichael, Mary. "Welcome to Max's World." *Newsweek*, May 26, 2008.

Cobain, Kurt. "Kurt Cobain's Suicide Note." Online: http://kurtcobainssuicidenote.com /kurt_cobains_suicide_note.html.

Davis, Julie. *Journey to the Fluted Mountain: Stories and Music From the Colorado Trail*. Nederland, Colorado: Winter Wind Music, 2007.

Decety, Jean, Kalina J. Michalska, Yuko Akitsuki, and Benjamin B. Lahey. "Atypical empathic responses in adolescents with aggressive conduct disorder: A functional MRI investigation." *Biological Psychology* (2008) doi:10.1016/j.biopsycho.2008.09.004 . Online: http://ccsn.uchicago.edu/events/Decety_BiologicalPsy2008.pdf.

Depression and Bipolar Support Alliance. Online: http://www.DBSAlliance.com.

Depression and Bipolar Support Alliance. "Introduction to Depression and Bipolar Disorder: Living with Depression or Bipolar Disorder." Online: http://www .dbsalliance.org/site/PageServer?pagename=about_publications_intro.

Fitzpatrick, Laura. "How We Fail Our Female Vets." *Time*, July 12, 2010.

Hittelman, Jan. "Asking the Tough Questions About Suicide: Surviving the Teenage Years." *Daily Camera*, D1, October 25, 2005.

———. "Internal Evaluation Affects External Moods." *Daily Camera*, Fit 9, July 29, 2008.

———. "What's on the Mind of Middle School Youth?" *Daily Camera*, Fit 9, May 27, 2008.

Hope Coalition. "A Letter from Colie's Mother." Online: http://www.hopecoalitionboulder .org/personal-stories.html.

International Schizophrenia Foundation. "About Schizophrenia" Online: http: //orthomed.org/isf/isfbrochure.html.

Jackson, P. Susan, and Jean Peterson. "Depressive Disorder in Highly Gifted Adolescents." *The Journal of Secondary Gifted Education* 14, no. 3 (Spring 2003) 182.

Jelinek, Pauline. "Soldier Suicides Hit Highest Rates." Associated Press. *Daily Camera*, 6A, May 30, 2008.

Johnson, Sheri. "Life Events and Bipolar Disorder: Preliminary Findings." Rutherford, CA: International Mental Health Research Organization, 1995. Online: http: //www.pendulum.org/treat/lifeevents.htm.

Johnston, L. D., P. M. O'Malley, J. G. Bachman, and J. E. Schulenberg. *Monitoring the Future: national survey results on drug use, 1975–2008*. Vol. 2. Bethesda, Maryland: National Institute on Drug Abuse, 2009. Online: http://www.eric.ed.gov/PDFS /ED508297.pdf.

Joiner, Thomas. *Why People Die by Suicide*. Cambridge, MA: Harvard University Press, 2005.

Jones, Dean. *Face to Face with Society's Lepers: Downtown Night Ministry*. Lima, Ohio: Fairway Press, 1991.

———. *A New Light: The Ecumenical Catholic Communion*. Boulder, Colorado: Woven Word Press, 2008.

———. *The Other Chamber: A Portrait of the Mentally Ill Offender*. Tacoma, Washington: MIO Publications, 1996.

Keating, Thomas. *Awakenings*. New York: Crossroad Publishing Company, 2000.

———. *The Daily Reader for Contemplative Living*. Compiled by S. Stephanie Iachetta. New York: Continuum, 2005.

———. *Intimacy with God: An Introduction to Centering Prayer*. New York: Crossroad Publishing Company, 2007.

Kehoe, Nancy. *Wrestling with Our Inner Angels: Faith, Mental Illness, and the Journey to Wholeness*. San Francisco: Jossey-Bass, 2009.

Klontz, Ted, Rick Kahler, and Brad Klontz. *The Financial Wisdom of Ebenezer Scrooge: 5 Principles to Transform Your Relationship with Money*. Deerfield Beach, Florida: Healthy Communities, 2006.

Kornblum, Janet. "Families Often Lost in Trauma of Mental Illness." *USA Today*, 10D, February 5, 2008.

Lerner, Michael. *The Left Hand of God: Healing America's Political and Spiritual Crisis*. San Francisco: Harper, 2006.

Loudon, Simi, ed. *Blue Jean Buddha: Voices of Young Buddhists.* Boston: Wisdom Publications, 2001.

Madkour, Rasha. "Florida Teen Abraham Biggs Live-Streams His Suicide on Internet." *Huffington Post,* November 21, 2008.

McGhee, Tom, and Kirk Mitchell. "Spate of teen suicides raises schools' alarms." *Denverpost.com,* November, 26, 2008. Online: http://www.denverpost.com/search /ci_11075115.

Mental Health America. "Factsheet: Conduct Disorder." Online: http://www.nmha.org /go/conduct-disorder.

Mental Health Ministries. Online: http://www.MentalHealthMinistries.net.

Mental Health Ministries. "Mental Health Illness and Families of Faith: How Congregations Can Respond." Online: http://www.mentalhealthministries.net /links_resources/study_guide/mental_illness_study_guide.pdf.

Merton, Thomas. *When the Trees Say Nothing.* Edited by Kathleen Deignan. Notre Dame, Indiana: Sorin Books, 2003.

Morgan, Murray. *Skid Road.* Sausalito, California: Comstock Editions, 1951.

Morra, Michelle. "The Power of Higher Powers." *Schizophrenia Digest* 6, no. 3 (Summer 2008) 19–23.

Mortenson, Greg. *Stones Into Schools: promoting peace with books, not bombs in Afghanistan and Pakistan.* New York: Viking Press, 2009.

MSNBC. "Trauma rampant after China Earthquake Zones." Online: http://www.msnbc .msn.com/id/24845043/.

National Alliance on Mental Illness. "Ministry, Mental Illness, and Communities of Faith." Online: http://www.nami.org/Content/ContentGroups/Helpline1 /Ministry,_Mental_Illness,_and_Communities_of_Faith.htm.

———. "What is Mental Illness?: Mental Illness Facts." Online: http://www.nami.org /template.cfm?section=about_mental_illness.

National Alliance on Mental Illness of Chicago. "Imagine What It's Like to Have a Mental Illness." Online: http://www.namigc.org/content/fact_sheets/mentalIllnesses /Depression/web-imagining%20what%20its%20like%20to%20have%20a%20 mental%20illness%200304.htm.

National Association of Cognitive-Behavioral Therapists. "Cognitive-Behavioral Therapy." Online: http://www.nacbt.org/whatiscbt.htm.

National Institute of Mental Health. Online: http://www.nimh.nih.gov.

———. "How can I help a friend or relative who is depressed?" Online: http://nimh.nih .gov/health/publications/depression/how-can-i-help-a-friend-or-relative-who-is -depressed.shtml.

———. "How can I help myself if I am depressed." Online: http://nimh.nih.gov/health /publications/depression/how-can-i-help-myself-if-i-am-depressed.shtml.

———. "Statistics." Online: http://www.nimh.nih.gov/health/topics/statistics/index .shtml.

———. "What are the symptoms of bipolar disorder?" Online: http://www.nimh.nih .gov/health/publications/bipolar-disorder/what-are-the-symptoms-of-bipolar -disorder.shtml.

———. "What is bipolar disorder?" Online: http://www.nimh.nih.gov/health /publications/bipolar-disorder/what-is-bipolar-disorder.shtml.

Nirvana. "Turnaround." Written by Mark Mothersbaugh and Gerald Casale. In *Incesticide* album. Los Angeles: David Geffen Company, 1992.

Nelson, James B. *Thirst: God and the Alcohol Experience.* Louisville, Kentucky: Westminster John Knox, 2004.

Office of National Drug Control Policy. "National Drug Control Policy Director Outlines plan of Action to Address Fast-growing Problem of Prescription Drug Abuse." Press Release, June 30, 2010. Online: http://www.whitehousedrugpolicy.gov/news /press10/063010.html.

Parker-Pope, Tara. "Taste for Quick Boost Tied to Taste for Risk." *New York Times*, Health, May 27, 2008. Online: http://www.nytimes.com/2008/05/27/health/27well .html.

Pinsky, Drew. *Cracked: Putting Broken Lives Back Together.* New York: William Morrow, 2003.

Psychology Information Online. "Bipolar Depression." No Pages. Online: http://www .psychologyinfo.com/depression/bipolar.htm.

Rasmussen, Brent. Online: www.CareerBuilder.com (accessed May 2, 2008).

RealtyTrac. "Foreclosure Activity Hits Record High in Third Quarter." No Pages. Online: http://www.realtytrac.com/foreclosure/foreclosure-rates.html.

Ries, Richard K., David A. Fiellin, Shannon C. Miller, and Richard Saitz, eds. *Principles of Addiction Medicine.* 4th ed. Philadelphia: Lippincott Williams and Wilkins, 2009.

Roth, Katherine. "Tragic cases bring tears to Santa helpers." Associated Press, December 2, 1999. Online: http://nl.newsbank.com/nl-search/we/Archives?p _product=APAB&p_theme=apab&p_action=search&p_maxdocs=200&s _dispstring=Dear%20Santa&p_field_advanced-0=&p_text_advanced -0=(%22Dear%20Santa%22)&xcal_numdocs=20&p_perpage=10&p_sort=YMD _date:D&xcal_useweights=no.

Simonson, Harold. *Through the Church Door.* Eugene, Oregon: Wipf and Stock Publishers, 2010.

Spradley, James. *You Owe Yourself A Drunk.* Boston, Massachusetts: Little Brown and Company, 1970.

Thich Nhat Hanh. *Please Call Me By My True Names: The Collected Poems of Thich Nhat Hahn.* Berkeley, California: Parallax Press, 1999.

Von Drehle, David. "The Broken States of America: How the financial crisis of the states affects all of us." *Time*, cover, June 28, 2010.

Wallace, Alicia. "Reviewing the First Quarter of Boulder's Economy." *Boulder Camera*, May 11, 2009.

Webb, Jim. "What's Wrong With Our Prisons?" *Parade*, cover story, March 29, 2009. Online: http://www.parade.com/export/sites/default/table_of_content /tableOfContent.html_529063710.html.

Weber, Max. *The Protestant Ethic and the Spirit of Capitalism.* New York: Scribner, 1930.

Willingham, Val. "Less stress helps breast cancer patients." *CNN Health.* Online: http: //pagingdrgupta.blogs.cnn.com/2010/06/08/embargoed-68-less-stress-helps- breast-cancer-patients/.

Wolff, Tobias. "Winter Light." *New Yorker*, June 9 and 16, 2008.

World Health Organization. "Lexicon of alcohol and drug terms published by the World Health Organization," Online: http://www.who.int/substance_abuse/terminology /who_lexicon/en/.